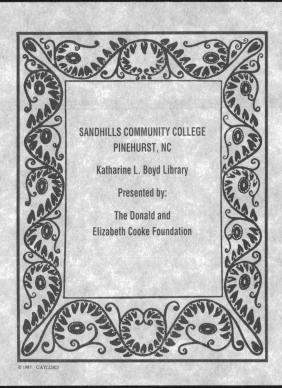

# The Career Training Sourcebook

## Other Books by Sara D. Gilbert

*Go for It—Get Organized* (Morrow)

*Get Help: Solving the Problems in Your Life* (Morrow)

*Lend a Hand: The How, Why, and Where of Volunteering* (Morrow)

# The Career Training Sourcebook

## Where to Get Free, Low-Cost, and Salaried Job Training

Sara D. Gilbert

**McGraw-Hill, Inc.**

New York St. Louis San Francisco Auckland Bogotá
Caracas Lisbon London Madrid Mexico Milan
Montreal New Delhi Paris San Juan São Paulo
Singapore Sydney Tokyo Toronto

Library of Congress Cataloging-in-Publication Data

Gilbert, Sara D.
The career training sourcebook : where to get free, low-cost, and salaried job training / by Sara D. Gilbert.
p. cm.
Includes index.
ISBN 0-07-023541-4. — ISBN 0-07-023540-6 (pbk.)
1. Occupational training—United States—Handbooks, manuals, etc.
2. Occupational retraining—United States—Handbooks, manuals, etc.
3. Career education—United States—Handbooks, manuals, etc.
I. Title.
HD5715.2.G55 1993
331.25'92'02573—dc20 92-28258
CIP



1 2 3 4 5 6 7 8 9 0 DOC/DOC 9 8 7 6 5 4 3 2

ISBN 0-07-023540-6 {PBK}
ISBN 0-07-023541-4 {HC}

*The sponsoring editor for this book was Theodore C. Nardin, the editing supervisor was Olive H. Collen, and the production supervisor was Donald Schmidt. The book was set in Palatino by McGraw-Hill's Professional Book Group composition unit.*

*Printed and bound by R. R. Donnelley & Sons Company.*

This book is printed on recycled, acid-free paper containing a minimum of 50% recycled de-inked fiber.

# Contents

# Quick Reference to Training Sources

# Preface

*The Career Training Sourcebook* provides access to training in skills needed for the 1990s and the twenty-first century.

Who needs training? You do. Here's why.

Five to eight careers or 6.5 careers on average—that's what employment experts say you can expect to experience as an American working your way through the technological, social, and economic shifts and surprises that are churning up the turn of this century. This means it's likely that you, right now, are facing or contemplating a career change. It also means that you need training:

> You may be one among the millions of technical, managerial, and production workers laid off or down-sized out of a job as the nation's economy jolted its way into the 1990s.
>
> Technical, managerial, production, administrative, or professional, you may still be employed at one of the nation's 10 million business organizations ...but you may also be experiencing earthquakes of structural and operational change.
>
> Employed or unemployed, you may be among the countless who are dissatisfied, restless to find more and different rewards from work and eager to take advantage of the prevailing attitude that career change is not only acceptable but expected.
>
> You may be nearing what used to be called "retirement" and seeking a new career for the second half of your life.

> You may be just entering (or reentering) this brave new job market and discovering either that you're not prepared for the work available or that you don't really like the career you prepared yourself to enter.

Even if you're not changing careers, your career—whether it is technical or administrative, in production or the professions—is changing, outmoding skills and expertise that until recently may have served you well. You may assume you're stuck, but never assume. You're not stuck—and you're not alone, either: During the next decade, according to the American Society of Training and Development (ASTD), 75 percent of the nation's work force will need retraining—in technical, managerial, and as yet unforeseeable skills.

But you may assume that you can't afford training, and your concern is not entirely unfounded. Because of the widespread need for career training, vast and growing sources for training exist: more than 3000 organizations promote and support training and development. ASTD has counted about 15,000 individual training and development professionals. Yet, because career training in the nineties has become such a major industry, much of it is devoted to creating a high-priced product. You may assume, in fact, that *all* career training is "too costly," in terms of money or time or both. With *The Career Training Sourcebook*, you will find sources for the training that fits *your* needs, whatever your career goals or situation. You will find expert sources, *free* sources, sources for training that allows you to earn while you learn—all obtained directly from the providers or through specialized information clearinghouses.

Unlike existing directories, the *Sourcebook* shows *all* the options for training, traditional and nontraditional. The examples and resources here will get you started in the direction that's truly best for you.

All chapters contain lists of resources for further information. This is a critical plus in today's rapid-change context, when corporations are constantly changing policy and schools are changing curriculums. The source lists here will always have up-to-date information.

At the beginning of each chapter is a brief section outlining the programs, the pros and cons, and the possibilities offered by each career-training source, followed by background facts, factors to consider in choosing a program, two sections on how to find the type of training offered, and some final advice about following up on opportunities and making decisions. You'll also find tips on getting into programs best suited to *your* needs.

After the background in Chapter 1 presents the context for the turn-of-the-century changes, Chapter 2 helps you to determine how you fit into that context and provides a simple formula and a checklist to help you make optimum use of the book's resources.

The material is organized according to the sources for free, low-cost, and salaried career training, from the most traditional to the least expected:

Chapter 3 covers apprenticeship and internship: These are the oldest forms of training for pay, but today's programs are filled with new opportunities.

Chapter 4 deals with formal education, listing sources that are low in cost and convenient for working adults.

Chapter 5 describes corporate training programs and tells how to gain access to them.

Chapter 6 lists government jobs that open the way to training opportunities.

Chapter 7 covers the government-sponsored training programs to which you have free access.

Chapter 8 covers free or low-cost programs provided by or through associations and other voluntary organizations.

Chapter 9 is about special training to which you're entitled as a member of a number of "exceptional" categories of workers.

Chapter 10 shows you how to volunteer your way to career training.

Chapter 11 gives the facts on how to find training where you least expect it.

Chapter 12 is a short guide for following up on the suggestions in the previous chapters.

Finally, in the appendix, called "Find Out More," general information about library, on-line, and bookstore sources is provided.

The first step toward making full use of the *Sourcebook* is to keep an open mind. Just as you'd be wrong to assume that you can't afford the training you need, you'd be wise not to assume that you know the career that's best for you; that assumption may be based on information about yesterday's workplace rather than tomorrow's.

Take a look at Chapter 1, which outlines the dramatic long- and short-term changes in the American work force, workplace, and marketplace that make training both necessary and available to you along career paths you may never have considered. "Never assume" could be the motto for this book, and it certainly holds true for our view of the workplace of the 1990s and our place in it. The *Sourcebook* addresses the changes that shook up our earlier assumptions—regarding that workplace—and opened the way to new career opportunities for which you can find free, low-cost, and salaried training.

## Acknowledgments

The information contained in the *Sourcebook* was drawn from material provided by a large number of associations, corporations, agencies, and individuals. The author gratefully acknowledges their help and particularly appreciates the use of the resources of New York University—notably the Center for Career and Life Planning of New York University's School of Continuing Education. Special thanks go to the center's director, Dr. Letitia Chamberlain, and, for their assistance in compiling the manuscript, to intern Anna Julia Cruz and to Maria Rivera and Alice Rosario.

## Author's Note

Although the information contained in *The Career Training Sourcebook* was accurate—and still being updated—at the time the manuscript was being readied for printing, corporations, organizations, and government agencies change addresses, phone numbers, and policies so frequently these days that data becomes rapidly outdated. Therefore, if referral or contact information in this book is not accurate, pursue your request by seeking revised instructions either from the specific source or from the more general sources listed in each section of the book. Also, since regular revisions of the *Sourcebook* are planned, please feel free to pass along to the publisher any valuable career-training resources that you think merit inclusion in subsequent editions of this book.

*Sara D. Gilbert*

# 1 Change, Training, and You

Change: the one fact of business life that can be predicted with any accuracy as America prepares to enter the twenty-first century. And the one response to change on which business, industry, government, and individuals agree is: training.

We know by now that we can never really predict what's coming next, as change ripples through America, set in motion by rapid-fire domestic and international economic and political forces.

Change may be most visible, perhaps, in the technological arena and the information-science forum, where yesterday's skills and expertise become outmoded at stopwatch speed. But change is also blowing through corporate boardrooms and managerial bureaucracies, as U.S. business and industry weather a sea change in both structure and philosophy.

Change also directs the current of our personal lives: today's Americans change homes, change styles, change jobs more frequently than in any previous era.

It's not simply the superficial patterns of society that are being reshaped. At a deeper level, our values and goals have undergone profound adjustments in recent years: we want more from life than work, more from work than a paycheck; our individual world views are widening, our attitudes are undergoing unprecedented processes of evolution.

The results of all this change in the workplace and work force? *More* change, of course, including the proliferation of career-related *training*—to meet and make the most of the changes that are a fact of both work and personal lives. Business, industry, and government recognize the critical need for training, and these providers spend billions of dollars on training a year.

And people just like you recognize the need for training, too: at least 25 million Americans of all educational backgrounds and levels of experience are involved in career training programs of every sort.

The bottom line is that change is a fact of life—and change demands training. As a result, resources for the training required to facilitate change are widespread. Sounds simple, doesn't it? But you know it's not so simple—and there are reasons for that.

Change can be unsettling for all of us. But you needn't simply grit your teeth as you are tossed along the rapids it creates: you can steer in your own direction by finding the kind of training *you* need most to chart your course through new career channels. That's what this book will do for you—beginning with this chapter, which provides the background information you will need to prepare yourself effectively to make the most of the new facts of working life for the 1990s.

In the next few pages you'll find snapshots of American business and society in a dramatic state of change; an overview of the kinds of training that result from those changes; and a focus on what "train for change" means for you.

## Pervasive Changes

As we move toward the twenty-first century, we're experiencing not just evolutionary processes, but a synergistic combination of economics, technology, demographics, and attitudes—a bundle of syllables that add up to one syllable: Change. Some are short-term changes, the results of events like recession or war; others are long-term, elements of historical trends—but temporary or permanent, they call for a response from you.

### The New Face of America

The face of change can be seen, quite literally, in the faces of the people who make up the U.S. work force: your coworkers on the job and your competition in the job market. An almost unbelievably short time ago, photos of American workers filling offices and factories showed white, male, young to middle-aged faces—and there were plenty of jobs available for that even-then narrow segment of our society. Today, the picture is dramatically different: The majority of the U.S. work force consists of what used to be called "minorities." By the year 2000, employment forecasters predict, these new-majority "minorities" and women will make up 82 percent of a work force which will also be considerably older, and decreasing in both size and competency.

In the mid-1980s, awareness of these demographics, combined with increasingly stiff international competition, galvanized government and industry into some major training action. By 1991 U.S. business alone was spending some $200 billion on the development or revamping of worker training programs. The underlying demographic trends—low birth rates, longer life spans, heightened diversity, and lower educational levels—remained true despite the temporarily enlarged "pool" in the recessionary early 90s caused by worker layoffs.

## New Economic Outlook

In the short space of less than a decade, from the 1980s into the 1990s, America and Americans have experienced high (very high) times and hard (very hard) times: the distance from the executive suite to the unemployment line was very short indeed for many people.

On the surface, those ups and downs could be seen as typical of the boom-and-bust cycle that's a regular feature of our economic system: a response to simple financial shifts and changes in market demand. At a deeper level, the "down" of rising unemployment may represent, according to economic forecasters, a permanent trimming of the work force. As one industry expert put it, "Jobs that are lost today are gone forever." The aim of most employers in every segment of American government, business, and industry is a "lean" work force, one that places a premium on efficient information processing, high-quality output, and a high level of customer and client satisfaction.

One of the driving forces behind this new attitude is the fact that as the work force is shrinking, so is the market for corporate goods. To get a piece of that smaller market, U.S. suppliers of products and services are competing with one another and with foreign competitors whose workers are more highly skilled. The focus on quality and a work force trained for quality is a natural response to such competition. In order to profit (or, in the case of smaller businesses and nonprofit organizations, to survive), providers must "do more with less"—a phrase which could be the economic motto for the 1990s. It could be yours, too: to profit in these new times, you need to make the most of everything available to you.

## New Responses

What these broad social and economic changes mean to *you* depends on your point of view, but wherever you fit into the picture, they should all point you toward training. For example:

If you're a white, male, native-born American, you can let your new "minority" status frustrate you—or you can acknowledge and accept the fact that training and retraining will keep you at least up to speed with your competition.

If you're a member of that new majority in the work force—female, nonwhite, and/or nonnative born—you indeed have wider opportunities than ever before, but you need training in order to take advantage of that status.

You can look at the numbers of unemployed—whether you're one of them or not—and see a hopeless situation. Or you can realize that it's enhancement of your capabilities through training—even and perhaps especially if you're unemployed or underemployed—that will help you stand out from the statistics.

## Specific Changes

Coinciding with these broad demographic and economic shifts are specific changes occurring in every workplace. In some instances, the changes are radical, involving alteration of the very structure of the workplace. These new settings make for new freedom, but also demand new skills of even experienced and highly trained employees.

### New Technology

The most obvious among these specific changes fall under the general heading of "technology." Technology has sharply reduced available production, clerical, and even managerial jobs in some industries; has created entirely new industries to deal with knowledge and communications; has thoroughly revamped the functions of many traditional jobs; and at every level, in every industry, trade, business, and profession, demands an unprecedentedly high degree of competence.

Virtually everyone is aware that today's offices and assembly lines are high-tech: but "technological change" means more—much more—than PCs or even robotics. It's not just that sophisticated technological advancement is proceeding at whirlwind pace; it's also that *effects* of technology are pervasive.

Today it's not only employees in technical fields who need high-tech skills. Seasoned workers on what used to be called assembly lines must now have sophisticated mathematical capabilities. Managers at all levels must now be "systems managers," facilitating the smooth flow, not of paperwork, but of "information." Even the most traditional of old-line organizations today rely as much on knowledge as on nuts and bolts.

Nor is it just in production, calculation, or record keeping that computer skills are in demand: high-tech communications networks are at the hub of virtually every operation today, from major corporations through nonprofit organizations to local enterprises and small businesses.

In a world where, by some estimates, new information is doubling every four years, where knowledge has become an almost tangible commodity, information-processing skills mean a lot more than simply the ability to input data. In the mid and even later 1980s, computer skills could give you an edge in the job market. Today, without computer skills, you may not be able to *get* many jobs. The majority of your competition is at least computer-literate, and basic computer skills are generally considered as important as literacy these days. Anything but unusually broad or highly specialized computers won't set you apart from the crowd.

But these days, technology isn't all that's new.

## New Globalization

One reason for the high-tech demands on the new American employee is the international networks that are kept humming by the global nature of business. "Globalization," spurred by the new markets and resources that have been opened by technological advances, by political and economic realignments, and by the old-fashioned need for new customers in an all-new internationally competitive environment, is perhaps *the* main business buzzword for the 1990s.

The term "globalization" may just as readily be applied to the new diversity in the work force. With immigrants making up an increasing portion of the U.S. population, and with pressure on employers to make use of the full range of the available work force, chances are good that the staffs of even domestic enterprises include members from a variety of cultural backgrounds.

These global developments put a premium on certain skills. You may need language skills or cultural expertise not only for pursuing an exotic globe-trotting career but for jobs right here at home. The more you simply *know* about the rest of the world, the better your chances to advance. Time was when no personnel office was interested in your high school French grade; today, corporations are not only interested, they're training employees in foreign languages. And whatever your job-seeking goals, international cross-cultural skills could make the difference.

## The New Workplace

Whatever your career dreams, prepare to pursue them in an all-new setting. Although this doesn't necessarily mean the science-fiction vision of pristine spaces where humans have been replaced by whirring machines, a new feature on the employment scene is the "virtual" workplace, where full-time employees "telecommute" by computer, modem, and FAX from their homes or satellite sites away from major hubs. There are also "virtual" work groups, made up of mobile independent contractors who conduct very real business, project-by-project, not in person but via computer networks.

Corporate America as well is undergoing what is no less than a revolution in structure and attitude. In response both to the new work force and the new marketplace, a new philosophy of and approach to operation and output are diffusing from some of the nation's leading businesses and business schools.

One of the hallmarks of this new philosophy is the "flat" organization, where there is no top or bottom to mark success or failure, but plateaus of teams, where emphasis is on overall quality and individual competencies rather than on carefully tracked career paths with "preset" rewards. In the "lean" environments of government and nonprofit institutions as well as corporations, the trend is to focus on "what individual employees can do for us and how we can keep them satisfied" rather than "how many people must we add to get the job done and then see who rises to the top." As this trend persists, the attainment of success will require not climbing, but moving laterally to areas where your special skills are in demand.

All this means, of course, training—training to develop those high-demand competencies and, perhaps, continual training, in interpersonal as well as technical skills. For just as most of today's and tomorrow's managers must be expert in information technologies, so must technical specialists be competent in people skills.

Figure 1.1 sums up the various elements of the changing workplace.

## Deep Changes

The overhaul of the very foundations of the American workplace is not occurring simply because of enthusiasm for new technology or alarm over the bottom line. Something even more fundamental is happening. Although restructuring is indeed triggered by the need for lean, quality-oriented, customer-focused management, it is responding to profound changes in the values and outlook of the work force: that is, *you*.

And "you" are new. Here's an important case in point. During the re-

| Elements of the Old Workplace | Elements of the New Workplace |
|---|---|
| ▪ Structured | ▪ Flexible |
| ▪ Stable, secure | ▪ Changing; little security |
| ▪ Employer will take care of employees | ▪ Employees responsible for themselves |
| ▪ Financial incentives | ▪ Variety of incentives |
| ▪ Work for others | ▪ Self-employment |
| ▪ Local or national economy | ▪ Global economy |
| ▪ White, male influence | ▪ Multiethnic, female influence |
| ▪ Large employers | ▪ Small employers/units |
| ▪ Labor-intensive | ▪ Knowledge-intensive |
| ▪ Worker as instrument | ▪ Worker as human resource |
| ▪ Hierarchical | ▪ Participatory |
| ▪ Education is completed | ▪ Lifelong learning |
| ▪ Clear definition of duties | ▪ Many duties, with cross training common |
| ▪ Focus on product | ▪ Focus on customer |
| ▪ Dollar driven | ▪ Value driven |

**Figure 1.1** A changing workplace.

cession of the early 1990s, personnel officers reported an interesting phenomenon. The conventional wisdom about the unemployed—that when times are tough in the employment market, a job seeker will take any available work—wasn't holding up. A significant number of people weren't just taking *any* job. They were willing to wait, for instance, for placements with benefits and other features that met their need for more than a paycheck. Nor were they automatically willing to relocate just to get work. Corporations whose massive layoffs made headlines say that regional firings needn't have been so large-scale, since openings existed for transfer to other parts of the country, but many employees simply weren't willing to move. More than a few individuals, it seems, would rather be out of work than totally disrupt the rest of their nonwork lives.

Contrast this trend indicator with the prevailing approach of the 1970s and 1980s, when up-and-coming managers and executives were willing, ready, and expected to go anywhere for the sake of staying on the fast track, and you get a glimpse of the 1990s approach to life and work. During the last decade the fast track lost its appeal for many, in favor of a path that is too deep, too personal to be called a "track" at all. Taking the new path means that each of us, increasingly, must take individual responsibility to train toward what we *want* to do. "I can't think of a career path that hasn't been transformed in the last 15 years," says Dr. Letitia Chamberlain, Director of New York University's Center for Career and Life Planning. "Today, people must be entrepreneurial, developing a portfolio of skills to carry along their own paths to career satisfaction."

This is not the "tune-in, turn-on, drop-out" mode of the 1960s. We know we need work. More of us are going it alone than even before and most couples and families require more than a single paycheck to provide their basic needs. But while more groups of us—old as well as young, women as well as men, "outs" as well as "ins"—are seeking work, we tend to seek work that is meaningful to us. Moreover, that "meaning" tends to change with each phase of life.

Career change is the norm these days. Corporations no longer expect lifetime loyalty from their workers: executives know that the typical career consists of "5 years here, 10 years there." This approach to work is at least as strongly an expression of internal attitudes toward work as it is a reaction to external changes in economics and technology.

True, in tough times, surveys show, we cling to jobs which we don't love but which offer some security—including the insurance package and other benefits that go with those jobs—rather than risk plunging into the choppy waters of the job-change sea. But even in those situations, signs are clear that we value much more than our jobs. Social researchers see the 1990s as a time of "nesting," of spiritual seeking, and of concern for family and extended family. Even at work, employees are signing up for available self-improvement programs in record numbers.

If that summary of social trends rings any bells for you, know that you are in harmony with an era. And what it means in practical terms is that to find expression for these new needs as you grow through your working life, even if you stay working in the same location for the same employer, you need training.

A changing economy, world, and workplace; changing technology, demographics, and demands for changing skills; changing personal values and goals: What all this means is that you may want to, need to, or have to train for changes that are generated from fast-paced external changes, or from deep-running internal changes.

What's more, you're *expected* to need training: if the often-made prediction that 75 percent of the work force will need retraining by the year 2000 is accurate, it should come as no surprise that training is available. In fact, a *Wall Street Journal* survey of corporate plans reported that "worker involvement and training dominate the agenda for the 90s...." Even in the face of recessionary tight finances, few of the nation's leading corporations cut back on their training operations.

## Career Training

Career training *is*. It is an integral part of the work force, the workplace, the economy, the culture, and educational institutions at every level.

"We don't need a work force, we need a learning force, an educated force—America needs a skillforce," as the National Alliance of Business puts it. The National Education Association notes, "If America's future work force must function differently than in the past, logic dictates that the education of that work force must be different as well."

### Career Training Is Whatever You Need

And "different" it is. In fact, the definition of "career training" is as varied as the number of careers—and even as the number of individuals pursuing careers. It means what *you* want and need it to mean.

Career training can mean anything from ongoing technical upgrades for on-line plant operatives to sophisticated executive seminars in management of diversity...from a workshop in sales techniques to a full course of study toward an undergraduate or graduate degree...from continuing education required to maintain certification in one's profession to a course in cross-cultural customs to enhance one's sensitivity to new customers' needs.

Career training programs can lead to a certificate, a diploma, or a degree, or simply to the setting of new goals after an exploration of new career possibilities. Career training can mean *retraining*, made critical by industry cutbacks, or it can mean enlightenment, made desirable by new prospects. It can be designed to enhance your competency for a lifelong employer, or to provide the foundation for an entirely new career. It can help you to enter or reenter the work force, or prepare you to extend your working life into a "retirement" career.

Career training can take place on the job, in a classroom or lab at a business or educational institution, or at home; it can be delivered via computer, video, or old-fashioned chalk and blackboard.

And career training is for everyone, from the plant operative to the CEO. It is for those who want to enter the work force and reap the benefits of the new workplace structure and for those who want to escape from it.

Career training doesn't mean going back to school with kids; rather, it means joining a group of other adults who share your interests. It doesn't mean learning one skill and being limited by it: rather, it means the ongoing process of opening up limitless possibilities.

Career training, in short, means whatever you need it to mean, and the career training you need *is* available to you, at little or no cost and often while you earn a salary. This book tells you where and how to get that learning.

## Career Training Is Where You Find It

Career training is offered by a huge range of providers, including high-priced seminar hustlers and self-styled experts, expensive high-class universities, and costly come-on "institutes" that advertise on late-night TV and on the backs of magazines.

*Free, lost-cost, or salaried* career training is available from literally millions of reputable providers, including the following:

*Business and industry.* The majority of American corporations, from small shops to the top-10, provide or provide *for* training and education for their paid employees through programs that range from orientation seminars for new hires and ongoing technical updates or tuition remission for job-related courses to regular paid-time seminars and full-curriculum "corporate colleges."

*Government.* The federal government sponsors, on its own and through state and local government, innumerable *free* career training programs offered in a variety of settings to those who meet various eligibility standards, as do state, local, and regional and community governments on their own. In addition, government agencies are even more likely than private businesses to offer in-depth training to new hires and job candidates while paying a salary.

*Associations and unions.* Most of the country's hundreds of thousands of professional and trade groups provide or arrange for training at no cost or a steep discount, on a wide variety of levels, for their dues-paying members. These programs generally address the specific needs of the business or industry represented by the group, but they also include training in more general skills, such as computer literacy or finance.

*Educational institutions.* Thousands of formal institutions of learning provide career-related training and education to adults. These accredited providers include licensed trade and technical schools, public school systems, and community colleges as well as major colleges and universities that are providing flexible schedules and curricula as a way of attracting adult students. Though most charge tuition, it isn't high (never anywhere near as high as the well-publicized figures for college costs) and it can also be reduced or eliminated through cooperation with employers or the government, or by use of private grants. At the very least, such training is tax deductible.

*Job-specific resources.* Anyone seeking temporary employment, from clerical through computer specialties, through any temporary agency receives training. The larger the agency, the more specific the training. Anyone joining a franchise operation—from tax preparation to restaurant management—whether as an employee, agent, or franchisee, also receives free or paid training. Though such training is designed specifically to meet the providers' needs, it can also give you skills that are transferable to your own choice of career.

"Free," "low-cost," or "salaried": these criteria apply to all the providers on the list above, as well as to all the specific sources listed in this book. Those words definitely represent general "pro's," or pluses, for any of the programs you'll find here. The training received from each type, however, also carries with it a set of specific minuses, or "con's," as well as a set of unique advantages. The chapters that follow detail the factors you need to take into consideration as you make your choices.

Of course, the scope and detail of specific training programs will vary and the numbers of programs offered by one segment of providers will change, depending on economic ups and downs and social and political currents. What will remain true well into the twenty-first century is that you will have a wide choice among providers for the career training that *you* need. All you have to do is find that training—which is what this book will help you do. First, you have to determine exactly what career training you *need*.

# 2

# The Career-Finding Formula

*Preview:* Training allows you to take charge of change. Take charge of *training* by filling in a four-point formula with information you'll gain in this chapter about yourself and career possibilities. Create a matrix to use in evaluating the programs you find through the *Sourcebook* to determine the optimum training—and career—for you.

Training is needed for virtually every twenty-first-century career path. It's acceptable. It's *expected.* It's available—as you'll find in great detail in the chapters that follow.

It's not, you see, that there are too few chances to find training you need at a price you can afford: rather, there may be too many.

In fact, you may find so many opportunities from the resources listed here that you may have a hard time choosing. But you can use a simple formula to find out which of all the possibilities fits your needs. It may look so simple that you assume you're too sophisticated for it. But never assume: You may be surprised at how much you learn from answering the questions in this four-point formula:

What do I want to do?
+What opportunities are available?
+What skills are demanded?
-What skills do I have?

---

=Career training to fill gap

As you'll see in the following pages, your answers to these four questions will help you to find the optimum career training resource.

## What Do I Want to Do?

You probably know why you want and need training. Your reasons are likely to be related to one or more of the "trigger events" for training and learning reported by adult education researchers: getting hired, getting promoted, getting fired, getting married, getting divorced, moving, or retiring. You probably have at least some idea of the *kind* of training you need—technical, managerial, financial, interpersonal—whether the training is to maintain your current status in a changing job, to advance in your career, or to embark on a new career or parallel career.

Training can take you in any direction you choose, but before you start the training, you're wise to be clear about that direction.

What do I want to do? This question sounds simple, but the answers to it will determine the training sources you'll turn to. So it's worth your while to take the following quick-check inventory. Use pencil or keyboard, and give short or long responses, but answer on paper these questions:

Why do I want training?

Why do I need training? (to maintain skills for current career? to change? what?)

Where am I now in my career?

Where do I want to go with it? Why?

What do I want from my career?

What do I need from my career?

What are my priorities for on-the-job satisfaction?

- Financial
- Security
- Other/personal:

What are my career goals:

- Immediate
- 5-year
- 10-year
- Lifetime

If you've given careful thought to your answers to this quick-check inventory, you should be ready to fill in part one of the four-point for-

**Complete each sentence below.**

1. In my free time, I like to ____________________
2. My most important possession is____________________
3. I am bored when ____________________
4. Something that really bugs me is ____________________
5. I daydream about ____________________
6. I am happiest when ____________________
7. My favorite people are those who ____________________
8. I work best when ____________________
9. I am not happy when ____________________
10. I'm proud of ____________________
11. I feel best about myself when ____________________
12. I find it difficult to ____________________
13. What I want most is ____________________
14. My friends would describe me as ____________________
15. I strongly believe in ____________________

**Figure 2.1** Some personality basics.

mula. If you are having trouble with some of the items, or prefer a more in-depth analysis, use the Department of Labor's forms shown in Figures 2.1 to 2.4. You may also seek professional guidance, as discussed in Chapter 12.

## What Opportunities Are Available?

Though you can pursue any career you want to, you'll most likely want to invest training time in a career with a future. The Bureau of Labor Statistics of the U.S. Department of Labor predicts 24 million job openings by 2010 A.D.— and only 16 million workers. That's a gap of 8 million that you can take particular advantage of if you train in the optimum direction.

The United States (subject, as if you didn't know, to change with little or no notice) sees bright outlooks for the service industries—especially:

Health-related enterprises, which have expanded far beyond hospitals and other professional medical facilities.

**Rating your values**

Mark how important each value is to you.

| Values | Highly Important | Important | Not Important |
|---|---|---|---|
| Geographic location | ______ | ______ | ______ |
| Adventure/excitement | ______ | ______ | ______ |
| Travel | ______ | ______ | ______ |
| Stable working hours | ______ | ______ | ______ |
| Autonomy | ______ | ______ | ______ |
| Change | ______ | ______ | ______ |
| Cooperation | ______ | ______ | ______ |
| Creativity | ______ | ______ | ______ |
| Dependence | ______ | ______ | ______ |
| Emotional well-being | ______ | ______ | ______ |
| Good health | ______ | ______ | ______ |
| Helping others | ______ | ______ | ______ |
| Honesty | ______ | ______ | ______ |
| Independence | ______ | ______ | ______ |
| Justice | ______ | ______ | ______ |
| Knowledge | ______ | ______ | ______ |
| Leadership/responsibility | ______ | ______ | ______ |
| Love | ______ | ______ | ______ |
| Adequate income | ______ | ______ | ______ |
| Loyalty | ______ | ______ | ______ |
| Physical appearance | ______ | ______ | ______ |
| Pleasure | ______ | ______ | ______ |
| Power | ______ | ______ | ______ |
| Recognition | ______ | ______ | ______ |
| Spiritual beliefs | ______ | ______ | ______ |
| Security | ______ | ______ | ______ |
| Skill | ______ | ______ | ______ |
| Solitude | ______ | ______ | ______ |
| Job stability | ______ | ______ | ______ |
| Wealth | ______ | ______ | ______ |
| Wisdom | ______ | ______ | ______ |
| Leisure time | ______ | ______ | ______ |
| Advancement potential | ______ | ______ | ______ |

**Figure 2-2.** Rating and prioritizing your values.

| Values | Highly Important | Important | Not Important |
|---|---|---|---|
| Family | ______ | ______ | ______ |
| Good fringe benefits | ______ | ______ | ______ |
| Pleasant work environment | ______ | ______ | ______ |
| Friendships | ______ | ______ | ______ |
| Political activities | ______ | ______ | ______ |
| Self-growth | ______ | ______ | ______ |
| Flexible working hours | ______ | ______ | ______ |

**Prioritizing your values**

Look in the "Most important" column and list below your top 10 values in order. Are the careers you're considering consistent with them?

**My 10 Top Values**

| | |
|---|---|
| 1. ______ | 6. ______ |
| 2. ______ | 7. ______ |
| 3. ______ | 8. ______ |
| 4. ______ | 9. ______ |
| 5. ______ | 10. ______ |

**Figure 2-2.** (*Continued*) Rating and prioritizing your values.

The knowledge industry: information management, information processing, and communications. Of the 24 million future job openings, 10 million are expected to be jobs that don't even exist yet. Most of those new openings will be in the information industry.

Small and mid-sized businesses, especially those dealing in the production and distribution of consumer goods rather than heavy machinery or electronics. Particularly important will be any with environmental expertise or international markets or connections.

For more detailed predictions, refer to Tables 2.1 and 2.2, or follow the government's occupational outlook predictions through directories such as the *Occupational Outlook Quarterly* you'll find at the library.

If you take any skill you have or can develop into the occupations listed in the table, you can expect a fairly smooth career path.

**Lifetime goals**

What do you want to accomplish in your lifetime of work? In what ways do you want to be remembered? How do you want to make the world better? Some mighty big questions, but now is the time to think big thoughts. So be as idealistic as you want and don't worry about how you are going to achieve your goals.

**Five-year goals**

To make this list easier, start by trying to imagine yourself in five years. Take a look at your lifetime goals list. Can any be achieved in five years? Write those here. Again, don't worry about how they will be achieved. Just select those you want to accomplish. Can you break any of your remaining lifetime goals into five-year chunks? Add those to this list as well.

**One-year goals**

From your five-year goals list, select your highest priorities. Then decide which parts of those goals you could accomplish in the next year.

**Figure 2-3.** "Timing" your goals.

This is a two-part exercise. First fill out part A, and then look at part B, which allows you to match your "like" characteristics with occupations requiring those interests, abilities, and work areas.

**Part A**

Check your feelings—your likes, your dislikes, your don't cares—for each of the personal characteristics listed below.

| Like | Don't Care | Dislike | Characteristics |
|---|---|---|---|
| | | | **Interests** |
| ☐ | ☐ | ☐ | 1. Dealing with scientific and technical ideas. |
| ☐ | ☐ | ☐ | 2. Being creative. |
| ☐ | ☐ | ☐ | 3. Making decisions. |
| ☐ | ☐ | ☐ | 4. Dealing with people in a business setting. |
| ☐ | ☐ | ☐ | 5. Influencing and sharing ideas with people. |
| ☐ | ☐ | ☐ | 6. Helping people. |
| ☐ | ☐ | ☐ | 7. Working with machines and equipment. |
| ☐ | ☐ | ☐ | 8. Working with things and objects. |
| ☐ | ☐ | ☐ | 9. Following an organized routine. |
| ☐ | ☐ | ☐ | 10. Understanding words and communicating. |
| | | | **Abilities** |
| ☐ | ☐ | ☐ | 11. Using numbers. |
| ☐ | ☐ | ☐ | 12. Understanding relationships of objects and ideas. |
| ☐ | ☐ | ☐ | 13. Seeing fine details in pictures or objects. |
| ☐ | ☐ | ☐ | 14. Seeing details in words and numbers. |
| ☐ | ☐ | ☐ | 15. Moving your hands and fingers rapidly. |
| ☐ | ☐ | ☐ | 16. Handling small objects rapidly. |
| ☐ | ☐ | ☐ | 17. Working with objects skillfully |
| ☐ | ☐ | ☐ | 18. Reacting to hand and foot move/ments. |
| ☐ | ☐ | ☐ | 19. Seeing differences in shades of the same color. |

**Figure 2.4** Matching your likes and dislikes with a career path.

| Like | Don't Care | Dislike | Characteristics |
|---|---|---|---|
| | | | **Work areas** |
| ☐ | ☐ | ☐ | 20. Participating in literary and visual arts and crafts. |
| ☐ | ☐ | ☐ | 21. Applying physical and life sciences such as medicine. |
| ☐ | ☐ | ☐ | 22. Caring for plants or animals. |
| ☐ | ☐ | ☐ | 23. Assuring the safety of others such as law enforcement. |
| ☐ | ☐ | ☐ | 24. Applying mechanical principles to practical situations. |
| ☐ | ☐ | ☐ | 25. Performing repetitive tasks such as in a factory. |
| ☐ | ☐ | ☐ | 26. Performing detailed tasks such as in an office. |
| ☐ | ☐ | ☐ | 27. Selling things to people. |
| ☐ | ☐ | ☐ | 28. Helping visitors, travelers, and customers. |
| ☐ | ☐ | ☐ | 29. Helping to care for the welfare of others. |
| ☐ | ☐ | ☐ | 30. Leading and influencing other people. |

**Part B**

Circle the "characteristics" numbers below that correspond with the "like" boxes you checked. This will show you which occupations require similar characteristics of interests, abilities, and work areas.

| Characteristics | Occupations | |
|---|---|---|
| 1. Scientific and technical | Computer programmers | Medical assistants |
| | Computer repairers | Medical laboratory Technicians/technologists |
| | Dental hygienists | Pharmacists' assistants |
| | Drafters | Physicians' assistants |
| | EEG technicians | Radiologic technologists |
| | ECG technicians | Registered nurses |
| | Electronics technicians | Respiratory therapists |
| | Emergency medical technicians | Soil conservation aides |
| | Engineering technicians | Systems analysts |
| | Health technicians/technologists | Technical illustrators |
| | Instrument repairers | Veterinary technicians |
| | Laboratory testers | |

**Figure 2.4** *(Continued)* Matching your likes and dislikes with a career path.

| Characteristics | Occupations | |
|---|---|---|
| 2. Creative | Chefs<br>Cosmetologists | Industrial designers<br>Technical illustrators |
| 3. Making decisions | Bill collectors<br>Claim adjusters<br>General office clerks<br>Legal assistants<br>Legal secretaries<br>Medical records technicians<br>Medical secretaries | Personnel officers<br>Recreation leaders<br>Secretaries<br>Stenographers<br>Teachers' assistants<br>Travel agents |
| 4. Dealing with people in business | Bank tellers<br>Bartenders<br>Bill collectors<br>Business managers<br>Buyers and purchasing agents<br>Cashiers<br>Claim adjusters<br>Cosmetologists<br>Dental assistants<br>Fashion merchandisers<br>Grocery checkers<br>Health aides<br>Hotel and motel managers<br>Legal secretaries | Office managers<br>Personnel officers<br>Radio and television announcers<br>Receptionists<br>Reducing salon attendants<br>Restaurant managers<br>Retail sales clerks<br>Secretaries<br>Security guards<br>Small business operatators<br>Travel agents<br>Waiters/waitresses |
| 5. Influencing and sharing ideas | Bill collectors<br>Buyers and purchasing agents<br>Fashion merchandisers | Radio and television announcers<br>Travel agents |
| 6. Helping people | Day care instructors<br>Emergency medical technicians<br>Health aides<br>Licensed practical nurses<br>Medical assistants<br>Nurse aides and orderlies<br>Physician assistants | Radiologic technologists<br>Recreation leaders<br>Registered nurses<br>Respiratory therapists<br>Teacher assistants<br>Therapists' assistants |

**Figure 2.4** (*Continued*) Matching your likes and dislikes with a career path.

| Characteristics | Occupations | |
|---|---|---|
| 7. Working with machines | Accounting and statistical clerks | Heating-cooling system mechanics |
| | Aircraft mechanics | Heavy equipment operators |
| | Appliance repairers | Instrument repairers |
| | Automobile and heavy equipment mechanics | Insulation workers |
| | Bakers | Irrigation technicians |
| | Body and fender repairers | Janitors |
| | Bookkeepers | Laboratory testers |
| | Building maintenance workers | Local truck drivers |
| | Cabinetmakers | Machinists |
| | Chefs | Meat cutters |
| | Clerk typists | Medical laboratory |
| | Computer operators | Technicians/technologists |
| | Computer programmers | Medical records technicians |
| | Computer repairers | Millwrights |
| | Data entry operators | Office machine repairers |
| | Dental assistants | Opticians |
| | Dental hygienists | Pest control workers |
| | Dental laboratory technicians | Pharmacists' assistants |
| | Dinner cooks | Photofinishers |
| | Drafters | Plumbers |
| | EEG technicians | Production assemblers |
| | ECG technicians | Radio and TV service technicians |
| | Electronics assemblers | Sewage plant operators |
| | Electronics technicians | Shipping and receiving clerks |
| | Engineering technicians | Systems analysts |
| | Equipment repairers | Technical illustrators |
| | Farm equipment mechanics | Travel agents |
| | Food service workers | Welders |
| | Glaziers | Word processing machine operators |
| | Grocery checkers | |
| | Health technicians/technologists | |

**Figure 2.4** (*Continued*) Matching your likes and dislikes with a career path.

| Characteristics | Occupations | |
|---|---|---|
| 8. Working with things and objects | Accounting and statistical clerks<br>Aircraft mechanics<br>Appliance repairers<br>Automobile mechanics<br>Bakers<br>Body and fender repairers<br>Bookkeepers<br>Building maintenance workers<br>Buspersons<br>Cabinetmakers<br>Cashiers<br>Dental laboratory technicians<br>Electronics assemblers<br>Electronics technicians<br>Farm equipment mechanics<br>Food service workers<br>Garbage collectors<br>Groundskeepers and gardeners<br>Heating-cooling system mechanics<br>Heavy equipment operators<br>Insulation workers<br>Irrigation technicians | Janitors<br>Laboratory testers<br>Pest control workers<br>Local truck drivers<br>Machinists<br>Meat cutters<br>Medical laboratory technicians/technologists<br>Opticians<br>Pharmacists' assistants<br>Photofinishers<br>Plumbers<br>Production assemblers<br>Sewage plant operators<br>Retail sales clerks<br>Room cleaners<br>Shipping and receiving clerks<br>Stock clerks<br>Travel Agents<br>Truck and heavy equipment mechanics<br>Veterinary technicians<br>Welders |

**Figure 2.4** (*Continued*) Matching your likes and dislikes with a career path.

## What Skills Are Demanded?

If you're an engineer, a paralegal, or a medical professional, you won't have trouble finding work between now and 2010. The down side is that all of those careers require specialized education—not the kind you're likely to find free, low-cost, or salaried.

The up side? Train yourself into a specialty that will make you valuable to businesses in those areas. Any technological skill you can develop, for example, will make you *in*valuable in any business or indus-

Table 2.1 The Changing Occupational Structure, 1984 –2000

| Occupation | Current jobs (000s) | New jobs (000s) | Rate of growth, %* |
|---|---|---|---|
| Service occupations | 16,059 | 5,957 | 37 |
| Managerial and management-related | 10,893 | 4,280 | 39 |
| Marketing and sales | 10,656 | 4,150 | 39 |
| Administrative support | 18,483 | 3,620 | 20 |
| Technicians | 3,146 | 1,389 | 44 |
| Health diagnosing and treating | 2,478 | 1,384 | 53 |
| Teachers, librarians, and counselors | 4,437 | 1,381 | 31 |
| Mechanics, installers, and repairers | 4,264 | 966 | 23 |
| Transportation and heavy equipment operators | 4,604 | 752 | 16 |
| Engineers, architects, and surveyors | 1,447 | 600 | 41 |
| Construction trades | 3,127 | 595 | 19 |
| Natural, computer, and mathematical scientists | 647 | 442 | 68 |
| Writers, artists, entertainers, and athletes | 1,092 | 425 | 39 |
| Other professionals and paraprofessionals | 825 | 355 | 43 |
| Lawyers and judges | 457 | 326 | 71 |
| Social, recreational, and religious workers | 759 | 235 | 31 |
| Helpers and laborers | 4,168 | 205 | 5 |
| Social scientists | 173 | 70 | 40 |
| Precision production workers | 2,790 | 61 | 2 |
| Plant and system workers | 275 | 36 | 13 |
| Blue collar supervisors | 1,442 | -6 | 0 |
| Miners | 175 | -28 | -16 |
| Hand workers, assemblers, and fabricators | 2,604 | -179 | -7 |
| Machine setters, operators, and tenders | 5,527 | -448 | -8 |
| Agriculture, forestry, and fisheries | 4,480 | -538 | -12 |
| Total | 105,008 | 25,952 | |

*The overall rate of growth will be 25%.

SOURCE: U.S. Department of Labor.

**Table 2.2** The Major Trends 1988–2000

| Occupation | Employment projected 1988 | 2000 | Change in employment 1988–2000 Number | % |
|---|---|---|---|---|
| **The Fastest-Growing Occupations** | | | | |
| Paralegals | 83 | 145 | 62 | 75.3 |
| Medical assistants | 149 | 253 | 104 | 70.0 |
| Home health aides | 236 | 397 | 160 | 67.9 |
| Radiologists—technologists and technicians | 132 | 218 | 87 | 66.0 |
| Data processing equipment repairers | 71 | 115 | 44 | 61.2 |
| Medical record technicians | 47 | 75 | 28 | 59.9 |
| Medical secretaries | 207 | 327 | 120 | 58.0 |
| Physical therapists | 68 | 107 | 39 | 57.0 |
| Surgical technologists | 35 | 55 | 20 | 56.4 |
| Operations research analysts | 55 | 85 | 30 | 55.4 |
| Securities and financial services sales workers | 200 | 309 | 109 | 54.8 |
| Travel agents | 142 | 219 | 77 | 54.1 |
| Computer systems analysts | 403 | 617 | 214 | 53.3 |
| Physical and corrective therapy assistants | 39 | 60 | 21 | 52.5 |
| Social welfare service aides | 91 | 138 | 47 | 51.5 |
| Occupational therapists | 33 | 48 | 16 | 48.8 |
| Computer programmers | 519 | 769 | 250 | 48.1 |
| Human services workers | 118 | 171 | 53 | 44.9 |
| Respiratory therapists | 56 | 79 | 23 | 41.3 |
| Correction officers and jailers | 186 | 262 | 76 | 40.8 |
| **Occupations with the Largest Job Growth** | | | | |
| Salespersons, retail | 3,834 | 4,564 | 730 | 19.0 |
| Registered nurses | 1,577 | 2,190 | 613 | 38.8 |
| Janitors and cleaners, including maids and housekeeping cleaners | 2,895 | 3,450 | 556 | 19.2 |
| Waiters and waitresses | 1,786 | 2,337 | 551 | 30.9 |
| General managers and top executives | 3,030 | 3,509 | 479 | 5.8 |
| General office clerks | 2,519 | 2,974 | 455 | 18.1 |
| Secretaries, except legal and medical | 2,903 | 3,288 | 385 | 13.2 |
| Nursing aides, orderlies, and attendants | 1,184 | 1,562 | 378 | 31.9 |
| Truck drivers, light and heavy | 2,399 | 2,768 | 369 | 15.4 |
| Receptionists and information clerks | 833 | 1,164 | 331 | 39.8 |
| Cashiers | 2,310 | 2,614 | 304 | 13.2 |
| Guards | 795 | 1,050 | 256 | 32.2 |
| Computer programmers | 519 | 769 | 250 | 48.1 |
| Food counter, fountain, and related workers | 1,626 | 1,866 | 240 | 14.7 |
| Food preparation workers | 1,027 | 1,260 | 234 | 22.8 |
| Licensed practical nurses | 626 | 855 | 229 | 36.6 |
| Teachers, secondary school | 1,164 | 1,388 | 224 | 19.5 |
| Computer systems analysts | 403 | 617 | 214 | 53.3 |
| Accountants and auditors | 963 | 1,174 | 211 | 22.0 |
| Teachers, kindergarten and elementary | 1,359 | 1,567 | 208 | 15.3 |

SOURCE: *Occupational Outlook Quarterly, April 1990.*

try. Technicians of all sorts represent the fastest-growing occupational category, according to the U.S. Department of Labor. Those in information technologies lead the list, followed by environmental and health-care technicians. Even within traditional trades and professions, high-tech skills are on the hot track. In manufacturing, for example, computer-aided drafting (CAD) is in great demand as companies that want to progress turn to computer-aided manufacturing (CAM). Finance and accounting now require sophisticated computer skills, and marketers with database and telecommunications expertise are in demand.

While workers with advanced skills and education have good prospects into the next century, the outlook for *un*skilled workers is extremely dim. By the year 2000, 70 percent of all jobs will require high school *plus* some college and/or specialized training. And even fairly basic career paths require new skills—enhanced English and math, for instance, to deal with the new technologies, and foreign languages to cope with the results of the newly globalized workplace.

In general, according to the U.S. Department of Labor, employers seek workers who

Know how to learn

Can read, write, and compute

Listen well and speak effectively

Can think creatively and solve problems

Take pride in their work

Have good self-esteem

Are able to set and meet goals, and manage their career well

Have good interpersonal skills, can negotiate with others, and are team players

The demand for employees with old-fashioned "basic" skills has dropped sharply—by more than 50 percent, some estimate—while the greatest need is for those with solid technical and/or managerial abilities.

And at a higher level, American Society for Training and Development (ASTD) reports that managers and executives must have in their skills portfolios not only an aptitude for dealing with technology and for managing technical workers but also these critical competencies:

Decision making

Planning and organizing

Problem solving and analysis

Adaptability

Innovativeness

Oral communication

Written communication

Teamwork

Supervision

Organizational knowledge

Personnel practices

Flexibility

Influencing others

Self-motivation

Tolerance of stress

Developing subordinates

Note that many of these "intangible" skills required of high-level managers are the same skills employers seek in all their workers. Be on the lookout for the opportunity to train not only for technical skills but for the skills listed above.

## What Skills Do I Have?

Before you begin to train for new skills, add up what you already have. Ask: Where have I been? How can I apply that past to my future?

Wherever you are in your career, you already have worthwhile experience and expertise.

You may want to use Figures 2.5 to 2.8, which were developed by the U.S. Department of Labor, to create an inventory of *all* your abilities.

## The Career Training Quotient

When you subtract what you have from what is needed in the fields you want to pursue, you know what training *you* need.

Your answers to those questions may show you that you need only a light brushup to clear your path toward career satisfaction or they may indicate a radical shift in your course. Either way, the more facts you have about yourself, the better use you'll be able to make of the facts you'll find in the chapters that follow.

Each chapter describes and lists free, low-cost, or salaried resources for career training available through different types of sources. Each begins with some *facts* about the training discussed and includes *factors* to consider in making a choice. You'll then read how to *find* specific train-

| Aptitudes | Abilities | Skills |
|---|---|---|
| Things you think you could do | Things you know you can do or can learn to do | Things you know you can do well and would enjoy doing |
| For example: Learn new sports | Ski downhill | Ski the expert slopes |

Don't worry too much about getting things in the proper columns. The main point of this list is to identify your real and potential capabilities. Take a look at your interests listed above to get some ideas. Be prepared to be pleasantly surprised when you start your lists.

| Aptitudes | Abilities | Skills |
|---|---|---|
| Things you think you could do | Things you know you can do | Things you know you can do well |
| ______ | ______ | ______ |
| ______ | ______ | ______ |
| ______ | ______ | ______ |
| ______ | ______ | ______ |
| ______ | ______ | ______ |
| ______ | ______ | ______ |
| ______ | ______ | ______ |
| ______ | ______ | ______ |
| ______ | ______ | ______ |

NOTE: Put an asterisk next to the aptitudes, abilities, or skills which you feel could lead to a satisfying career.

**Figure 2.5**

Skills from Life Circumstances

1. Take a few minutes to list five things you would like to do.
   1. ______
   2. ______
   3. ______
   4. ______
   5. ______
2. What are your hobbies and special interests?
   A. ______
   B. ______
3. Now list jobs related to your hobbies or interests.
   A. 1. ______ B. 1. ______
   2. ______ 2. ______

**Figure 2-6.**

Skills from Work Experience

Make a worksheet like this for each of the jobs you have held—including part-time or voluntary.

Employer's Name: ______

Employer's Address: ______

______

Supervisor's Name: ______

______

Date Worked: From ______

To ______

Reason You Left Job: ______

Machines or Vehicles You Operated: ______

______

Name of Job Held: ______

Tasks You Did: ______

1. ______
2. ______
3. ______
4. ______
5. ______

Now prioritize (1, 2, 3, etc.) each task to determine how satisfying the job was to do. Would you like another job like this one?

**Figure 2-7.**

ing programs, with exemplary ones described and many other likely prospects listed. Each chapter ends with a section on making decisions—*following up* on applications and *deciding* which opportunity is for you. Often, *tips* are offered for making the most of your opportunities.

As you go through the information in the book, you'll be able to rate the available options in terms of your own needs if you apply this *career-change checklist* to each possibility:

What do I want or need to learn? (What can I learn?)

Where will it get me? (Will it get me where I want to be?)

Is it suited to me? (*Why* is it suited to me?)

How much can I manage? (Can I devote full time? Can I devote part time? Can I live on the stipend or half pay? Can I afford it?)

Skills from Education

List each of the schools you have attended, dates, courses of study, and degrees received. If you have not completed your education, write your plans as well as how you will finance continued education.

| Training or Education | Dates | Degrees | What jobs has this training prepared you for? |
|---|---|---|---|
| 1. High School or GED: | | | |
| 2. Community or Junior College: | | | |
| 3. University: | | | |
| 4. Vocational or Technical Training: | | | |

Other Training: *List any special training you have received—dates, places, and skills you obtained. Include business and trade schools, correspondence courses, military training, or special courses you completed through your employer.*

**Figure 2-8.**

# 3
# Learning On the Job

## Preview

*Programs:* Internships are *not* just for students or scientists, nor are apprenticeships limited to trades and crafts. You can intern at government agencies and major corporations, and apprentice yourself in the arts and professions. Thousands of formal programs exist, and you can also make individualized arrangements.

*Pros and Cons:* Though most internships and apprenticeships pay less than regular employment, and many come with study requirements attached, they offer a chance to get the inside track on a career that may interest you while learning the ropes and testing the waters at no cost. Whether joining a formal program or creating your own, you're likely to find stiff competition—so you'll need a clear focus on career goals and a strong presentation of your assets.

*Possibilities:* This chapter describes the scope of programs available to anyone in almost every field, lists numerous sources, and suggests ways to create your own on-the-job training programs.

Apprenticeships and internships—the original form of "career training"—are an appropriate opening for this volume of training sources. And, even on the eve of the twenty-first century, when "training" itself has been elevated to the loftier status of "human resource development," these basic systems of career training are holding their own, in traditional as well as updated forms. In fact, they are so up to date that they've acquired a jargon of their own: apprenticeship is now often called "work-based learning"; interning may be termed "experiential education."

Apprenticeship is required for the skilled trades, and internship is for the sciences—but the systems work equally well for the aspiring photographer who apprentices to a professional, the homemaker reentering the job market who turns volunteer work into a formal internship, or the career changer who gains credentials during a summer's stint at a government agency.

## A Few Facts

At least 400,000 apprenticeship positions exist in some 800 fields, from the blue-collar trades into managerial occupations and the service sector, in a trend that is increasing strength through government support. The arts, professions, businesses, associations, and government agencies offer thousands of formalized internships. You'll find samples of those openings described or listed here, as well as the means of access to countless others. You will also find, at the end of the chapter, suggestions for creating you own on-the-job training opportunities.

"On-the-job training" is often employers' code for "no training worth mentioning." Here it refers to training where the *focus* is on learning. On-the-job training that offers opportunities for serious career-change learning is usually one of two types: apprenticeships or internships.

> *Apprenticeship* is defined by the government as "structured on-the-job training combined with related theoretical instruction."
>
> *Internship,* as defined by the National Society for Internships and Experiential Learning (NSIEE), is: "Any carefully monitored work or service experience in which an individual has intentional learning goals and reflects actively on what s/he is learning throughout the experience."

You can find or establish these work-and-learning relationships through unions, associations, public agencies, nonprofit organizations, and businesses, especially small businesses.

You don't pay for this training, and most of it pays *you*. Sounds good. Is it for you?

## Some Factors to Consider

Apprenticeships and internships are an excellent source of training in many careers for those with a little extra time and income. Though you may lose some income, you can gain resume credentials and network contacts.

Before deciding on this potentially valuable form of free or salaried on-the-job training, you'll need clear answers to the career-change checklist.

### What Do I Need or Want to Learn?

Answer this question carefully! Apprenticeships and internships in general provide an opportunity to try out a new career firsthand, but because these programs, by definition, offer specialized training, you'll need to choose your programs with care in order to gain the specific knowledge that you know you want or need. While an apprenticeship is more likely to teach a given set of skills, an internship offers more general insights as you perform often low-level tasks within the context of a business or profession.

A well-managed apprenticeship or internship will also provide practice with those important basic competencies in high demand for the twenty-first century:

- Understanding different cultures and environments
- Acquiring generic skills in verbal communication
- Gaining interpersonal skills—the ability to interact and to cope with difficult and/or ambiguous situations
- Working in groups
- Setting goals and managing time

### Where Will It Get Me?

Landing a learning position in the field of your choice is an outstanding means of opening the gateway toward a career in that field, because of the contacts you immediately make and the experience that automatically registers on your resume. Though you can't count on it, many apprenticeships and internships lead directly to a job with the same organization, and any career path such training involves can be worthwhile, as long as your interests in the new direction are strong.

### Is It Suited to Me?

You're more likely to get into—and gain from—an internship or apprenticeship if...

You're venturing into a whole new area and need experience and credentials—especially if you have some general skill to contribute to the learning relationship.

You are a woman or a member of a minority group and can find programs where you will be given preference over other candidates.

You have the patience and personality to be a beginner, working under someone else's direction. (Think about this one hard if you're at mid-career.)

You've gone back to school and are seeking ways to earn extra credit and help pay tuition.

### How Much Can I Manage?

If you're paid for this training, you won't be paid much. Though data shows that completion of an internship or apprenticeship leads to higher-than-beginner's pay when you begin a "real" job in the field, that can be anywhere from one to five years down the road. So before you commit to—or even consider—apprenticeship or internship as a training option, you'll need to work out a budget of both time and money to be sure that you can afford it. Have you savings? Can you take an extra job?

## Where to Find Apprenticeships and Internships

Keeping all that background about the field and about yourself in mind, you're ready to choose from among the following possibilities: examples and contacts for entering apprenticeships in hundreds of fields; the *leading* companies, associations, government agencies, and cultural organizations offering paid internships to adults; and contacts for several hundred other providers and coordinating groups.

### Apprenticeships

**Programs.** In the past apprenticeships were primarily for young people entering a blue-collar trade or craft. Today apprenticeships are in place for broader age groups seeking to enter any of over 800 skilled or service occupations. Recently the government, through its Apprenticeship 2000 and Work-Based Learning projects, has extended efforts to increase the numbers of apprenticeship openings in each state and to expand structured work-based learning programs outside the traditional construction and manufacturing trades by encouraging corporations of all sorts to open apprenticeship programs in a variety of service fields and other occupations that require specific skills.

Apprenticeships are growing especially rapidly in such service occupations as paramedics, computer programming, health care (workers and technicians), banking (tellers), commercial design, and child care.

Some professions—architecture, engineering, and real estate brokerage, for example—require an apprenticeship period prior to licensing, and in some states, you can once again apprentice to become a lawyer.

The jobs most commonly associated with apprenticeship are the skilled trades, generally in public utilities, construction, and manufacturing, and include electricians, machinists, carpenters, auto mechanics, painters, laborers, and other well paid skilled workers. Examples are:

Air conditioning, heating, and refrigeration mechanic

Auto body repairer

Auto mechanic

Baker

Barber

Boilermaker

Bookbinder

Brickmason/stonemason

Cabinetmaker

Carpenter

Construction painter

Cook/chef

Cosmetologist

Diesel mechanic

Dispensing optician

Drafter

Dry-wall applicator

Electrical and electronic technician

Electrician

Furniture and wood finisher

Heavy equipment mechanic

Instrument repairer

Insulation worker

Operator

| | |
|---|---|
| Machinist | Shipwright |
| Maintenance mechanic | Ship electrician |
| Meat cutter | Ship outside machinist |
| Millwright | Ship painter |
| Office machine repairer | Ship pipefitter |
| Pattern and model maker | Ship rigger |
| Photoengraver and lithographer | Small engine repairer |
| Plumber and pipefitter | Structural iron worker |
| Printing press operator | Surveyor (party chief) |
| Psychiatric aide | Tool and die maker |
| Rigger | Utilities lineperson |
| Sheet metal worker | Wastewater treatment |
| Shipfitter | Welder |

Note that women might particularly want to consider apprenticeship in the skilled trades. According to the Department of Labor, which has developed and implemented an aggressive enforcement, outreach, and education program to increase the recruitment and retention of women in apprenticeship, "These skilled trades jobs have the potential for greatly improving the economic status of women—higher wages, better fringe benefits, a wider variety of work schedules, greater job security and more opportunities for advancement." Although the number of women working has increased significantly over the past 20 years and is expected to increase further, 80 percent of working women are in traditionally female jobs, many of which are low paying.

While it's often thought that only unions offer apprenticeships, in fact, the decision to sponsor an apprentice may also be made by employers, employer associations, joint employer-union apprenticeship committees, or an organization of employees registered with a state or trades apprenticeship council. The UAW/Ford National Education Training program is a prime example of a case in which employers and employees have joined to create apprenticeship.

Other major corporations that pay particular attention to apprenticeship are:

- AT&T
- Ball Publishing Company
- Boeing
- Diamond-Star Motors
- Dresser-Rand
- Dunlop Tire
- Harman International
- HF Henderson Industries
- Ingersoll Milling Machine Company
- KLM
- Manth-Brownell
- Metcraft
- Northwestern Steel and Wire Company
- Polaroid
- Robert A. DeMattia Company
- Rohr Industries
- Shell Oil Foundation
- SJS Incorporated
- 3M Corporation
- Unicadd
- US WEST, Inc.

**Pay-Plus.** Formalized programs, such as those offered by unions, provide a set sliding salary scale, usually beginning at one-half the going rate. Others, especially more casual arrangements, pay anything from nothing to full salary; some arrangements may include other benefits, and many offer educational programs in conjunction with the training.

**Prerequisites.** Though some of the most physically demanding trades establish a maximum age for apprentices, in most cases, as long as you're at least 16 years old you're eligible. Individual programs often have, in addition to predetermined guidelines, more subjectively determined requirements.

**Procedure.** Obtain information from the branch of the Federal Bureau of Apprenticeship and Training that serves your state (see list below) or apply directly to the specific organization you are interested in. (Remember: Competition can be stiff for apprenticeship slots! Some industries report 10 times the number of applicants for the openings available, and unions may take on apprentices one by one, especially where demand is down for skilled labor.)

You may also inform your present employer of your interest in an apprenticeship and find out the qualifications and demands of the job to determine if you want to proceed. Your goals may be questioned, especially if you have changed careers before, so be prepared to present yourself positively.

Ask all the questions you need to about the terms of the program! Ask for all written materials that you need for your decision. You may need to take a general aptitude test and pass it with a satisfactory score, and to pass a physical examination that meets the requirements of the occupation.

If you meet all these qualifications and want to proceed, your next step would be an interview with the company's or union's apprenticeship training committee. The committee will further help you decide if an apprenticeship is really for you. If you are selected for training, your name is then placed on a list and when work becomes available, you will be called. Prior to reporting to work, you may be required to sign an "apprenticeship agreement" card, which registers you with the state as an apprentice.

Most apprenticeships have a probationary period. (Now's the time to quit if you don't like this work!) If you satisfactorily complete your probationary period, if you finish the necessary classroom training, and if you meet all the other requirements of the terms of your apprenticeship agreed upon when you were first indentured, you will reach journey level. (In a union this can take as long as five years, with salary going up regularly.) You'll now be eligible for full-fledged employment, and will have under your belt a new career which you earned while learning.

## Apprenticeship Listings

For current apprenticeship information, contact the regional office of the Federal Bureau of Apprenticeships and Training or a union of your interest. Those lists follow.

Your state's employment office is also a valuable resource; a list of state employment offices is given at the end of Chapter 7.

### Federal Bureau of Apprenticeship and Training Regional Offices

| Region | Jurisdictions served |
|---|---|
| **I—Boston**<br>Regional Director<br>One Congress Street, 11th Floor<br>Boston, MA 02114<br>(617) 565-2288 | Connecticut, Maine, Massachusetts, New Hampshire, Rhode Island, Vermont |

| | |
|---|---|
| **II—New York**<br>Regional Director<br>Federal Building, Room 602<br>201 Varick Street<br>New York, NY 10014<br>(212) 337-2313 | New Jersey, New York,<br>Puerto Rico,<br>Virgin Islands |
| **III—Philadelphia**<br>Regional Director<br>Gateway Building, Room 13240<br>3535 Market Street<br>Philadelphia, PA 19104<br>(215) 596-6417 | Delaware, District of<br>Columbia, Maryland,<br>Pennsylvania, Virginia,<br>West Virginia |
| **IV—Atlanta**<br>Regional Director<br>Room 200<br>1371 Peachtree Street N.E.<br>Atlanta, GA 30367<br>(404) 347-4405 | Alabama, Florida,<br>Georgia, Kentucky,<br>Mississippi, North<br>Carolina, South<br>Carolina, Tennessee |
| **V—Chicago**<br>Regional Director<br>Room 758<br>230 South Dearborn Street<br>Chicago, IL 60604<br>(312) 353-7205 | Illinois, Indiana,<br>Michigan, Minnesota,<br>Ohio, Tennessee |
| **VI—Dallas**<br>Regional Director<br>Federal Building, Room 502<br>525 Griffin Street<br>Dallas, TX 75202<br>(214) 767-4993 | Arkansas, Louisiana,<br>New Mexico, Oklahoma,<br>Texas |
| **VII—Kansas City**<br>Regional Director<br>Federal Office Building<br>911 Walnut Street, Room 1100<br>Kansas City, MO 64106<br>(816) 426-3856 | Iowa, Kansas,<br>Missouri, Nebraska |
| **VIII—Denver**<br>U.S. Custom House, Room 476<br>721 19th Street<br>Denver, CO 80202<br>(303) 844-4791 | Colorado, Montana,<br>North Dakota,<br>South Dakota, Utah,<br>Wyoming |
| **IX—San Francisco**<br>Regional Director<br>Federal Building, Room 715<br>71 Stevenson Street<br>San Francisco, CA 94105<br>(415) 744-6580 | Arizona, California,<br>Hawaii, Nevada |

**X—Seattle**
Regional Director
1111 Third Avenue, Room 925
Seattle, WA 98101-3212
(206) 442-5286

Alaska, Idaho,
Oregon, Washington

## Major Unions Offering Apprenticeships

Brotherhood of Railway Carmen
4929 Main Street
Kansas City, MO 64112
(816) 561-1112

Communications Workers of America
1925 K Street N.W.
Washington, DC 20006
(202) 434-1100

Internat'l Brotherhood of Electrical Workers
1125 15th Street N.W.
Washington, DC 20005
(202) 833-7000

International Brotherhood of Teamsters, Chauffeurs, Warehousemen, and Helpers
25 Louisiana Avenue N.W.
Washington, DC 20001
(202) 624-6800

Internat'l Ladies Garment Workers Union
1710 Broadway
New York, NY 10019
(212) 265-7000

International Longshoremen's Association
17 Battery Place, Room 1530
New York, NY 10004
(212) 425-1200

International Union of Hotel and Restaurant Employees
1219 28th Street N.W.
Washington, DC 20007
(202) 393-4373

Transport Workers Union of New York
80 West End Avenue, 6th Floor
New York, NY 10023
(212) 873-6000

United Food & Commercial Workers International Union
1775 K Street N.W.
Washington, DC 20006
(202) 223-3111

United Mine Workers of America
900 15th Street N.W.
Washington, DC 20005
(202) 842-7200

Utility Workers Union of America
815 16th Street N.W., Room 605
Washington, DC 20006
(202) 347-8102

## Internships

**Programs.** Internships are less formal in structure than apprenticeships, but they also combine work and learning components. Many internships involve students working for little or no pay in return for education or educational credit—but you do not *have* to be a student. The National Society for Internships and Experiential Education (NSIEE) lists these widely varying characteristics for internships:

- Part-time or full-time
- 1 month to 2 years
- Paid or unpaid
- Sponsored through an educational institution or arranged independently by a learner and a host organization
- Evaluated for academic credit or not credited
- For learners from high school age through senior citizens
- Varying learning goals (academic development, ethical development, citizenship development, career development, personal and social development)

**Pay-plus.** Many internships pay nothing, but those listed here provide at least a small stipend. If you are or want to be a student (no matter what your age), an internship can be a way to keep a career path open during your return to school—and it can also be a way to help finance that education (see Chapter 4 for details).

**Prerequisites.** Many (but not all) internships are designed for students, but since "students" can mean anyone of any age, plenty of internships are available for adults as well, especially but not exclusively with nonprofit and service organizations.

All the internships offered by the government, corporations, associations, and arts organizations listed in the following pages are open to career changers and older students as well as the young.

**Procedure.** If you're a student seeking credit, it's best to apply through your school. Otherwise, contact and apply directly to the programs you are interested in.

**Government Internships**

The federal government offers numerous internship opportunities—*many with full salary* and benefits. For information on internships with a particular agency, see the contact list in Chapter 7. Most government agencies require a college degree or some college, and the intern must be willing to relocate to the site of the agency for the internship.

Programs range from the prestigious two-year Presidential Management Intern program at the White House, open to graduate students only, to short-term jobs in congressional offices in Capitol Hill (contact your representative). There are *lots* of opportunities.

For example, the General Services Administration's one-year Management Intern Program consists of rotational assignments in several services and staff offices followed by permanent assignment. Training is available in accounting, architecture, auditing, computers, and engineering and is designed for college graduates with backgrounds in accounting, auditing, architecture, computer programming, or engineering.

GSA
18th and F Streets N.W.
Washington, DC 20405
(202) 501-1231

The Agency for International Development's International Development Internship program trains interns in Washington, D.C., for overseas assignments. Its target jobs include agricultural economist, capital development loan officer, education advisor, engineer, financial manager, health/nutrition officer, population officer, program officer, rural development assistant, and urban development/regional officer. AID seeks college graduates in agriculture, agricultural economics, public health, nutrition, population, education administration, economics, finance, business administration, accounting, civil engineering, rural sociology, or urban development/regional planning. Interns must have a foreign language proficiency or receive training after employment. (Preferred languages are Spanish and French, but others are considered.)

AID
320 21st Street N.W.
Washington, DC 20523
(202) 663-1451

Other federal programs worth looking into:

The Department of State offers several internships, including the Presidential Management Intern Program, Summer Internship Program, and the College Cooperative Education Program Office of Personnel Management.

1900 E Street N.W.
Washington, DC 20415
OPM General Information: (202) 606-2424

The Central Intelligence Agency

CIA
Box 1925
Washington, DC 20505
(703) 482-1100

National Aeronautics and Space Administration

NASA
Goddard Space Flight Center
Greenbelt, MD 20771
(202) 453-1000

The Department of Energy offers a Management Intern Program.

DOE
1000 Independence Avenue S.W.
Washington, DC 20585
(202) 586-8495

The Federal Bureau of Investigation offers various internships.

FBI
10th and Pennsylvania Avenue N.W.
Washington, DC 20535
(202) 324-3020

National Security Agency

NSA
Attn: M322 (AAP)
Fort George G. Meade, MD 20755-6000

The National Institutes of Health offers one-year management internships in nontechnical as well as technical fields.

NIH
Bethesda, MD 20014
(301) 496-4000

Social Security Administration

SSA
Division of Personnel
6401 Security Boulevard
Baltimore, MD 21235
(301) 965-1234

The Department of Housing and Urban Development

USD-HUD
Personnel Department
451 7th Street S.W.
Washington, DC 20410
(202) 708-1112

Management Analysis Center

MAC
Personnel Office
Massachusetts Avenue
Cambridge, MA 02140

U.S. Naval Weapons Center

Naval Weapons Center
Commander (Code 09201)
China Lake, CA 93555

In addition, the U.S. Army offers several types of internships; for example, the Army Material Command in Texarkana, Texas, offers training in communications and electronics engineering, and the Army Corps of Engineers offers a number of internships. For information contact the U.S. Army Civilian Personnel Office, (202) 697-0335.

To find out about interning at a federal agency of interest to you, see the contact list in Chapter 7.

**Corporate Internships**

Company-sponsored internships range from short-term stints during college break periods to elaborate long-term plans designed for anyone. Some examples:

Turner Communication (1 CNN Center, Atlanta, GA 30348)—owner and operator of the three top U.S. commercial cable networks, CNN, TBS, and TNT—offers recent grads as well as career changers with a college degree the opportunity to learn (at a moderate salary) video journalism firsthand. The popular program leads to a career ladder in either TV operations or editorial work.

Farrar, Straus & Giroux publishers (19 Union Square West, New York, NY 10003) has an all-year-round internship program which puts interns into all departments where they are needed, doing the work that is needed, to "learn a good deal about the company in particular and publishing in general." But they do not pay.

The Weyerhaeuser Company (Tacoma, WA 98401) offers paid summer internships, manufacturing internships, and professional intern programs to students *or* career changers with degrees.

Other companies offering internships are listed on the following pages.

Airwork Corp.
Municipal Airport
Milville, NJ 08332
(609) 825-6000

Alexander & Alexander Services Inc.
1211 Avenue of the Americas,
44th Floor
New York, NY 10036
(212) 840-8500

AMP Incorporated
470 Friendship Way
Harrisburg, PA 17105-3608
(717) 564-0100

AMS Consultants Inc.
655 Third Avenue
New York, NY 10017
(212) 867-1777

Amcast Industrial Corp.
P.O. 3931
South Dixie Drive
Dayton, OH 45401
(513) 298-5251

American Appraisal Associates
525 East Michigan Street
Milwaukee, WI 53202
(414) 271-7240

American Automobile Association
1000 AAA Drive
Lake Mary, FL 32746
(407) 444-7272

American General Finance Inc.
601 N.W. 2d Street
Evansville, IN 47708
(812) 424-8031

American General Life Insurance Co.
2727 Allen Parkway
Houston, TX 47708
(713) 522-1111

American Trading and Production Corp.
1 North Charles Street
Baltimore, MD 21201
(410) 347-7000

Amsouth Bancorporation
P.O. Box 11007
1900 5th Avenue
Birmingham, AL 35203
(205) 320-7151

ARA Leisure Services Inc.
1101 Market Street
ARA Tower
Philadelphia, PA 19107
(215) 238-3000

ARA Living Centers Inc.
15415 Katy Freeway, Suite 800
Houston, TX 77094
(713) 578-4600

Arkla Inc.
525 Milam
Shreveport, LA 71101-3539
(318) 429-2700

Atlantic Research Corp.
5390 Cherokee Avenue
Alexandria, VA 22312
(703) 642-4000

Atlantic Richfield Co.
515 South Flower Street
Los Angeles, CA 90071
(213) 486-3511

Austin Co.
3650 Mayfield Road
Cleveland, OH 44121
(216) 382-6600

Autoclave Engineers Inc.
2930 West 22d Street
Erie, PA 16506
(814) 838-2071

BASF Corp.
8 Campus Drive
Parsippany, NJ 07054
(201) 397-2700

BankAmerica Corp.
555 California Street
San Francisco, CA 94104
(415) 622-3456

Barnett Banks Inc.
50 North Laura Street
Jacksonville, FL 32202
(904) 791-7720

Barrett Paving Materials Inc.
5800 Cherry Hill Road
Ypsilanti, MI 48198
(313) 483-4775

Briggs Stratton Corp.
P.O. Box 702
Milwaukee, WI 53201
(414) 259-5333

Brigham Women's Hospital
75 Francis Street
Boston, MA 02115
(617) 732-5500

Burger King Corp.
P.O. Box 17777
Old Cutler Road
Miami, FL 33157
(305) 378-7011

Burlington Industries Inc.
1345 Avenue of the Americas
New York, NY 10105
(212) 621-3000

Burns and Roe Inc.
700 Kinderkamack Road
Oradell, NJ 07649
(201) 265-2000

Centerior Energy Corp.
6200 Oakfree Boulevard
Cleveland, OH 44131
(216) 447-3100

Charles Stark Draper Laboratories Inc.
555 Technology Square
Cambridge, MA 02139
(617) 258-1000

Children's World Learning Centers
573 Park Point Drive
Golden, CO 80401
(303) 526-1600

Chrysler Corporation
12000 Chrysler Drive
Highland Park, MI 48288-1919
(313) 956-5741

CIGNA Corp.
1601 Chestnut Street
Philadelphia, PA 19192
(215) 761-1000

Cincinnati Bell Telephone Co.
201 East 4th Street, Room M10
Cincinnati, OH 45202
(513) 397-9900

Circuit City Stores Inc.
9950 Maryland Drive
Richmond, VA 23233
(804) 527-4000

Citicorp
399 Park Avenue
New York, NY 10022
(212) 559-1000

Consumers Power Company
212 West Michigan Avenue
Jackson, MI 49201
(517) 788-0550

Contraves Goerz Corp.
610 Epsilon Drive
Pittsburgh, PA 15238
(412) 967-7700

DAKA International Inc.
3 Lakeside Office Park
Wakefield, MA 01880
(617) 246-2525

Days Inns of America Inc.
2751 Buford Highway N.E.
Atlanta, GA 30324
(404) 325-4000

Dayton Walther Corp.
2800 East River Road
Dayton, OH 45439
(513) 296-3113

Depository Trust Co., Inc.
55 Water Street
New York, NY 10041
(212) 898-1200

Dictaphone Corp.
3191 Broadbridge Avenue
Stratford, CT 06497
(203) 381-7000

Dobbs Houses Inc.
5100 Poplar Avenue
Memphis, TN 38137
(901) 766-3600

Eastman Kodak Company
343 State Street
Rochester, NY 14650
(716) 724-4000

Ebasco Services Inc.
2 World Trade Center
New York, NY 10048
(212) 839-1000

Ecology and Environment Inc.
368 Pleasant View Drive
Lancaster, NY 14086
(716) 684-8060

EG&G Rotron Inc.
7 Hasbrouck Lane
Woodstock, NY 12498
(914) 679-2401

El Camino Resources Ltd.
8550 Balboa Boulevard
Northridge, CA 91325
(818) 895-6600

El Paso Electric Co.
303 North Oregon Street
El Paso, TX 79904
(915) 543-5711

Electronic Associates Inc.
185 Monmouth Park Highway
West Long Branch, NJ 07764
(908) 229-1100

Emerson Electric Co.
8000 West Florissant Avenue
St. Louis, MO 63136
(314) 553-2000

Emery Worldwide
3350 West Bayshore Road
Palo Alto, CA 94303
(415) 855-9100

Equitable Life Insurance Co. of Iowa
604 Locust Street
Des Moines, IA 50306
(515) 245-6911

Eurotherm Corp.
11485 Sunset Hills Road
Reston, VA 22090
(703) 471-4870

Farmland Industries Inc.
3315 North Oak
Kansas City, MO 64116
(816) 459-6000

Federal Home Loan Bank Board
1700 G Street
Washington, DC 20552
(202) 906-6000

Fisher Price Co.
636 Girard Avenue
East Aurora, NY 14052
(716) 687-3000

Ford Motor Company
American Road
Dearborn, MI 48121
(313) 322-3000

Imperial Hotels Corporation
1000 Wilson Boulevard
Arlington, VA 22209
(703) 524-4880

Intalco Aluminum Corp.
4050 Mountainview Road
Ferndale, WA 98248
(206) 384-7061

International Paper Co.
2 Manhattanville Road
Purchase, NY 10577
(914) 397-1500

James River Corp. of Virginia
120 Tredegar Street
Richmond, VA 23217
(804) 649-5411

Jefferson Hospital Association Inc.
1515 West 42d Avenue
Pine Bluff, AR 71603
(501) 541-7371

Jerricho Inc.
101 Jerricho Drive
Lexington, KY 40579
(606) 263-6000

Kenner Products
1014 Vine Street
Cincinnati, OH 45202
(513) 579-4000

Kohler Co.
444 Highland Drive
Kohler, WI 53044
(414) 457-4441

Levitz Furniture Corp.
6111 Broken Sound Parkway N.W.
Boca Raton, FL 33487
(407) 994-6006

Lincoln National Corp.
1300 South Clinton Street
Fort Wayne, IN 46802
(219) 455-2000

Liz Claiborne Inc.
1441 Broadway
New York, NY 10018
(212) 354-4900

Lockheed Sanders Inc.
95 Canal Street
Nashua, NH 03060
(603) 885-4321

Lufkin Industries Inc.
601 South Racquet
Lufkin, TX 75901
(409) 634-2211

Marshall & Ilsley Corp.
770 North Water Street
Milwaukee, WI 53202
(414) 765-7801

Marshall Field & Co.
111 North State Street
Chicago, IL 60602
(312) 781-1000

Marshalls Inc.
200 Brickstone Square
Andover, MA 01810
(508) 474-7000

National Engineering & Contracting Company
12608 Alameda Drive
Cleveland, OH 44136
(216) 238-3331

National Forge Co.
1 Front Street
Irvine, PA 16329
(814) 563-7522

National Railroad Passenger Corp. (AMTRAK)
50 Maine Avenue N.E.
Washington, DC 20002
(202) 484-7540

O'Connells Daniel Sons Inc.
480 Hampton Street
Holyoke, MA 01040
(413) 534-5667

Rosemount Inc.
12001 Technology Drive
Eden Prairie, MN 55344
(612) 941-5560

RR Donnelley & Sons Co.
2223 South Martin Luther King Drive
Chicago, IL 60616
(312) 326-8000

Ruan Transport Corp.
666 Grand Avenue
Des Moines, IA 50309
(515) 245-2500

Schlage Lock Co.
2401 Bay Shore Boulevard
San Francisco, CA 94134
(415) 467-1100

Seafirst Corp.
10500 NE 8th Street
Bellevue, WA 98154
(206) 358-5400

Season-All Industries Inc.
1480 Wayne Avenue
Indiana, PA 15701
(412) 349-4600

Soo Line Railroad Co.
105 South 5th Street
Minneapolis, MN 55402
(612) 347-8000

Steelcase Inc.
P.O. Box 1967
Grand Rapids, MI 49501
(616) 247-2710

Stone & Webster Engineering Corp.
P.O. Box 2325
Boston, MA 02107
(617) 589-5111

Thomas Somerville Co., Inc.
4900 6th Street N.E.
Washington, DC 20011
(202) 635-4321

Toro Co., Inc.
8111 Lyndale Avenue South
Bloomington, MN 55420
(612) 888-8801

Walgreen Company
200 Wilmot Road
Deerfield, IL 60015
(708) 940-2500

### Associations, Special-Interest Groups, and Foundations

Associations and other special-interest groups provide internships either with their organizations or for groups they serve. For example:

> The Environmental Careers Organization [68 Harrison Avenue, Boston, MA 02111, (617) 426-4375] arranges over 300 *salaried* 3- to 12-month internships in environmental, community development, and public affairs projects in the Northeast, West Coast, and Great Lakes regions. Salaries are high enough to live on; housing aid is available; and career counseling and some permanent placements are offered. Some college is preferred, but jobs are open to adult career changers of any age.

At the United Way of America [801 North Fairfax Street, Alexandria, VA 22314, (703) 836-7100] 24 salaried one-year programs are designed to develop skills in social service work and management. The minimum salary is $12,000, plus benefits and travel expenses. Regular employment follows. Internships begin in the Washington, D.C., area, but participants are later assigned to United Way agencies elsewhere. Interns must accept employment in one of many and varied United Way agencies after training. The programs are for college graduates, ages 21 to 30, and acceptance is competitive.

The International Foundation of Employee Benefits Plans [P.O. Box 69, Brookfield, WI 53008-0069, (414) 786-6700] *provides* college-student interns to corporate members of the group. Each intern works for two successive summers for the sponsoring employer and must attend nine full-day education seminars which are sponsored by the International Foundation. Some of the interns go on to full-time work with the sponsor company.

The Virginia Poverty Law Center, Inc. (9 West Main Street, Richmond, VA 23220), a resource center for legal aid and pro bono lawyers, has two or more unsalaried positions for work with attorneys or trainers. Duties include legal research, factual research, summarizing documents, and planning training. These internships are open to law students, career changers, and people reentering the work force, with an interest in law and a concern for low-income citizens.

Four broad areas that offer internships are the arts, communications, environmental action, and research. Some specific examples are given in the following list.

*Arts*

Arena Stage
6th and Maine Avenue S.W.
Washington, DC 20024
(202) 554-9066

Work with theater directors, designers, administrators at nonprofit residential repertory. 20 to 25 interns per year; 2–12 months, full-time; year-round openings.

New York State Theatre Institute
1400 Washington Avenue
Albany, NY 12205
(518) 442-5825

Work in technical theater production, arts management, performing, and education for performing arts/education center. 75 interns per year; 1 semester, full- or part-time; year-round openings.

North Carolina Arts Council
Department of Cultural Resources
Raleigh, NC 27601-2807
(919) 733-7897

Openings statewide at local arts councils in planning, fund raising, financial management, programming, publicity, marketing, promotion. 3 interns per year; 3 months, full-time, September–June.

Spoleto Festival USA
P.O. Box 15
Charleston, SC 29402
(803) 722-2764

Administrative and production positions for nonprofit visual and performing arts organization. 50 interns per year; full-time, May–June.

Wolf Trap Foundation for the Performing Arts
1624 Trap Road
Vienna, VA 22182
(703) 255-1939

Administrative and technical interns for nonprofit theater organization. 25 to 30 interns per year; 3 months: full-time summers, part-time fall and spring; year-round openings.

*Communications*

Alliance of Motion Picture and Television Producers
14144 Ventura Boulevard, Room 255
Sherman Oaks, CA 91423
(818) 995-3600

Positions as "second assistant directors"; help conduct business of set or location. 10 to 20 interns a year; program takes approximately 2 years, full-time; year-round openings.

Center for Investigative Reporting
530 Howard Street, 2d Floor
San Francisco, CA 94105
(415) 543-1200

Internships in Washington, D.C. and San Francisco: contribute to stories and research; participate in seminars on investigative techniques. 12 to 15 interns per year; 3 to 7 months part-time; openings January–June, June–December.

*Environmental Action*

Center for Science in the Public Interest
1875 Connecticut Avenue N.W., Room 300
Washington, DC 20004
(202) 332-9110

Background research, fact checking, and administrative work for national consumer organization. 20 interns per year; 10 weeks, full- part-time; year-round openings.

Community Environmental Council Inc.
930 Miramonte Drive
Santa Barbara, CA 93109
(805) 963-0583

Research, writing, program design, and implementation on new ways to solve environmental problems. 8 interns per year; 6 months, openings January–June and June–January.

Critical Mass Energy Project of Public Citizen
215 Pennsylvania Avenue S.E.
Washington, DC 20003
(202) 546-4996

Work to oppose nuclear power and promote safe energy. 1 to 10 interns per year; 10+ weeks, full-time; year-round openings.

National Audubon Society
950 Third Avenue
New York, NY 10022
(212) 822-3200

Positions around the country for environmental protection organization, in wildlife sanctuary research and maintenance or in government relations research and lobbying. 50 to 80 interns per year; 3 to 12 months, full- or part-time; year-round openings.

National Wildlife Federation
1400 16th Street N.W.
Washington, DC 20036
(202) 797-6819

Research, lobby, write for environmental organization in Washington, D.C. 12 interns per year; full-time, 6 months; year-round openings.

Sierra Club
408 C Street N.E.
Washington, DC 20002
(202) 547-1141

Research, monitor congressional hearings, develop issues background for conservation organization. 60 interns per year; 3 months, full-time; year-round openings.

*Research*

Essential Information
P.O. Box 19405
Washington, DC 20036
(202) 387-8030

Research and writing for public interest group. 6 to 8 interns per year; 9 weeks, full- and part-time; year-round openings.

Women's Sports Foundation
342 Madison Avenue, Room 728
New York, NY 10173
(212) 972-9170

Research, provide information on topics in women's sports. 12 interns per year, 3–12 months, full- or part-time; year-round openings.

Whatever your special interests, you can find (or create) an internship with large and small nonprofit organizations. And if you *are* "special," many opportunities are open *only* to minorities, women, or people with disabilities (see Chapter 9).

**Create Your Own Internship**

You needn't limit yourself to even the tens of thousands of established learning opportunities: you can create your own. You won't, in all likelihood, get paid for these self-initiated arrangements, but you'll get all the training you can manage, and you can set your own schedule to fit your paying work. For example, at the beginning of a sabbatical, an English teacher with a long-time interest in theater approached a small professional theater in his area and offered to help out in any capacity. For a year, he was able to do something new and to learn if he wanted to devote *all* his energies to theater work.

Small businesses are the fastest-growing enterprises in the country. They are likely to operate on tight staffs and budgets—and few are likely to have formal training programs. But because they need help, they're good candidates for training trades.

Even in large businesses or organizations, where you've been employed for a while, you can learn a new career on the job by approaching possible mentors in the aspects of the job you'd like to learn. In any case, keep in mind the four-point formula:

What do I want to do?

\+ What opportunities are available?

\+ What skills are demanded?

− What skills do I have?

= Career training needed to fill gap

To look for internship sources for the training you need, do your homework. Keep abreast of what's going on in your corporation locally in the fields you'd like to learn. Find out all you can about them. Associations are a good source of information and ideas, as are networks of personal contacts. Focus on a few businesses, arts organizations, or social service operations that seem likely to match your values and goals, and find out what they need. Then create a focused resume and send it with a cover letter explaining what you want to do for the organization, and why—and what you could contribute to its operation.

Don't be surprised if any of these potential "trainers"—whether arts administrators, small business owners, or social service providers—are a bit suspicious or reluctant to participate in your plan. Though most of us are flattered by interest in our work, and certainly willing to have help with hard projects, we aren't used to getting something for free—and we *do* look "gift horses" in the mouth. You may have to sell yourself as hard as you would in a competitive job interview. But it's worth it if you can learn for free a job now that you'd like to do for pay later.

## Find Out More

For more (*lots* more) information about interning, contact these resources:

Council on International Educational Exchange (CIEE)
205 East 42d Street
New York, NY 10022
(212) 661-1414

Specializes in international internship programs.

Dynamy, Learning Through Internships
57 Cedar Street
Worcester, MA 01609
(508) 755-2571

An educational program which seeks to develop committed, knowledgeable, self-confident, and civically active adults.

Energize Associates
5450 Wissahicken Avenue
Philadelphia PA 19144
(215) 438-8342

Specializes in social service and volunteer groups.

The Foundation Center
79 5th Avenue
New York, NY 10003
(212) 620-4230

Source for *all* activities, including internships, funded by foundations.

National Endowment for the Arts
1100 Pennsylvania Avenue N.W.
Washington, D.C. 20506

For formal museum training programs, internships, and apprenticeships, call (202) 682-5442. For jazz study apprenticeships for aspiring performers and professionals, call (202) 682-5445.

National Society for Internships and Experiential Education
3509 Haworth Drive, Suite 207
Raleigh, NC 27609

Nonprofit organization "to support the use of internships and other forms of experiential learning as an integral part of education. NSIEE is concerned with the integration of academic, career, and personal development of learners through internships and experiential education programs in all their forms." Publishes directories of internship opportunities.

## Making Decisions

Here's how to get the internship or apprenticeship that best serves your training needs.

Pick a list of possibilities from the lists here and from directories provided by clearinghouses and agencies.

Write or phone them for information and ask for an application.

You may want to ask about restrictions on the internship you're inquiring about—age, or special qualifications (minority, or disabled status). Be prepared to counter potential discouragements, such as "it's only for students" by saying "I'm a lifelong learner" or by politely *insisting* on having an application sent.

When applying, remember that these positions are extremely competitive, so present yourself well. And remember that the sponsoring organization cares less about the fact that you are now a corporate vice president with responsibility for a multimillion dollar budget, or the mother of five, than about what you can bring to the specific organization or to the profession in general.

Whether it's an internship or an apprenticeship, formal or informal, that best fits your career training needs, acceptance into the position requires application with a special emphasis. In addition to completing the application according to instructions and submitting it by any deadline date (basic but important!), you'll need to sell yourself by showing not only what you want to gain from the arrangement, but what you can *bring* to it—and why the goal matters to you.

Beware of organizations that say they have internships but are really looking for low-paid drudges. It's a good idea to come to a formal agreement about the *terms* of apprenticeship or internships. Be sure you're clear about:

Pay

Duties

Length of time

Learning and/or credits

Possibility of regular employment following the program

A good way to find out about the possibility of post-training employment is to ask, "How many interns are hired full time?"

You may also want to know about:

Qualifications of supervisor

Any tests to be passed

Form of evaluation

Apprenticeships are likely to follow guidelines established by the state or by the professional or trades organizations concerned, so it's wise for you to get a copy of those guidelines. Internships are more open-ended, but it's a good idea, in accepting the position, to do so in writing, covering all the above points as your understanding of the relationship.

You'll want to gain as much as possible from your on-the-job training experiences, so before you sign on, check that the possibilities match your answers to the career-change checklist.

What do I want or need to learn? (What can I learn?)

Where will it get me? (Will it get me where I want to be?)

Is it suited to me? (Why is it suited to me?)

How much can I manage? (Can I devote full time? Can I devote part-time? Can I live on the stipend or half-pay? Can I afford it?)

If, during the program, you find you are not gaining all that you expected or that was promised, talk to your supervisor.

Whichever type of on-the-job resource you use, when the program is complete, be sure to get an evaluation form or letterhead recommendation from your supervisor as the "credential" that will open career doors.

# 4
# Don't Skip School

## Preview

*Programs:* Nearly 300 colleges and universities offering special adult education programs; 1400 community colleges; 2000 accredited trade and technical schools; almost countless for-profit seminars providing career training; a huge variety of correspondence and "distance learning" institutions—they're all out there, offering training, degrees, certificates, or hands-on experience in anything and everything you could possibly want to learn.

*Pros and Cons:* You may be turned off by high-hype sells for "career training institutes," or convinced that all worthwhile education carries a high price tag. But the facts are that with a few guidelines, you can find educational courses that exactly suit your needs—and if there's any cost, deduct it or let someone else foot the bill. The only real drawbacks? Making the right choice and finding the time to study.

*Possibilities:* Since the possibilities are almost infinite, you'll find here descriptions of the *types* of adult education institutions, with guides to how to decide which type best suits your needs. You'll also find lists of associations, agencies, and other resources to contact for the providers that are nearest and most appropriate to you.

Forget the stereotypes about "going back to school": adult education comes in a lot of different packages. It's a big business and it's a buyer's market, so you'll have a lot to choose from—and it doesn't have to cost you a lot in time or money. Nor is school "just for kids." Lifelong learning is a necessity, and no matter how much or how little schooling you've had, no matter what your age, you'll feel right at home in the classrooms of today and tomorrow.

## A Few Facts

25 million American adults annually enroll in 50 million education courses—and during the past decade, this number has increased at a rate of 2.5 times the rate of population growth. The majority of these programs are job-related; this is not surprising, since for the first time in history the majority of U.S. jobs require more than a high school education. Most require some kind of specialized schooling, and advancement in many, as you may have learned, require postgraduate study.

So you're never "too old": In fact, 1 in 4 undergraduate college students is over 30 years old, and there are many more adult learners and trainees in noncollege classrooms than there are students in their late teens and early twenties. Similarly, there are many more nontraditional forms of post-high school education than ever before. And even lofty institutions of formal higher education have adapted their schedules and curricula to meet the needs of the adult, part-time students who now form the *majority* on their campuses.

This combination of demand and supply means that at this stage of your life and career, you have even more choices than when you were of "school age." You can choose your format, your schedule, your coursework, and your classmates.

## Some Factors to Consider

Certificates...degrees...technical training...managerial seminars...corporate colleges...telecourses....If you choose an educational program as your optimum career training resource, you have a lot of options.

Don't assume that education means college or graduate school and all the time and effort those imply: *most* of the career paths of the next two decades will require some college education but not necessarily a degree. But don't assume that education *doesn't* mean college: formal higher education may be just what you need to develop or change your career. You have such a variety of possibilities, in fact, that you'll need to consider carefully the *type* of education you want to sign up for.

Here are the ways that working adults go back to school for degrees, diplomas, or certificates, often at little or no cost to themselves:

At any of the nearly 2000 colleges, universities, and community colleges, using funds from scholarships, grants, or employer tuition remission

At graduate schools, on your own or through cooperative programs provided by government and businesses

At "corporate colleges," where your way is paid and you get a salary too

At any of 2000 accredited trade and technical schools, using public or private grants

At seminars designed for your specific needs

At home—in front of your computer or TV set

And you can get that schooling at little or no cost, as you'll discover in these pages.

In researching the resources available and deciding which is best for you, keep your answers to the four-point formulas in mind. The following list gives an idea of the *scope* of courses from which you could choose.

Agricultural business and production

Agricultural sciences

Architecture and related programs

Biological sciences/life sciences

Business management and administrative services

Communications

Communications technologies

Computer and information sciences

Conservation and renewable natural resources

Construction trades

Education

English language and literature

Engineering

Engineering-related technologies

Ethnic, cultural, and area studies

Foreign languages and literatures

Health professions and related sciences

Home economics

Interdisciplinary and multidisciplinary studies

Law and legal studies

Liberal arts and sciences, general studies and humanities

Library science

Marketing and distribution

Marketing operations

Mathematics

Mechanics and repairers

Military technologies

Parks, recreation, leisure, and fitness studies

Personal and miscellaneous services

Philosophy and religion

Physical sciences

Precision production trades

Protective services

Psychology

Public administration and services

Science technologies

Social sciences and history

Theological studies and religious vocations

Transportation and materials moving workers

Visual and performing arts

Vocational home economics

## How to Find Educational Resources

You can join the 7 million other American adults who are attending college part-time working toward their undergraduate degree. Or you can work toward a graduate degree at one of the many schools that arrange class times to fit job schedules. Or, of course, you can attend any institution of higher education you're qualified for, since some 2000 colleges and community colleges offer adults-only programs, as listed below.

A plus factor of choosing a degree program is the prestige that accompanies a degree (if it's a degree you actually need). In addition, you're likely to meet a lot of other folks with whom you share common interests. So if a course of study wider in range than that demanded by your specific career needs is what you *want*, then it's indeed what you should go for.

The minuses include cost and time.

Though employer-sponsored tuition remission or veterans' benefits or special scholarships for adult students can cover most of the costs, you'll still need to consider the money factor. Do, however, keep in mind that job-related education costs are tax-deductible.

You'll need to find time in your schedule—either while you're working full- or part-time, or during a hiatus from work. But you needn't work toward an academic degree—whether or not you already have one. The schools listed below also offer career-specific diplomas or certificates, which can be impressive credentials for employers or potential employers.

## Academic Programs for Adults

Any institution of higher education will accept qualified adults as students. But if you're past "college age" or there has been a time gap since you were last in class, you may need some special considerations, and you may get more from the experience if you're in a classroom with other adults, rather than with 18-year-olds, if only because your age and/or experience mean that you *learn* differently.

So here are lists of institutions that offer special programs for older students.

Adams State College
Alamosa, CO 81102

Alabama A&M University
Normal, AL 35762

American University
4400 Massachusetts Avenue N.W.
Washington, DC 20016

Armstrong State College
11935 Abercorn Street
Savannah, GA 31419

Appalachian State University
Boone, NC 28608

Arizona State University
Tempe, AZ 85721

Auburn University
Auburn, AL 36849

Augusta College
2500 Walton Way
Augusta, GA 30910

Ball State University
Muncie, IN 47306

Barry University
11300 N.E. 2d Avenue
Miami Shores, FL 33161

Baylor University
500 Speight Street
Waco, TX 76798

Bethune-Cookman College
640 2d Avenue
Daytona, FL 32114

Boise State University
1910 University Drive
Boise, ID 83725

Boston College
140 Commonwealth Avenue
Chestnut Hill, MA 02167

Bowling Green State University
Bowling Green, OH 43403

Bradley University
1501 W. Bradley Ave.
Peoria, IL 61625

Brigham Young University
Administration Building
Provo, UT 84602

Bryant College
450 Douglas Pike
Smithfield, RI 02912

California State University
400 Golden Shore Street
Long Beach, CA 90802

Carthage College
2001 Alford Drive
Kenosha, WI 53140

Central Michigan University
Mount Pleasant, MI 48859

Central Washington University
Ellensburg, WA 98926

Chapman College
333 North Glassell Street
Orange, CA 92666

Clarion University of Pennsylvania
836 Wood Street
Clarion, PA 16214

Clayton State College
5900 North Lee Street
Morrow, GA 30260

College of Charleston
66 George Street
Charleston, SC 29424

College of Saint Catherine
2004 Randolph Avenue
Saint Paul, MN 55105

Colorado State University
Fort Collins, CO 80401

Columbia College
10001 Roger Street
Columbia, MO 65216

Columbus College
Columbus, GA 31993

Concordia College of Saint Paul
275 Syndicate Street North
Saint Paul, MN 55104

Dartmouth College
Hanover, NH 03755

Delaware State College
1200 North Dupont Highway
Dover, DE 19901

Drexel University
32d and Chestnut Streets
Philadelphia, PA 19104

Duke University
Durham, NC 27706

East Carolina University
1000 East 5th Street
Greenville, NC 27858

East Stroudsburg University
East Stroudsburg, PA 18301

East Tennessee State University
Boundry Road
Johnson City, TN 37614

East Texas State University
East Texas Station
Commerce, TX 75428

Eastern Illinois University
Charleston, IL 61920

Eastern Kentucky University
521 Lancaster Avenue
Richmond, KY 40475

Eastern Michigan University
Ypsilanti, MI 48197

Eastern Montana College
1500 North 30th Street
Billings, MT 58201

Eastern New Mexico University
Portales, NM 88130

Eastern Oregon State College
1410 L Avenue
La Grande, OR 97850

Eastern Washington University
Cheney, WA 99004

Edward Waters College
1658 Kings Road
Jacksonville, FL 32209

Elmhurst College
190 Prospect Avenue
Elmhurst, IL 60126

Embry-Riddle Aeronautical University
600 South Clyde Morris Boulevard
Daytona Beach, FL 32114

Emporia State University
12th and Commercial Streets
Emporia, KS 66801

Fashion Institute of Technology
227 West 27th Street
New York, NY 10001

Ferris State University
901 South State Street
Big Rapids, MI 49307

Florida A&M University
Martin Luther King Jr. Boulevard
Tallahassee, FL 32307

Florida Atlantic University
500 N.W. 20th Street
Boca Raton, FL 33431

Florida International University
Tamiami Trail
Miami, FL 33199

Florida State University
600 West College Avenue
Tallahassee, FL 32306

Franklin and Marshall College
P.O. Box 3003
Lancaster, PA 17601

Franklin Pierce College
Dover Campus
7½ Somersworth Road
Dover, NH 03820

George Mason University
4400 University Drive
Fairfax, VA 22030

George Washington University
2121 I Street N.W.
Washington, DC 20052

Georgia State University
University Plaza
Atlanta, GA 30303

Governors State University
Governors Highway and University Parkway
University Park, IL 60466

Hamilton College
College Hill Road
Clinton, NY 13323

Harvard University
1350 Massachusetts Avenue
Cambridge, MA 02138

Howard University
2400 6th Street N.W.
Washington, DC 20059

Humboldt State University
Plaza Avenue
Arcata, CA 95521

Idaho State University
741 South 7th Street
Pocatello, ID 83209

Illinois State University
Normal, IL 61761

Indiana State University
217 North 6th Street
Terre Haute, IN 47809

Indiana University
813 East 3d Street
Bloomington, IN 47405

Indiana University of Pennsylvania
Pratt Hall, 216B
Indiana, PA 15705

Iowa State University
Ames, IA 50011

Johns Hopkins University
3400 North Charles Street
Baltimore, MD 21218

Kansas State University
Manhattan, KS 66506

Keene State College
229 Main Street
Keene, NH 03431

Kent State University
Kent, OH 44242

Lake Superior State University
1000 College Drive
Sault Sainte Marie, MI 49783

Lamar University
4400 Martin Luther King Parkway
Beaumont, TX 77710

Lincoln University
820 Chestnut Street
Jefferson City, MO 65101

Linfield College
900 South Baker Street
McMinnville, OR 97125

Louisiana State University
99 University Lakeshore Drive
Baton Rouge, LA 70803

Loyola College
4501 North Charles Street
Baltimore, MD 21210

Loyola University of Chicago
820 North Michigan Avenue
Chicago, IL 60611

Mary Baldwin College
Stauton, VA 24401

Mary Washington College
Fredericksburg, VA 22401

Mesa State College
P.O. Box 2647
Grand Junction, CO 81502

Metropolitan State College
P.O. Box 17362
Denver, CO 80217

Miami University
Hamilton Campus
1601 Peck Boulevard
Hamilton, OH 45011

Michigan State University
John A. Hanna Building
East Lansing, MI 48824

Mississippi State University
Starkville, MS 39762

Missouri Western State College
4525 Downs Drive
Saint Joseph, MO 64507

Morgan State University
Hillen Road and Cold Spring Lane
Baltimore, MD 21239

Murray State University
University Station
Murray, KY 42071

National University
University Park
San Diego, CA 94102

New Mexico State University
Las Cruces, NM 88003

New School of Social Research
66 West 12th Street
New York, NY 10011

New York University
50 West 4th Street
New York, NY 10012

North Carolina State University
2205 Hillsborough Street
Raleigh, NC 27695

North Dakota State University
1301 12th Avenue North
Fargo, ND 58105

North Park College and Seminary
3225 West Foster Avenue
Chicago, IL 60625

Northeastern University
360 Huntington Avenue
Boston, MA 02115

Northern Michigan University
Marquette, MI 49855

Northern State University
12th Avenue and J Street South
Aberdeen, SD 57401

Nova University
3301 College Avenue
Fort Lauderdale, FL 33314

Ohio State University
1800 Cannon Drive
Columbus, OH 43210

Ohio University
Athens, OH 45701

Oklahoma State University
Stillwater, OK 74078

Oakland University
Walton and Squirrel Streets
Rochester, MI 48309

Old Dominion University
Hampton Boulevard
Norfolk, VA 23529

Pacific Lutheran University
Tacoma, WA 98447

Pennsylvania State University
University Park, PA 16802

Pittsburg State University
1701 South Broadway Street
Pittsburg, KS 66762

Portland State University
724 S.W. Harrison Street
Portland, OR 97231

Purdue University
West Lafayette, IN 49707

Regis College
West 50th Avenue and Lowell
Boulevard
Denver, CO 80221

Rhode Island College
600 Mt. Pleasant Avenue
Providence, RI 02908

Rollins College
1000 Holt Avenue
Winter Park, FL 32789

Roosevelt University
430 South Michigan Avenue
Chicago, IL 60605

Rutgers University
Van Nest Hall
New Brunswick, NJ 08903

Saint Joseph's College
Windham, ME 04062

Saint Louis University
221 North Grand Boulevard
Saint Louis, MO 63103

Saint Xavier College
3700 West 103 Street
Chicago, IL 60655

Seton Hall University
400 South Orange Avenue
South Orange, NJ 07079

South Dakota State University
Brookings, SD 57007

Southern Illinois University
Carbondale, IL 62901

Southern Methodist University
6425 Boaz Lane
Dallas, TX 75275

Southern Oregon State College
1250 Siskiyou Boulevard
Ashland, OR 97320

Southwest State University
North Highway 23
Marshall, MN 56258

Southwest Texas State University
San Marcos, TX 78666

Stetson University
421 North Woodland Boulevard
De Land, FL 32720

Stockton State College
Jimmy Leeds Road
Pomona, NJ 08240

Stonehill College
320 Washington Street
North Easton, MA 02357

State University of New York (SUNY)
350 Broadway
Albany, NY 12246

Syracuse University
Syracuse, NY 13244

Temple University
Broad and Montgomery Avenues
Philadelphia, PA 19122

Tennessee State University and
Community College System
3500 John A. Merritt Boulevard
Nashville, TN 37209

Texas A&M University
College Station, TX 77843

Texas Christian University
2800 University Drive
Fort Worth, TX 76129

Texas Tech University
Broadway and University
Lubbock, TX 79409

Thomas A. Edison State College
101 West State Street
Trenton, NJ 08625

Towson State University
York Road
Towson, MD 21204

Transylvania University
300 North Broadway Street
Lexington, KY 40508

Trinity University
715 Stadium Drive
San Antonio, TX 78212

Troy State University
Troy, AL 36082

Tufts University
Medford, MA 02155

Union College
Schenectady, NY 12308

University of Oklahoma
660 Parrington Oval
Norman, OK 73069

University of Alabama
401 Queen City Avenue
Tuscaloosa, AL 35401

University of Alaska
Anchorage, AK 99508

University of Arizona
Tucson, AZ 85721

University of Arkansas
433 North Garland Avenue
Fayetteville, AR 72701

University of California—Berkeley
120 Sproul Hall
Berkeley, CA 94720

University of California—Los Angeles
405 Hilgard Avenue
Los Angeles, CA 90024

University of Chicago
5801 South Ellis Avenue
Chicago, IL 60637

University of Cincinnati
2624 Clifton Avenue
Cincinnati, OH 45221

University of Connecticut
Admissions Building
Storrs, CT 06269

University of Dayton
300 College Park Avenue
Dayton, OH 45469

University of Florida
Gainesville, FL 32611

University of Georgia
114 Academic Building
Athens, GA 30602

University of Hartford
200 Bloomfield Avenue
West Hartford, CT 06117

University of Hawaii
Hilo Campus
Manoa Campus
2444 Dole Street
Honolulu, HI 96822

University of Houston
4800 Calhoun Road
University Park
Houston, TX 77044

University of Illinois—Urbana-Champaign
506 South Wright Street
Urbana, IL 61801

University of Iowa
Iowa City, IA 52242

University of Kansas
Lawrence, KS 66045

University of Kentucky
Lexington, KY 40506

University of Maine
Chadborne Hall
Orono, ME 04469

University of Maryland
3300 Metzerott Road
Adelphi, MD 20783

University of Massachusetts
Goodell Building
Amherst, MA 01003

University of Michigan
503 Thompson Avenue
Ann Arbor, MI 48109

University of Minnesota
Minneapolis, MN 55455

University of Mississippi
Library Loop
University, MS 38677

University of Missouri
Jesse Hall, Room 320
Columbia, MO 65211

University of Montana
Missoula, MT 58112

University of Nebraska—Omaha
60th and Dodge Streets
Omaha, NE 68182

University of Nebraska—Lincoln
501 North 14th Street
Lincoln, NE 68583

University of Nevada—Reno
9th Virginia Street North
Reno, NV 89557

University of Nevada—Las Vegas
4505 South Maryland Parkway
Las Vegas, NV 89154

University of New Hampshire
Durham, NH 03824

University of New Haven
300 Orange Avenue
West Haven, CT 06516

University of New Mexico
Scholes Hall, Room 160
Albuquerque, NM 87131

University of New Orleans
Lake Front
New Orleans, LA 70148

University of North Carolina—Asheville
1 University Heights
Asheville, NC 28804

University of North Dakota
University Station
Grand Forks, ND 58202

University of Notre Dame
Notre Dame, IN 46556

University of Pennsylvania
Millersville, PA 17551

University of Pittsburgh
4200 5th Avenue
Pittsburgh, PA 15260

University of Rhode Island
Kingston, RI 02881

University of Saint Thomas
2115 Summit Avenue
Saint Paul, MN 55105

University of South Carolina
Columbia, SC 29208

University of South Dakota
414 East Clark Street
Vermillion, SD 57069

University of Southern Indiana
8600 University Boulevard
Evansville, IN 47712

University of Southern Mississippi
Hardy Street
Hattiesburg, MS 39406

University of Tennessee
Student Service Building, Room 305
Knoxville, TN 37996

University of Texas—Arlington
800 South Cooper Street
Arlington, TX 76019

University of Tulsa
600 South College Avenue
Tulsa, OK 74104

University of the District of Columbia
4200 Connecticut Avenue N.W.
Washington, DC 20017

University of Utah State College
1340 E. 200 South
Salt Lake City, UT 84102

University of Vermont
85 Prospect Street
Burlington, VT 05405

University of Virginia
Miller Hall
McCormick Road
Charlottesville, VA 22906

University of Washington
Administrative Offices AH-30
Seattle, WA 98125

University of Wisconsin
1220 Linden Drive
Madison, WI 53706

University of Delaware
Hullian Hall
Newark, DE 19716

University of Southern California
University Park
Los Angeles, CA 90089

Utah State University
Logan, UT 84322

Virginia Commonwealth University
910 West Franklin Street
Richmond, VA 23284

Virginia Polytechnic Institute and State University
Blacksburg, VA 24061

Virginia State University
Petersburg, VA 23803

Washington State University
Pullman, WA 99164

Wayne State University
5980 Cass Avenue
Detroit, MI 48202

West Virginia University
Morgantown, WV 26506

Western Montana College
710 South Atlantic Street
Dillon, MT 58725

Western Carolina University
Cullowhee, NC 28723

Western Illinois University
900 West Adams Street
Macomb, IL 61455

Western Oregon State College
345 Monmouth Avenue North
Monmouth, OR 97301

Western State College of Colorado
College Heights
Gunnison, CO 81231

Wheeling Jesuit College
316 Washington Avenue
Wheeling, WV 26003

Your local community college is also specially geared to working adult students—and costs may be lower than at a private school. There are over 1000 community colleges around the country: if your county doesn't have one, probably the neighboring county does. In addition, many thousands more localities have programs offering free or nearly free educational programs for adults. For a complete listing, contact:

Adult and Continuing Education Network
1550 Hayes Drive
Manhattan, KS 66502
(913) 539-5376

At even less cost, you can attend class at a local public school: many school systems offer evening classes for adults. The curriculum may be limited, but it's worth checking out. Call the school system's headquarters—or contact your local Occupational Information Coordinating Committee (OICC). You'll find details on OICC's services in Chapter 7: they can provide a list of schools and colleges of *all* types in your area.

## Trade and Technical Schools

There are some 2000 accredited trade and technical schools in the country, teaching skills in over 120 occupations, from accounting to X-ray technology. Don't make the mistake of lumping all of these institutions together with the type of "institutes" hyped on late-night or mid-day

TV. Instead, these schools can give you the specialized skills you may need to point your career in a specific direction—in a short-term, hands-on format, at a cost that should be considerably lower than that of a full-fledged college. Another plus is that you can find out fairly quickly if you really like the skill they're teaching you.

On the con side: You'll need to choose carefully. Many trade schools promise much more than they deliver—and they may talk you into a program that's unsuitable, often because of arrangements that allow them to receive federal funds according to the number of their enrollees. So beware of any that overpromise or pressure you to enroll. Get a registration agreement in writing that includes full disclosure of costs. Ask to talk with graduates about job placement successes. Ask to see their accreditation certificate. And if you have any doubts (or even if you don't), check with one of these two accrediting organizations:

The Career College Association
750 First Street, N.E.
Washington, DC 20007
(202) 336-6700

Accreditation Council, Continuing Education and Training (ACCET)
600 East Main Street
Richmond, VA 23219
(800) 648-6742

Those same organizations will send you, at very low cost, a list of their member schools. You'll find that you can study any of these skills:

| Skill | Terms, weeks |
|---|---|
| Accounting | 24–30 |
| Actor | 150 |
| Air-conditioning/refrigeration technician | 12–73 |
| Animal trainer | 3–6 |
| Appliance repairer | 12–72 |
| Architectural engineering technician | 60–100 |
| Artist, commercial | 52–136 |
| Artist, fine | 104–152 |
| Auto body repairer | 26–52 |
| Automotive technician | 14–50 |
| Aviation maintenance technician | 33–84 |
| Bank teller | 32 |
| Barber/hairstylist | 32–52 |
| Bartender | 2 |
| Blueprint reader | 3–40 |
| Boat design | 42–84 |
| Brickmason | 102 |
| Broadcaster | 13–48 |
| Broadcasting technician | 10–92 |
| Building maintenance technician | 52–60 |
| Cabinetmaker | 60 |
| Cardiac technician | 12–48 |
| Carpenter | 102 |
| Chiropractic assistant | 28–32 |
| Civil engineering technician | 18–104 |

| | |
|---|---|
| Computer-aided drafting | 52 |
| Computer graphics | 10–12 |
| Computer operator | 24–32 |
| Computer programmer | 26–208 |
| Computer service technician | 30–120 |
| Construction technologist | 32–104 |
| Cosmetologist | 52 |
| Culinary arts specialist | 26–52 |
| Data entry specialist | 26–52 |
| Data processor | 21–100 |
| Dealer | 4–16 |
| Dental assistant | 12–50 |
| Dental laboratory technician | 26–72 |
| Desktop publishing | 10–24 |
| Diesel mechanic | 10–48 |
| Dietetic technician | 13–52 |
| Diver | 8–15 |
| Drafter | 17–88 |
| Dressmaker and designer | 3–88 |
| ECG technician | 12–16 |
| Electrician | 21–104 |
| Electrologist | 12 |
| Electronics technician | 24–108 |
| Emergency medical technician | 28–34 |
| Engraver | 12 |
| Equestrian trainer | 8 |
| Fashion designer | 33–96 |
| Fashion illustrator | 52–136 |
| Fashion merchandiser | 34–72 |
| Flower arranger | 10 |
| Food service specialist | 52 |
| Gemologist | 26 |
| Graphic designer | 12–30 |
| Gunsmith | 69 |
| Heating mechanic | 12–24 |
| Heavy equipment operator | 3–10 |
| Horsemanship specialist | 8 |
| Horticulturist | 40 |
| Hotel-motel manager | 15–16 |
| Illustrator | 136 |
| Industrial design technology | 88 |
| Instrumentation specialist | 78–80 |
| Interior designer | 64–108 |
| Jewelry designer | 12–40 |
| Legal assistant/paralegal | 24–52 |
| Legal secretary | 16–72 |
| Locksmith | 10 |
| Loss prevention/security officer | 16 |
| Machinist | 14–102 |
| Makeup artist | 8–52 |
| Massage therapist | 52 |
| Mechanical engineering technician | 64–108 |
| Medical administrative assistant | 22–30 |
| Medical assistant | 12–48 |
| Medical/dental receptionist | 16–27 |

| | |
|---|---|
| Medical lab technician | 48–72 |
| Medical office manager | 14–28 |
| Medical secretary | 52 |
| Motion pictures/television/video production | 12–150 |
| Motorcycle mechanic | 12–33 |
| Musical instrument maker/repairer | 16 |
| Nanny | 10–18 |
| Nurse's aide | 10–49 |
| Office machine repairer | 15–50 |
| Optometric assistant | 24 |
| Painter | 102 |
| Paperhanger | 10 |
| Pet groomer | 10–16 |
| Pharmacy technician | 20–32 |
| Phlebotomy technician | 12–25 |
| Photographer | 12–150 |
| Physical therapy aide | 38 |
| Pilot, commercial | 12–69 |
| Plumber | 26 |
| Printer | 24–72 |
| Programmer analyst | 34–208 |
| Psychiatric assistant | 32 |
| Real estate agent | 6 |
| Receptionist | 12–24 |
| Recording specialist | 52 |
| Respiratory therapist | 26–52 |
| Retailer | 36–45 |
| Seaman/marine technician | 16 |
| Secretary/transcriptionist | 24–38 |
| Shorthand reporter | 104 |
| Skin care specialist | 26 |
| Surgical technician | 52 |
| Surveyor | 15–72 |
| Tailor | 5–60 |
| Taxidermist | 15 |
| Theater production specialist | 60 |
| Tool and die designer | 28–108 |
| Travel personnel specialist | 6–34 |
| Truck driver | 1–8 |
| Upholsterer | 10–26 |
| Veterinarian assistant | 28–72 |
| Vocational nurse | 48 |
| Watchmaker and repairer | 52 |
| Welder | 2–72 |
| X-ray technician | 100 |

You can learn similar skills, for free, at the vocational schools of your community's public school system: 14 million people do each year—many of them adults. In fact, with the workplace demand for specialized skills beyond the high school level, vocational schools of all sorts are making a comeback. Many are now called "career colleges," and their offerings can be quite sophisticated. (The Career College Association was, until recently, the National Association of Trade and Technical Schools. It merged with an independent college association.) Many corporations are becoming involved with the schools in their communities, both to improve the quality of the schools and to train their own workers. Is your company so involved? If so, you could get the skills training you seek at no cost, and on salary.

### Professional Seminars

Professional seminars are also a way to learn a specific skill in a short-term format. But the costs are likely to be steep—and there's no accreditation system for these profit-making enterprises. The fashionable topics for most of these "high power" 1990s workshops involve sales, self-marketing, self-presentation, and communications of all sorts. Most are very expensive—so unless you've heard raves from people you trust about an in-person career seminar (and until you've talked with the sponsor's other clients), you're probably better off finding a program on a similar topic offered by a college or other established institution.

See Chapter 8 to learn what associations have to offer along these lines. Many professional seminars that could have value for you are offered at reasonable cost through professional and trade associations—or for *free,* through your employer.

### At Home

Correspondence schools will still teach you skills you need, by mail, at a distance. But these days "distance learning" encompasses a wide range of high-tech educational delivery systems, via video, telecommunications, and computer. From the right institution, and with the right equipment, in fact, you can earn a complete college degree without ever leaving home.

Though costs aren't necessarily low (see if your employer or other funding source will help foot the bill for this kind of education), it can be a great convenience if your schedule isn't flexible enough to fit in class attendance or if you live far away from the institution offering the programs you want.

Here's a list of regular, accredited academic institutions that offer distance learning of all types in a variety of subject matter:

#### Colleges and Universities Offering Distance Education

Adams State College
Office of Extension and Field Service
Alamosa, CO 81102

Ann Arundel Community College
Special Sessions, Extended Learning Division
101 College Parkway
Arnold, MD 21012

Appalachian State University
Instructional Service Center
155 Whitener Hall
Boone, NC 28608

Arizona State University
Correspondence Study Office
Off-Campus Academic Services
Farmer 404
Tempe, AZ 85287

Armstrong/Savannah State College
Center for Continuing Education
305 West Broad Street
Savannah, GA 31401

Auburn University
Off-Campus Instruction
202 Ramsay Hall
Auburn University, AL 36849

Augusta College
Continuing Education
2500 Walton Way
Augusta, GA 30910

Ball State University
School of Continuing Education
Carmichael Hall
Muncie, IN 47306

Boise State University
Continuing Education
1910 University Drive
Boise, ID 83725

Bowling Green State University
Off-Campus Program
Continuing Education
Bowling Green, OH 43403

Brigham Young University
Independent Study
206 Harmon
Provo, UT 84602

California State University, Chico
The Center for Regional and Continuing Education
Chico, CA 95929-0250

California State University, Los Angeles
ITFS Extension Center
Continuing Education
5151 State University Drive
Los Angeles, CA 90032

Central Michigan University
Continuing Education and Services
Independent Study
Rowe Hall 125
Mt. Pleasant, MI 48859

Colorado State University
Division of Continuing Education
Fort Collins, CO 80523

East Tennessee State University
Office of Academic Program Development
Box 23, Room 980A
Johnson City, TN 37614

Eastern Kentucky University
Division of Extended Programs
Coats Box 27-A
Richmond, KY 40475

Eastern Michigan University
Division of Continuing Education
Ypsilanti, MI 48197

Eastern Oregon State College
Continuing Education and Regional Programs
8th and K Avenues
La Grande, OR 97850

Embry-Riddle Aeronautical University
Department of Independent Studies
Daytona, FL 32014

Florida State University Center for Professional Development and Public Service
Tallahassee, FL 32306

George Mason University
Division of Continuing Education
4400 University Drive
Fairfax, VA 22030

George Washington University
GW Television Station
801 22d Street N.W.
Suite T-306
Washington, DC 20052

Governors State University
Office of Extended Learning
University Parkway
University Park, IL 60466

Home Study International
6940 Carroll Avenue
Takoma Park, MD 20912

Indiana State University
Independent Study
Alumni Center 124
Terre Haute, IN 47809

Indiana University
Division of Extended Studies
Owen Hall 001
Bloomington, IN 47405

Iowa Lakes Community College
Television Center
300 South 18 Street
Estherville, IA 51334

Iowa State University
Office of Continuing Education
102 Scheman Building
Ames, IA 50011

Johnson County Community College
Television Operations EMC/TV
12345 Colle at Quivira
Overland Park, KS 66210

Kansas Regents Network
Division of Continuing
Education
312 Umberger Hall
Manhattan, KS 66506

Kansas State University
Academic Outreach
Division of Continuing Education
314 Umberger Hall
Manhattan, KS 66506

Louisiana State University
Office of Independent Study
Baton Rouge, LA 70803

Memorial University of Newfoundland
Division of Continuing Studies
G.A. Hickman Building
St. John's, Newfoundland, AIB3X8

Metropolitan State College
Extended Campus Credit Programs
1006 11th Street, Box 6
Denver, CO 80204

Mississippi State University
Independent Study Program by
Correspondence
P.O. Box 5247
Mississippi, MS 39762

Missouri Western State College
Continuing Education
4525 Downs Drive
St. Joseph, MO 64507

Murray State University
Independent Studies Program
Center of Continuing Education
Sparks Hall
Murray, KY 42071

New York Institute of Technology
American Open University
New York Institute of Technology,
Room 66
211 Carlton Avenue
Central Islip, NY 11722

North Carolina State University
Public Service
Box 7401
Raleigh, NC 27695-7401

North Dakota Division of Independent Studies
Box 5036
State University Station
Fargo, ND 58105

Northern Kentucky University
Credit Continuing Education and Experiential Learning
1401 Dixie Highway
Covington, KY 41011

Ohio University
Director of Independent Study
302 Tupper Hall
Athens, OH 45701

Oklahoma State University
Independent and Correspondence Study Department
001 Classroom Building
Stillwater, OK 74078

Old Dominion University
Center for Instructional Development
Hughes Hall 101
Norfolk, VA 23508

Oregon State System of Higher Education
Portland State University
P.O. Box 1491
Portland, OR 97207

Pennsylvania State University
Department of Independent Learning
128 Mitchell Building
P.O. Box 3207
University Park, PA 16802

Purdue University
Self-Directed Learning Programs
116 Stewart Center
West Lafayette, IN 47907

Radford University
Continuing Education Office
P.O. Box 5814
Radford, VA 24142

Rochester Institute of Technology
Instructional Media Services
Electronic Learning Systems
One Lomb Memorial Drive
Rochester, NY 14623-0887

Roosevelt University
College of Continuing Education
External Studies Program
430 South Michigan Avenue, Room 124
Chicago, IL 60605

Saint Joseph's College
External Degree Program
White's Bridge Road
North Windham, ME 04062

Savannah State College
Coastal Georgia Center for Continuing Education
Correspondence Study
P.O. Box 20436
Savannah, GA 31404

Southeastern College of Assemblies
Independent Study by Correspondence
1000 Longfellow Boulevard
Lakeland, FL 33801

Southern Illinois University at Carbondale
Division of Continuing Education
Individualized Learning Program
Washington Square C
Carbondale, IL 62901

Southwest Texas State University
Correspondence and Extension Studies
118 Medina Hall
San Marcos, TX 78666

Temple University
Office of Television Services
632 Gladfelter Hall
Philadelphia, PA 19122

Texas Tech University
Independent Study by Correspondence
Division of Continuing Education
P.O. Box 4110
Lubbock, TX 79409

Thomas A. Edison State College
Center for Learning Through Telecommunications
101 West State Street, CN 545
Trenton, NJ 08625

University of Alabama
Independent Study Division
College of Continuing Studies
P.O. Box 870388
Tuscaloosa, AL 35487

University of Alaska
Center of Distance Education
Room 130, Red Building
Fairbanks, AK 99775-0900

University of Arizona
Correspondence/Independent Study
Babcock Building 1201
1717 East Speedway
Tucson, AZ 85719

University of Arkansas
Department of Independent Study
2 University Center
Center for Continuing Education
Fayetteville, AR 72701

University of California Extension
Student Services
Oakland, CA 94612

University of California—San Diego
Communications and Marketing
University Extension X-001
La Jolla, CA 92093

University of Cincinnati
Continuing Education
Mail Location 146
Cincinnati, OH 45221

University College of Medicine
Texas A&M
Biomedical Communications
College Station, TX 77843

University of Colorado at Boulder
Independent Study Program
Division of Continuing Education
Box 178, 1221 University
Boulder, CO 80309

University of Florida
Independent Study by Correspondence
Division of Continuing Education
Gainesville, FL 32611

University of Georgia
Georgia Center for Continuing Education
Division of Telecommunications and Media Services
Athens, GA 30602

University of Houston
Instructional Television
Houston, TX 77204

University of Idaho
Correspondence Study in Idaho
Continuing Education Building, Room 116
Moscow, ID 83843

University of Illinois
Guided Individual Study
302 East John Street, Room 1406
Champaign, IL 61820

University of Iowa
Guided Correspondence Study
Center for Credit Programs
116 International Center
Iowa City, IA 52242

University of Kansas
Independent Study
Division of Continuing Education
Lawrence, KS 66045

University of Kentucky
Independent Study Program
Room 1, Frazee Hall
Lexington, KY 40506

University of Louisville
Office of Continuing Studies
Instructional Communications Center
Strickler Hall West, 106
Louisville, KY 40292

University of Maryland
Instructional Telecommunications
University Boulevard at Adelphi Road
College Park, MD 20742

University of Massachusetts
Video Instructional Program
113 Marcus Hall
Amherst, MA 01003

University of Michigan
Independent Study
Extension Service
200 Hill Street
Ann Arbor, MI 48104

University of Minnesota
Department of Independent Study
45 Westbrook Hall
77 Pleasant Street S.E.
Minneapolis, MN 55455

University of Mississippi
Department of Independent Study
Center for Public Service
E.F. Yerby Center, Room 2
University, MS 38677

University of Missouri—Columbia
Center for Independent Study
136 Clark Hall
Columbia, MO 65211

University of Missouri—St. Louis
Continuing Education
Video Instruction
355 Marillac, 8001 Natural Bridge Road
St. Louis, MO 63121

University of Nebraska—Lincoln
Independent Study Program
269 Nebraska Center for Continuing Education
33d and Holdege Streets
Lincoln, NE 68583-0900

University of Nevada—Reno
Independent Study by Correspondence
Division of Continuing Education
333 College Inn
Reno, NV 89557

University of New Brunswick
Extension and Summer Session
P.O. Box 4400
Fredericton, New Brunswick, E3B 5A3

University of New Mexico
Independent Study by Correspondence
1634 University Boulevard N.E.
Albuquerque, NM 87131

University of New Orleans
Division of Academic Extension and Public Service
New Orleans, LA 70148

University of North Carolina
Independent Study
Division of Extension and Continuing Education
Abernethy Hall, CB #3420
Chapel Hill, NC 27599

University of North Dakota
Department of Correspondence Study
Box 8277
University Station
Grand Forks, ND 58202

University of Northern Colorado
Independent Study
Division of Statewide Programs
Frasier Hall, Room 11
Greeley, CO 80639

University of Northern Iowa
Credit Programs
Guided Correspondence Study Programs
Cedar Falls, IA 50614

University of Notre Dame
Center for Continuing Education
P.O. Box 1008
Notre Dame, IN 46556

University of Oklahoma
Independent Study Department
1700 Asp Avenue, Room B-1
Norman, OK 73037

University of Rhode Island
College of Continuing Education
119 Promenade Street
Providence, RI 02908

University of South Carolina
Telecommunications Instruction and Independent Learning
915 Gregg Street
Columbia, SC 29208

University of South Dakota
Independent Study Division
414 East Clark
Vermillion, SD 57069

University of South Florida
Open University
4202 Fowler Avenue, SVC 116
Tampa, FL 33620

University of Southern Mississippi
Division of Lifelong Learning
Southern Station Box 5056
Hattiesburg, MS 39406

University System of New Hampshire
School for Lifelong Learning
Durham, NH 03824

University of Tennessee—Knoxville
Center of Extended Learning
420 Communications Building
Knoxville, TN 37996

University of Texas at Austin
Extension Instruction and Materials Center
P.O. Box 7700
Austin, TX 78713

University of Tulsa
Division of Continuing Education
600 South College Avenue
Tulsa, OK 74104

University of Utah
Division of Continuing Education
Extension Program
1152 Annex Building
Salt Lake, UT 84112

University of Virginia
Department of Telecommunications
P.O. Box 3697
Charlottesville, VA 22903

University of Washington
Distance Learning
5001 25th, NE GH 23
Seattle, WA 98195

University of Wisconsin—Extension
Independent Study
432 North Lake Street
Madison, WI 53706

University of Wisconsin—La Crosse
Office of Extended Education
1725 State Street
La Crosse, WI 54601

University of Wisconsin—Madison
Outreach Development
356 Bascom Hall
Madison, WI 53706

University of Wisconsin—Milwaukee
Division of Outreach and Continuing Education
P.O. Box 413
Milwaukee, WI 53201

University of Wisconsin—Stevens
Continuing Education and Outreach
Media-Based Programs
103 Main Building
Stevens Point, WI 54481

University of Wyoming
Correspondence Study Department
Box 3294, University Station
Laramie, WY 82071

Utah State University
Life Span Learning Programs
Computer Center Building, Room 201
Logan, UT 84322

Virginia Commonwealth University
Media Instruction
Box 2041
Richmond, VA 23284

Virginia Polytechnic Institute
State University
Learning Resources Center
135 Smyth Hall
Blacksburg, VA 24061

Washington State University
Graduate and Professional Programs
Extended University Services
202 Van Doren Hall
Pullman, WA 99164

Weber State College
Independent Study Program
Continuing Education
Odgen, UT 84408-4005

Webster University
Media Studies and Communications
470 East Lockwood
St. Louis, MO 63119

West Virginia University
Center for Extension and Continuing Education
812 Knapp Hall
Morgantown, WV 26506

Western Carolina University
WCU MicroNet
Cullowhee, NC 28723

Western Illinois University
Independent Study Program
School of Continuing Education
5 Horrabin Hall
Macomb, IL 61455

Western Michigan University
Self-Instructional Program
Ellsworth Hall, Room B-102
Kalamazoo, MI 49008

Western Oregon State College
Division of Continuing Education and Summer Programs
Monmouth, OR 97361

Western Washington University
Independent Study
Continuing Education
Old Main 400
Bellingham, WA 98225

Wichita State University
Division of Continuing Education
Academic Outreach
1845 Fairmount, Box 22
Wichita, KS 67208

## Employer-Paid Education

Nice work if you can get it—and nice education too. Why not get a job at a college, university, or other educational institution that offers programs you need? Most of these provide free or nearly free education at their own institutions to their employees. Of course, you'll have to get a job there first—but since these institutions need employees of all sorts, from security guards to financial administrators, you should be able to angle your experience to fit (it might even be worth your while to take a job below your qualifications). And, of course, you'll have to stay on the job as long as your education lasts. But why not look closely at the institutions in your area (or in the area where you want to live), find ones that offer programs of interest, target your resume, and apply.

## Business-Education Partnerships

| Institution | Sponsor | Degrees |
|---|---|---|
| American College (Bryn Mawr, Pa.) | National Association of Life Underwriters | M.S.: Financial services Management |
| Arthur D. Little Management Education Institute (Cambridge, Mass.) | Arthur D. Little, Inc. | M.S.: Administration Management |
| Boston Architectural Center School of Architecture (Boston, Mass.) | Boston Architectural Center | I. Bachelor of Architecture |
| DeVry Institutes of Technology (Chicago, Ill.) | Bell & Howell Company, DeVry, Inc. | B.A. and A.A.S.: ▪ Electronics engineering technology ▪ Computer information systems |
| G.M.I. Engineering and Management Institute (Flint, Mich.) | General Motors Corporation | Bachelor of: ▪ Mechanical engineering ▪ Industrial engineering ▪ Electrical engineering ▪ Industrial management Master of manufacturing management |
| McDonald's Management Institute (Oak Brook, Ill.) | McDonald's Corporation Hamburger University | A.A.S.: Business management |
| National Technological University (Central office, Fort Collins, Col.) | Major business corporations, U.S. government, and Association of Mechanical, Computer, and Electrical Engineers | M.S.: Computer engineering Engineering management Electrical engineering Industrial engineering Mechanical engineering |
| Northrop University (Inglewood, Calif.) | Northrop Corporation | B.S. and M.S.: Engineering (aerospace electronics, etc.) Business administration M.S. Systems Logistics management and technology Masters in: ▪ Taxation ▪ Procurement Acquisition J.D. |

Another way to get a higher education at your employer's expense is to work for an employer that will foot the bill—whether at corporate colleges like those listed on the previous page, or through generous tuition remission that many employers offer. (There'll be more on those possibilities in the next chapter.)

## Find Out More

To find out more about going back to school, contact these sources for information and referral.

### General Information

American Association for Adult and Continuing Education
2101 Wilson Boulevard
Arlington, VA 22201
(703) 522-2234

Lists of noncredit lifelong learning programs, including list of occupational and professional certificate courses nationwide.

Association for Continuing Higher Education
18 Lincoln Avenue
Evansville, IN 47714
(812) 479-2472

List of some 300 colleges with adult programs.

College Board Office of Adult Learning Services
45 Columbus Avenue
New York, NY 10023
(212) 713-8000

Variety of information on finding and making the most of adult education programs.

Council for Noncollegiate Continuing Education
530 East Main Street
Richmond, VA 23219
(804) 648-6742

Network and directory of adult training and education programs offered by trade associations, unions, and professional organizations.

The federal government's Educational Resource Information Clearinghouse (ERIC)
(800) 848-4815

The ERIC Clearinghouse on Adult, Career, and Vocational Education is an invaluable source of information.

National University Continuing Education Association (NUCEA)
1 Dupont Circle
Washington, DC 20036
(202) 659-3130

Guides to for-credit adult learning, including home study programs.

## Specialized Information

Electronic Networking Association
2744 Washington Street
Allentown, PA 18104
(215) 821-7777

An association of people primarily interested in computer conferencing.

International Teleconferencing Association (ITCA)
1299 Woodside Drive, Suite 101
McLean, VA 22102
(703) 556-6115

An association of people primarily interested in business television.

National University Teleconference Network (NUTN)
332 Student Union
Oklahoma State University
Stillwater, OK 74078
(405) 744-5191

A pioneering consortium of course providers.

*Teleconference*
Applied Business TeleCommunications
Box 5106
San Ramon, CA 94583
(415) 820-5563

Primarily aimed at business television.

United States Distance Learning Association (USDLA)
Box 5129
San Ramon, CA 94583
(415) 820-5845

Publishes a monthly newsletter and maintains a database of available programming.

## Making a Decision

In some sense, going back to school is easy: call or write for a catalog and application pack from the schools that seem most likely. Follow the application procedure, which may include collecting records of previous education and may include a test of some kind (which won't be as scary as the SAT), and sign on with the best school that accepts you.

But because it does represent an investment of time and money, you'll want to put a lot of care and thought into choosing the right school. The four-point formula applies:

What do I want to do?

+ What opportunities are available?

+ What skills are demanded?

− What skills do I have?

= Career training needed to fill gap

Here are some tips to help you decide what—if any—classroom training is needed to fill that gap:

Check the help-wanted ads in newspapers and trade or professional journals to see what education is called for in the jobs and careers you hope to enter.

Look through career directories at the library or bookstore for guidelines on educational levels required in your career choice.

Talk to librarians in the "careers" section of the library, and go through their resource files.

Contact the professional or trade associations that represent the occupations you're aiming at, to learn what training their members have—and also to get referrals to the training and education programs they recommend.

Finally, match your career-change checklist against the education resources you're considering. Take the checklist with you to interviews at the school or schools you're considering, as a reminder to get satisfactory answers for your questions:

What do I want or need to learn? (What can I learn?)

Where will it get me? (Will it get me where I want to be?) Is it suited to me? (Why is it suited to me?)

How much can I manage? (Can I devote full time? Can I devote part time? Can I live on the stipend or half pay?)

That last question may be especially important to be clear about. Before you sign up with any kind of college or training school, a professional adviser at the school should be available to suggest the best course of study for you.

No matter how much money or encouragement you get, don't sign on for more education than you need. Remember—they want you, and will do everything they can to make it possible for you to fill a seat in their classrooms and labs. They also want you to be able to stay—and a legitimate institution won't pressure you beyond your capacity.

## Finding Out About Financial Aid

Financial aid is available to adult students, but it may be limited, so know your resources. Following is a summary of generally available sources. However, if you are studying in a specific area, associations and individual government agencies may be able to provide funding. Be sure to ask for referrals from all organizations that may have a particular interest in promoting your field of study.

And the schools to which you're applying will, for sure, be happy to provide lists and suggestions.

You'll most likely be able to deduct any job-related educational expenses from your income tax. Check it out.

### Financial Aid Sources for Adult Students

*College Work-Study (CWS).* CWS funds provide campus-sponsored jobs to both undergraduate and graduate students to help them pay for college. The amount of CWS monies you may earn depends upon your financial need, the amount of funds available through your college, and the institution's hourly wage scale for your particular job.

*Employer-Provided Assistance.* An increasing number of employers provide educational assistance benefits to their employees. Generally, three out of four employees receiving employer-provided educational assistance take job-related courses, and work in mid- to lower-level corporate positions. However, there are employers who are willing to finance baccalaureate and graduate degree study for their employees. Employees will not be taxed for financial assistance received for job-related courses.

*Institutional Aid.* Many colleges and universities offer individual grant, scholarship, or other assistance programs that are available to part-time students. Some schools offer special benefits such as reduced tuition for senior citizens, tuition waiver, or reimbursement programs. You may qualify to receive assistance from a mix of federal and institutional aid programs.

*Pell Grants.* A Pell grant is an undergraduate, needs-based award that does not have to be repaid. Currently, such grants range between $200 and $2,300 per academic year, and are awarded to students regardless of attendance status. Pell grants are given to the students with the greatest financial need.

*Perkins Loans.* Perkins Loans are low interest, needs-based loans available to undergraduate and graduate students attending full-time or less than full-time. The size of a loan depends upon your financial need, the amount of funds available through your college or university, and the number of years of college you have completed when you apply. Loan maximums range from $4,500 for undergraduates who have completed fewer than two years of a program leading to a baccalaureate degree; to $9,000 for students who have completed two years or more of a baccalaureate program (the total includes any Perkins Loan amount borrowed during the first two years; and $18,000 for graduate-level or professional study (including any Perkins Loan amount borrowed for undergraduate study).

*PLUS and SLS Loans.* A PLUS loan is a market-rate, non-needs-based loan made by a bank, credit union, or savings and loan association to a student's parents to pay for undergraduate- or graduate-level study. PLUS loans cannot exceed $4,000 per year, and the total amount borrowed cannot exceed $20,000. Supplemental Loans for Students (SLS) are available only to graduate students or to financially independent undergraduate students. SLS loans also cannot exceed $4,000 per year, and the total amount borrowed cannot exceed $20,000, including any amounts previously borrowed through the Stafford Loan program.

*SEOGs.* If you attend less than full-time, you may be eligible to receive a Supplemental Educational Opportunity Grant (SEOG), a needs-based, nonrepayable award of up to $4,000 per year for undergraduate-level study.

*Stafford Loans.* A Stafford Loan is a low interest, needs-based loan made through a bank, credit union, or savings and loan association for undergraduate- or graduate-level study. Loans are available only to students attending on at least a half-time basis. Loan maximums range from $2,625 per year for the first two years of undergraduate study; to $4,000 per year for students who have completed at least two years of undergraduate study; and $7,500 per year for graduate-level or professional study.

*State Programs.* A growing number of states, such as Minnesota, Massachusetts, Michigan, New York, Vermont, and Connecticut, offer financial aid programs specifically designed for part-time students. For example, in 1984 New York initiated the Aid for Part-Time Study Program (APTS) to provide awards to state residents attending college at least half-time. The Minnesota Part-Time Student Grant program provides assistance to Minnesota residents attending less than half-time. In addition, most states offer programs for which less-than-full-time students are eligible.

*Veterans Programs.* If you are a veteran, reservist, or active member of the United States armed forces, contact your local veterans office or speak with your education services officer about military educational assistance benefits. The New GI Bill, made permanent by the United States Congress in 1987, provides extensive educational benefits to military personnel. Also, many states now offer additional educational assistance programs for veterans and military personnel who attend college on a part-time basis.

## Some Final Tips

1. *Know where you're going:* Evaluate and clarify your career and life goals. Courses for your personal satisfaction require a different approach from training aimed toward a job promotion. Professional counseling can help: Do your goals make sense? What level of education is actually required to achieve them?

2. *Be realistic:* A step-by-step approach to education suited to you is likely to be more satisfying than a sudden plunge into deep academia. Try one course before signing on for a long-term program. Or consider a noncredit transitional course designed to refresh rusty study skills. Then sit near the front of the classroom exchange phone numbers with a classmate (in case of absence), know how to reach your instructor, and build your vocabulary. Remember that studying takes time; there are no instantaneous results. That's also a good way to get a clear view of how much time, money, and motivation you have.

3. *Shop carefully:* Compare thoroughly the programs offered by the schools in your area. Is the school convenient to your home or your office? Are classes scheduled to fit your already busy day? What financial aid is available to you? Are courses designed for more "traditional" college students comfortable for you? What guidance and support are available for you?

4. *Count your pennies:* Financial aid for part-time students is available. Will your employer pay for some or all of your training? Veterans, union members, and others with special backgrounds or affiliations may be eligible for funding, too. Some educational expenses are tax-deductible. If your plans seem too costly, set a more limited goal, such as a diploma program, which may fit your needs and your budget.
5. *Build support:* It's important that your family, friends, and coworkers understand what your educational program means to you—and to them. They may need to bend to give you the time and space you need to achieve your goal. Make them partners in your success, rather than competitors for your energy.
6. *Speak up:* If the program, course, or instructor is not what you expected or won't help you reach your goals, talk with someone who can effect a change. As an adult, you bring something special to the classroom, so don't be timid about making your own contributions to the course.
7. *Get organized:* Create space and time for your studies. A corner of your home (office) devoted exclusively to your books, papers, and supplies will greatly help your concentration. Choose some time each day when you do nothing but schoolwork, and allow no interruptions (especially beware the telephone). If that's impossible at home, try going to work early or staying late; or stake out a carrel or study room in the library.
8. *Ask for help:* Don't expect to know it all. Take advantage of any counseling or remedial help your school makes available. Cultivate classmates who can benefit your studies. Discuss any confusing points with your instructor. And if you feel yourself floundering, seek an adviser's suggestions.
9. *Stretch your flexibility:* When you add school to your daily life, it's likely you will have to forgo housework, overtime, or socializing. Maybe someone else can help at home or work; maybe you'll need to let it go. If you've signed up for more courses than you can reasonably handle, reevaluate: Take fewer courses over a longer period so that you can comfortably cope with your life while you're pursuing your education.
10. *Don't worry about anxiety:* Virtually every adult who returns to school experiences anxiety or a wavering of self-confidence. This applies to the wildly successful business executive as well as to the young person who dropped out only recently. A return to school is a significant change—so it's no wonder that you may feel nervous. Remember that you're not alone. Just take a deep breath and give yourself credit.

# 5
# Tapping the Corporate Source

## Preview

*Programs:* Whether from lofty idealism or bottom-line practicality, increasing numbers of employers are training and retraining their employees. Managers can learn technical skills; technicians, managerial skills. Curriculums vary from word processing to foreign languages, from courses in interpersonal skills to graduate degrees.

*Pros and cons:* In most cases, you must be an employee of a training-oriented company to tap into this source—but you also receive pay and benefits. You may have to push a new or present employer to get the training *you* want, but that very willingness makes you look good. Is it worth changing jobs? Maybe. Though you'll have to stay on that job for a while, your skills portfolio can benefit in the long run.

*Possibilities:* In this chapter are a descriptive list of the most comprehensive corporate training programs, a listing of other likely prospects, a discussion of tuition remission for education, and suggestions on how to find and pursue corporate training that serves *your* purposes.

*Stop!* If you think this chapter is not for you—think again. "Most employees get ahead by leveraging what they learn in the current job into a new and better job," according to The American Society for Training and Development (ASTD). That leverage is even greater in a job where you can learn a *lot*—that is, a job with an employer who puts a priority on training.

## A Few Facts

U.S. corporations spend $210 billion on training annually. That's greater than the expenditures of all the nation's public school systems. Of that, $120 billion goes to what the government calls "informal" training, but *$80 billion* goes for formalized training and education programs. That equals the amount spent by the nation's 2000 colleges and universities and is four times the amount spent by individual adults on continuing education courses.

Though average corporate training expenditures represent only 1.4 percent of payroll costs, companies really committed to employee education spend a much higher percentage than that. And although on average, according to the U.S. Bureau of Labor Statistics, only 10 percent of employees benefit from formal training programs, training-oriented companies offer *all* their employees a wide scope of programs.

Still, you may assume that corporations are the last place to look for usable individual career training, especially if (1) you're looking to train your way out of a company or a job you don't like, (2) you've been laid off from a major corporation—perhaps one that boasts of its training program, or (3) you're familiar enough with the business pages to know that the layoffs and "downsizing" of the early nineties were not temporary cutbacks but permanent alterations in corporate structure. Well, never assume.

## Some Factors to Consider

Corporations are an outstanding resource for career training and, in fact, excellent free education of all sorts. The reasons for that? Business has discovered that it *must* provide training, in part because the worker pool is undertrained in general, but also because revolutionary technological *and* cultural changes demand training (see Chapter 1).

It is true that the downturn of the early nineties caused training cutbacks in some companies. A number of organizations once known for good training—among them CBS, Capital Cities/ABC, Federal Mogul, and General Motors—contacted for this chapter reported the dismantling of their programs. A few others brushed the question aside with comments like "Who needs to train, when we have thousands practically begging for work here?" But you don't want to work for a company with an attitude like that.

Where you likely *do* want to work is at the kind of company that is actually expanding and revamping its training program despite short-term economic concerns. And many are—including and sometimes especially those that have downsized. In what it called "the hidden upside in all the downsizing," the *New York Times* reported that "what staff is left gets more attention, greater freedom, and better training." Those companies are focused on increasing quality, productivity, and efficiency, so they have to teach their remaining employees how to achieve those ends.

In 1991, AT&T reported that, with 140,000 fewer employees, training was more extensive than in the past. This is only in part because of new technologies and a need for greater efficiency; it's also due to a new, sharper focus on the customer and on employees' personal and professional development—and to a restructuring that has put, according to one description, "the chairman of the board at the bottom of the organizational structure."

Even during downsizing phases, it should be noted, companies still hire—up to 20 percent of the work force of companies that cut back are new employees. But if you assume that it's tricky to find the right corporate training source, you're right. First you have to find one among the relative few whose training goes beyond basic, company-focused "orientation." Then, from those, you must single one out whose programs fit your training needs. Finally, of course, you have to land a job with the one that's best for you.

Adding to the difficulty is the fact that corporations (even ones that boast of their involvement with grade school education) don't promote their training programs to the public and potential employees. Even surveys conducted by major industry membership groups like the National Association of Business and the International Foundation of Employee Benefits Plans have gathered little information on training by corporations. Why? Because they don't want to promise this benefit? Because they, like too many individuals, are embarrassed to admit they need training? Or just because their educational offerings change frequently? Whatever the reasons, you won't find training described in any widely available directories to corporate careers or to adult education. It's not even detailed in the data banks of the federal government or the ASTD.

You'll find it here: information about and access to excellent, relevant training and education provided by the same people who are also paying your salary.

Find the right source and you can gain everything from basic computer skills to college and postgraduate degrees, in settings that range from one-day seminars to entire corporate colleges. You can study at home, during working hours, or over days and weeks away from the job. And you can learn from professional, experienced educators and trainers.

For training has become a profession (and a major industry) in itself: a far cry from just two generations ago, when formal career training is said (by an NCR spokesman, it should be noted), to have been invented by NCR's founder, John H. Paterson. Countering the contemporary belief that good salesmen were "born" with the skill, Paterson instituted a training program for his salesmen which at first consisted simply of having the company's outstanding salesmen pass on their techniques to the others on the staff. Then he developed a primer which was required study for all those who joined the sales staff. If must have worked: more than a century later, his company is still selling.

Much corporate training today is similar to John Paterson's first approach: it consists of workers passing their expertise along to others. In fact, an estimated 95 percent of companies provide this kind of training only.

But in *smart* enterprises—ones that seek the tangible rewards of TQM (total quality management), as exemplified by the Baldrige Award, or value the ideal of what Peter Senge calls "the learning organization," or, in what researcher Robert Rosen calls "the *healthy* corporation," recognize the significance of a holistic approach to business—you'll find a revolution in the attitudes and activities related to learning.

You can be a winner in this revolution if you take advantage of all the training and educational benefits your employer offers. If that's not much, consider moving to a "smarter" or "healthier" employer. Even if you have no thought of changing jobs, training should be in your work plan. These days, training is *expected*. It is necessary just to keep up; it makes you look good; it prepares you to move into other corporate positions—and keeps you in shape for a fast getaway in case the "revolution" causes an upheaval in your own work area. In short, you'd better make the most of training opportunities. Career-guidance experts on today's work arena recommend that you be an "entrepreneur," that you mind your own "business" first rather than plan on a lifetime of loyalty to someone else's business so that your only reward is a "solid" pension. Keep your skills portfolio updated and you'll be ready to travel—and remember that it's also to your employer's benefit to maintain the value of that portfolio, which is why wise companies are willing to spend as much as they do on training.

Yes—of course the corporations are doing it for their own good, and in the majority of companies the focus of training is narrow, addressing only skills specific to the company itself. But many others, recognizing that the corporate good is served by enhancing employees' general competencies and overall well-being, provide a surprisingly wide range of training and educational opportunities. And it's from these that you can benefit.

You may want to completely change careers. Why not take a flyer with the airlines, for instance? Even those that are cutting back on overall staff are still looking for flight attendants, and several, including the still-profitable USAIR and Delta, are actively seeking *older* ones to train—especially people whose work experience relates to personal service of some kind.

Or, if you don't need a career change, but just want to enhance your competencies and then to match your skills to a company's needs, remember that enterprises of all kinds need employees with every kind of skill. Pepsico, for instance, is noted for its training, and all its varied divisions provide both specific training and training that has longer-term value.

## How to Find Corporate Training Resources

Pursue employment at a company with training that's right for you, and walk away a few years later with not just a notch on your resume but a new set of skills in your portfolio. Or explore what training your current employer offers, and get as much of it as you can.

That approach sounds absolutely simpleminded to some: Its outcome seems so unlikely to be valuable that they dismiss the possibility. But before you assume that corporate training isn't worth your consideration, consider what some of these corporations have to offer. Then make your own moves.

### The Benchmark Approach to Training

This is the *new* corporate America, the one where you can find not only a job or a career, but career training and personal development. Two companies in particular exemplify the 1990s training approach in terms of purpose, philosophy, and practice, companies whose programs and philosophies can serve as benchmarks (to use the TQM term) as you explore the corporate world as a training resource—Levi Strauss and Company and the 3M Corporation.

Levi Strauss, a century-old manufacturer of blue jeans and other sportswear, is in what one spokesperson calls a "continuous learning mode," for the benefit of the company and its employees. Having recently reorganized into the contemporary "flat" style of organization, Levi Strauss is focusing on "building a culture where employees have to take responsibility to improve and enhance both the company's output and their own value." The company's mission is to make a profit from quality products using ethical practices in a work environment that is "safe and productive and characterized by fair treatment, teamwork, open communications, personal accountability, and opportunities for growth and development."

Once virtually the only manufacturer of blue jeans, which were worn by a limited market, today Strauss is one among many which makes jeans, now a worldwide phenomenon. How can the company maintain its size and quality in a context of competition and the possible fadeout of what could be a fad? "To lead change through continuous improvement," says management. Of course Strauss has an eye on the bottom line, but it seems to be one of those companies which understands that the bottom line rests on its employees.

Participation in specific education and development courses is largely left to the employee's sense of responsibility and involvement, but the whole organization is moved by what it calls "the empowering 'we'," and the company provides resources, from GED classes through tuition remission for college.

Levi Strauss and Co.
1155 Battery Street
San Francisco, CA 94111
(415) 544-6000
Fax: (415) 544-3939

In contrast with Levi Strauss, which concentrates on one basic product, 3M has a list of products that goes on for pages, yet its attitude toward training and development is similar. 3M states its philosophy this way:

> Our key corporate strategies, as we head into the 1990s, will be based on innovation, continuous productivity improvement, a focus on quality, and expansion and refinement of our global reach....We will be able to implement these strategies only through our people.

Expressing those goals in somewhat less lofty terms, 3M offers a thick catalog of wide-ranging courses, including communications skills, customer service, managing change, engineering, foreign languages, and personal development. It also offers some degree programs, including marketing, and has a generous tuition-refund policy.

3M provides information about and access to adult education programs and self-study materials, and it backs up its statement that "development is looked on very seriously as important at all levels" by requiring a certain amount of training annually for all new hires and most other employees at general, supervisory, management, directorial, and executive levels.

3M Corporation
3M Center
Saint Paul, MN 55144-0001
(612) 733-1110
Fax: (612) 733-9973

## Corporate Resource Lists

By no means all—or even most—businesses operate with the attitude expressed by Levi Strauss and 3M. But below are listed more than 100 companies whose programs may be of interest to you as you explore the training resources of the corporate world.

**Programs.** All the companies listed offer programs that cover company-related and more general topics, specially taught, in both managerial and technical areas. There are five lists:

1. A directory of benchmark companies with the most generous and innovative approach to training of employees.
2. A directory of companies or groups of companies that offer benchmark training to nonemployees—to employees of other organizations and, in some cases, to the general public.
3. A directory of companies with full training programs of general value, but not of benchmark quality.
4. A directory of corporations that offer for-credit courses.
5. A name and address list of other companies known to have training programs that go beyond the basic company-focused minimum.

**Pay-Plus.** All the programs described come with the company's standard salary and benefits, and all the companies listed in the first three sections below offer tuition reimbursement for outside study.

**Prerequisites.** Unless otherwise stated, all programs require employment with the company. Some have a minimum term of employment prior to eligibility for any but "orientation" training. In some of these organizations, a supervisor determines and approves enrollment in a training course. In most of the courses described, training is open to employees at all levels. All of the programs for employees provide salary and benefits during training.

### Benchmark Training

The following question was put to nearly 1000 of the nation's leading corporations: "If I came to your company with some work experience but an interest in changing the direction of my career...or with good basic education but no specialized training...or an employee who wanted more from my job...What could I expect?

In the following sections headed "training philosophy" you will read some of their answers.

***AGWAY.*** Farmer-owned farm supply and food marketing cooperative with 8000 employees in sales, production, transportation, research, and all areas of management.

*Training Philosophy.* "We have learned over time that training is one of the best investments we can make, both in terms of cost-saving on the job, in retaining valued employees, and in attracting new people."

*Scope.* Formal courses including computer skills, communications, sales techniques, and interpersonal skills. Offers a one-year on-the-job management development program for up to 100 candidates for management annually.

AGWAY
333 Butternut Drive
Syracuse, NY 13214-1879
(315) 449-7061
Fax: (315) 449-6078

***Air Products and Chemicals.*** One of the largest international suppliers of industrial gases, chemicals, and environmental and energy systems.

*Training Philosophy.* "As the business environment becomes more complex, more international, and more competitive, our success will depend increasingly on the ability of our people to apply their talents. Our efforts at empowerment include...broader training in leadership and skills development.

*Scope.* Average of 40 hours a year training programs in management skills and individual development, MIS, and sales—open to all levels. Also offers technical training, particularly in environmental safety.

Air Products and Chemicals
7201 Hamilton Boulevard
Allentown, PA 18195-1501
(215) 481-4911
Fax: (215) 481-5900

***Amoco.*** International leader in oil drilling and refining and chemical manufacture and production.

*Training Philosophy.* "We will enable everyone to realize his or her potential by offering development opportunities, personal challenge, and growth."

*Scope.* Job-specific training offered by the Production, Chemical, and Oil divisions. In addition, Amoco's corporate human resources operation offers over 100 courses, including writing and communications and general management skills.

Amoco Oil Co.
200 East Randolph Drive
Chicago, IL 60601-7125
(312) 856-6111
Fax: (312) 856-2460

***Beckman Instruments.*** International manufacturer of scientific and medical laboratory equipment and supplies.

*Training Philosophy.* "We place a high importance upon the individual, and each person's contribution to our team. We strive to maintain an...environment that allows us to pursue personal career satisfaction....More than ever before, development of our personal skills and talents is crucial to success.

*Scope.* Management development courses covering general topics such as positive influence, personal computing, and business writing, led by internal and external experts.

Beckman Instruments
2500 North Harbor Boulevard
Frillerton, CA 92635-2600
(714) 871-4848
Fax: (714) 773-8283

***Computer Sciences Corporation (CSC).*** Computer hardware and software research, development, marketing, and production; plus credit services.

*Training Philosophy.* "CSC's commitment to developing the full potential of its employees is reflected in...programs designed to empower employees to take charge of their own career development."

*Scope.* A full series of in-house technical, professional, and managerial development programs; skills development in marketing, sales, finance, and human resources; foreign language and cultural adaptation courses.

Computer Sciences Corporation (CSC)
2100 East Grand Avenue
El Segundo, CA 90245-5098
(310) 615-0311
Fax: (310) 640-2648

***Ford Motor Corporation.*** One of the country's leading auto makers (the one that began reshaping itself earliest), with diverse interests in aerospace, finance, and other areas around the world.

*Training Philosophy.* "We will still be measured by how well we handle our financial resources, but we will also be measured by how well we handle our human resources."

*Scope.* 2.5 percent of payroll spent annually on education, from production-specific skills through graduate degrees, including management and high-tech training, under the auspices of an extensive education, development, and training program in cooperation with the United Auto Workers that includes career planning and life management guidance; 55 regional in-plant learning centers offering everything from GEDs to master's degrees; national programs in Detroit for management and salaried employees.

Ford Motor Corporation
American Road
Dearborn, MI 48126
(313) 322-3000
Fax: (313) 845-8981

***General Electric.*** The nation's largest conglomerate, with nearly 300,000 employees in its appliance, credit, aerospace electronics, nuclear, manufacturing, power, and other divisions.

*Training Philosophy.* "Our philosophy is that *everyone* gets trained."

*Scope.* Extensive training programs offered at GE's Management Development Institute in Crotonsville, New York, and at individual plants throughout the nation and the world, providing generalized training in managerial, interpersonal, and business skills as well as high-tech specializations. The emphasis in on quality, creativity, and individual career development, with a focus on business objectives. Contact:

General Electric
3135 Eastern Turnpike
Fairfield, CT 06431-0001
(203) 373-2211
Fax: (203) 373-3131

***GTE.*** An international telecommunications company with an emphasis on information services and cellular communications.

*Training Philosophy.* "There are choices in leadership; foremost among them is the freedom to decide how to move forward, how to grow, how to learn, how to achieve personal goals."

*Scope.* Wide range of courses and programs in every area of management, marketing, and finance, as well as self-initiated, self-planned educational path under professional guidance, at management development centers around the country.

GTE
1 Stamford Forum
Stamford, CT 06901-3500
(203) 965-2000
Fax: (203) 965-2277

***Hallmark.*** A leading producer of greeting cards and other stationery and gift products.

*Training Philosophy.* "We firmly believe the success of the organization depends on the ability of employees to grow professionally."

*Scope.* Training for employees at all levels, including courses in business writing, time management, and life management, as well as company-focused programs, offered by the Leadership Development Institute, a corporate education and training resource center.

Hallmark
2501 McGee Street
Kansas City, MO 64108-2615
(816) 274-5111

***IBM.*** International company for the research, developing, manufacture, and marketing of computer hardware and software, office systems, typewriters, and telecommunications systems.

*Training Philosophy.* "IBM is committed to the personal and professional growth of its employees—and recognition for work well done. It invests heavily in employee education, development and training programs to help IBM people achieve a high level of proficiency from the start and maintain or improve that level throughout their careers."

*Scope.* Comprehension courses in engineering specialties, computer sciences, mathematics, and physics—plus managerial training, finance, and accounting—offered at New York State institute and centers around the country as well as individual plant and laboratory sites.

IBM
1 Old Orchard Road
Armonk, NY 10504-1783
(914) 765-1900
Fax: (914) 765-4190

**Ingersoll Rand.** A leading manufacturer of machinery and tools.

*Training Philosophy.* "Our employees mean the world to us....The company is committed to achieving excellence by investing in the development of its greatest asset—its employees."

*Scope.* For sales staff and middle and senior managers, courses ranging from company-specific skills through creativity and career development to cross-cultural training; for technical employees, a career ladder that includes educational support; all with accompanying career guidance.

Ingersoll Rand
200 Chestnut Ridge Road
Woodcliff Lake, NJ 07675-7700
(201) 573-0123
Fax: (201) 573-3054

**Johnson & Johnson.** One of the leading producers and distributors of health-related products.

*Training Philosophy.* "Johnson & Johnson believes that employee development is the cornerstone of business success....Formal training, which supplements on-the-job development, represents an important opportunity for all employees to enhance both knowledge and skill for their own growth and the growth of the business."

*Scope.* Area-specific training available to employees of each of Johnson & Johnson's 24 operating companies; courses in virtually every aspect of management given at the corporation's Education and Conference Center at the New Brunswick, New Jersey, headquarters; courses for selected managers featuring professional instruction in "world class manufacturing" given by the company's Operations Institute in conjunction with Duke University's Fuqua Business School.

Johnson & Johnson Consumer Products
199 Grandview Road
Skillman, NJ 08558-9418
(908) 874-1000
Fax: (908) 874-1506

**Kaiser Permanente.** One of the nation's leading and oldest health-care providers.

*Training Philosophy.* "The mission of the Center for Professional Development is to develop excellence in leadership and management skills by providing relevant, innovative, timely, high-quality training and coaching services which support the organization's vision and strategic direction."

*Scope.* A wide range of workshops and courses for all personnel categories, including business writing, stress management, negotiation, communications, and presentation skills, as well as training for technicians who need "bridging" into health-related specialties.

Kaiser Permanente Medical Center
2800 West MacArthur Boulevard
Oakland, CA 94611-5693
(510) 596-1000
Fax: (510) 596-6672

***McDonald's Corporation.*** The country's leading fast-food restaurant chain.

*Training Philosophy.* "McDonald's is a place where people `grow their careers....The CEO and all top management came up through the restaurants and know first-hand the value of training.'"

*Scope.* Hamburger University pioneered a new type of training program and attitude when it opened in 1961, and today serves as a model for the kind of training enterprises to which many of today's corporations aspire. McDonald's offers courses in everything from how to make french fries to sophisticated management techniques. Training, which is open to all employees and required for managers, opens paths to executive positions.

McDonald's Corporation
1 McDonald's Plaza
Oak Brook, IL 60521
(312) 575-3000

***Mason and Madison Inc.*** A medium-sized advertising and public relations agency with a large-sized training program.

*Training Philosophy.* "We understand that you may not spend the rest of your life here, but while you're here, we will train you and support your education."

*Scope.* This "problem-solving" company offers a wide range of programs to aid managers in developing programs for their own staffs; an in-house job-specific curriculum on technology and communications; social styles workshops for personal development; ongoing support for attendance at seminars. Tuition remission for education is 100 percent—from GED to graduate degrees.

Mason and Madison Inc.
23 Amity Road
Bethany, CT 06524-3433
(203) 393-1101
Fax: (203) 893-2813

***Merrill Lynch.*** A leading retail stock brokerage firm which is now expanding into lending and insurance.

*Training Philosophy.* "We don't just give our financial consultants a training program. We give them a graduate school."

*Scope.* Well known and respected for its finance-related training, the firm trains over 4000 "financial consultants" in its formal programs, which include a two-year Professional Development Program and training in advanced professional management, given at the company's corporate training center in Princeton, New Jersey.

Merrill Lynch
250 Vesey Street
World Financial Center
New York, NY 10281
(212) 449-1000

***Motorola.*** A top-ranking electronics and telecommunications equipment company.

*Training Philosophy.* "Our goal is `total quality' because quality pays."

*Scope.* Motorola's training programs are so well respected that academics and training professionals publish studies on them and even competitors solicit advice from Motorola. Motorola has spent $100 million on employee managerial and technical education designed to train employees in Motorola's new, highly effective "zero defects" administrative and production techniques.

Motorola
1303 East Algonquin Road
Schaumburg, IL 60196-1079
(708) 397-5000
Fax: (708) 576-3258

***Pfizer.*** An international research, manufacturer, and marketer of pharmaceutical, health care, and personal products.

*Training Philosophy.* "Pfizer's fundamental strength depends upon the continuous development of its people, both as individuals and as members of organizational teams. The development of self, subordinates and organization is the responsibility of every manager. Because research is the core of the enterprise, a `learning community' must be created."

*Scope.* Many intensive, team-focused management development seminars, open to all levels, with an emphasis on personal-assessment techniques; problem-solving seminars; an evolving, ongoing curriculum of intensive one-topic workshops and personal development training.

Pfizer
235 East 42 Street
New York, NY 10017-5755
(212) 573-2323
Fax: (212) 573-7851

***Polaroid Corporation.*** A developer, manufacturer, and distributor of photographic and high-tech equipment.

*Training Philosophy.* "We continue to be committed to developing our human resource potential through education, training, and retraining."

*Scope.* In-house, work-hours courses in technical and managerial skills, as well as self-management and personal development; courses in communications, computers, and mathematics; career guidance and vocational interest testing.

Polaroid Corporation
549 Technology Square
Cambridge, MA 02139-3589
(617) 577-2000
Fax: (617) 577-2000

***Steelcase, Inc.*** The world's leading producer of office furniture.

*Training Philosophy.* "If we can help build the essential human spirit, we will benefit and you will feel more rewarded."

*Scope.* Wide range of courses, with emphasis on individual leadership, creativity, flexibility, sensitivity, and problem-solving techniques; computer-based training for self-initiated, self-paced learning; workshops in personal management and development; managerial skills training.

Steelcase, Inc.
P.O. Box 1967
Grand Rapids, MI 49501-1967
(616) 247-2710

***Trinova.*** An international manufacturer and distributor of engineered components and systems for industry, distributed to industrial, aerospace, defense, and automotive markets.

*Training Philosophy.* "We genuinely believe that education is a vital tool to achieve our goals and that it is an important investment in our future." In a change from attitudes that prevailed during the 1980s, Trinova offers courses to all managerial employees and requires education on the plant floor, where "it was never thought about until manufacturing changed."

*Scope.* Required, company-specific training; a variety of management development courses at several levels; general business and foreign-language courses taught by outside university faculty at Trinova's Management Education Center.

Trinova
3000 Strayer Avenue
Maumee, OH 43537
(419) 867-2200
Fax: (419) 867-2547

***Universal Foods.*** International manufacturer and marketer of selected products for the food ingredient, consumer food, and biotechnology markets.

*Training Philosophy.* "The Universal Way concentrates on improving the system by which all work gets done in an environment that nurtures the growth and contribution of all employees....Through education and support, employees are empowered to make decisions and to make changes."

*Scope.* Full curriculum of management development courses, with TQM focus, open to all employees.

Universal Foods
433 East Michigan Street
Milwaukee, WI 53202-5106
(414) 271-6755
Fax: (414) 347-3785

***Westinghouse.*** An international manufacturer and distributor of electrical and electronic equipment and supplies.

*Training Philosophy.* "The Employee Development mission at Westinghouse, a diverse corporation with many different training needs, is to provide broad services in the areas of management development, individual development, organizational effectiveness, and marketing."

*Scope.* Management-oriented courses at headquarters and in regional divisions; advanced management program; personal development; other specialized programs offered at universities and institutions around the country.

Westinghouse
11 Stanwix Street
Pittsburgh, PA 15222-1384
(412) 244-2000
Fax: (412) 642-3404

**Benchmark Corporate Training for Nonemployees**

Perhaps the best known of the companies that offers training for nonemployees is the Walt Disney Company. Disney, known in the business world for the high level of training and morale of its work force, operates the Disney University on five "campuses" at its theme parks around the world. At these campuses, it not only trains "its most valuable asset—its people" but also provides business programs for service industry executives who want to learn the secrets of Disney's success.

The Walt Disney Company
500 East Buena Vista Street
Burbank, CA 91521-0001
(818) 560-1000
Fax: (818) 560-1930

Five other companies that provide training for employees and nonemployees are listed below.

***Allen Bradley Corporation.*** A subsidiary of Rockwell International specializing in computer controls, networks, and software.

*Scope.* Provides extensive and supportive training for its own employees and presents a full range of in-class and videotaped courses for its customers and clients, particularly in the area of computer-integrated manufacturing systems.

Allen Bradley Corporation
1201 South 2d Street
Milwaukee, WI 53204-2498
(414) 671-2000
Fax: (414) 382-4444

***Autodesk.*** A leading developer of computer-aided design (CAD) software.

*Scope.* See NCR, below.
Autodesk
2320 Marinship Way
Sausalito, CA 94965-2818
(415) 332-2344
Fax: (415) 491-8302

***NCR.*** Manufacturer of high-tech equipment.

*Scope.* A wide-ranging, in-depth system of employee training. Its Customer and Support Education (CASE) program delivers technical and professional or managerial training to its customers.
NCR
1700 South Patterson Boulevard
Dayton, OH 45479
(513) 445-5000
Fax: (513) 445-1238

***New England Telephone.*** A major east coast telephone network.

*Scope.* Managerial and technical education (including 100 percent tuition reimbursement for outside programs) at five special centers for its own 24,000 employees, as well as training for the 80,000 others employed in the NYNEX region.
New England Telephone
185 Franklin Street
Boston, MA 02110-1585
(617) 743-9800

***Safeco.*** A leading group of insurance companies based in Seattle, Washington.

*Scope.* Runs an "agent school" for its own employees; presents workshops that provide detailed, professionally led training and study programs in insurance techniques to independent agents.
Safeco
15411 N.E. 51st Street
Redmond, WA 98052
(206) 867-8000
Fax: (206) 867-8796

**Focused Training**

Other business organizations have extensive training programs, but ones which focus more narrowly on specific corporate needs. The utilities industry, for example—phone companies and power, water, and gas companies—provide extensive and usually excellent training, but with an almost exclusive emphasis on meeting the company's specific production or managerial needs. But even in those industries, as at the companies listed below, you can find valuable crossover training.

The following list includes organizations that not only provide good training but are also from industries with good job and growth outlooks—so if the training possibilities meet your needs and background, you may just want to stay.

***AETNA Life and Casualty.*** Among the largest U.S. insurance companies.

*Scope.* Wide training in insurance-related needs, especially in the "hire and train" program, bringing in "nontraditional" employees.

AETNA Life and Casualty
151 Farmington Avenue
Hartford, CT 06156
(203) 273-0123
(203) 273-0079

***American Standard.*** International manufacturer and distributor of plumbing supplies.

*Scope.* Formalized training in sales, production, and relations with customer groups.

American Standard
1114 Avenue of The Americas
19th Floor
New York, NY 10036-7776
(212) 703-5100
(212) 703-5177

***Amtrak.*** The nation's passenger railway.

*Scope.* Companywide commitment to progressive career development: ongoing in-house leadership and management training, plus strong skills development and on-the-job training, with focus on promotion from within.

Amtrak
60 Massachusetts Avenue, N.E.
Washington, DC 20002-4225
(202) 906-3000
(202) 906-3865

***ARA Services.*** Institutional catering and maintenance, health-care facilities, Living Centers.

*Scope.* Trains 150,000 employees in "taking time to care."

ARA Services
1101 Market Street
Philadelphia, PA 19107-2988
(215) 238-3000
Fax: (215) 238-3333

***Arthur Andersen and Company.*** The world's largest accounting consulting firm: about 50,000 employees at locations worldwide.

*Scope.* Trains up to 1200 students a day at its Minnesota Center for Professional Education in accounting, computer systems, and customer service—to "provide highest quality services to our clients."

Arthur Anderson and Company
69 West Washington Street
Chicago, IL 60602-3094
(312) 580-0069 *or* (312) 507-2548

***Banc One.*** Profitable bank holding company.

*Scope.* Skills and customer-service training throughout system; Bank One College, with intensive residential sessions for managers and executives.

Banc One
100 East Broad Street
Columbus, OH 43271
(614) 248-5800
Fax: (614) 248-5624

***Becton Dickinson.*** Manufacturer of high-tech medical equipment.

*Scope.* Training for new-style company organization plus ongoing updates for technical and scientific workers.

Becton Dickinson
1 Becton Drive
Franklin Lakes, NJ 07417-1880
(201) 847-6800
Fax: (201) 847-6475

***Brown and Root.*** Leading supplier of construction, maintenance, and engineering services.

*Scope.* General quality-focused training; special programs for engineers in various specialties.

Brown and Root
4100 Clinton Drive
Houston, TX 77020
(713) 676-3011
Fax: (713) 676-4109

***Browning-Ferris Industries.*** A major waste-disposal, recycling, and landfill business.

*Scope.* Intensive, professionally led programs in such areas as accounting and sales for 700+ district managers; "CARE" quality management training program focused on environmental safety.

Browning-Ferris Industries
757 North Eldridge Parkway
Houston, TX 77079-4435
(713) 870-8100
(713) 870-7844

***Caterpillar Inc.*** International manufacturer and marketer of heavy equipment.

*Scope.* Plant with a future program trains employees in state-of-the-art technology for its computer-integrated manufacturing systems.

Caterpillar Inc.
100 N.E. Adams Street
Peoria, IL 61629
(309) 675-1000
Fax: (309) 675-6155

***Citibank.*** Leading banking, financial service, and bank holding company.

*Scope.* Extensive (and intense) specialized training for those employees who seek success in its various enterprises.

Citibank
399 Park Avenue
New York, NY 10022
(212) 559-1000

***Corning, Inc.*** Manufacturer of glass and glass-related products.

*Scope.* Requires "quality" training; has a formalized system of career-development networks providing expertise in company operations and production technologies.

Corning, Inc.
Herrington Road
Corning, NY 14831
(607) 974-9000
(607) 974-8150

***Dayton Hudson Corp.*** One of the country's largest retailing chains.

*Scope.* Wide range of training programs for both in-store personnel and managerial staff.

Dayton Hudson Corp.
777 Nicollet Mall
Minneapolis, MN 55402-2055
(612) 370-6948
Fax: (612) 370-5502

***Domino's Pizza, Inc.*** One of the top 10 fast-food restaurant chains.

*Scope.* College of Pizzerology trains employees in pizza making and store management techniques during year-long part-time program.

Domino's Pizza, Inc.
P.O. Box 997
Ann Arbor, MI 48106-0997
(313) 930-3030
Fax: (313) 668-0342

***Ethyl Corporation.*** Major chemical manufacturing and development corporation.

*Scope.* Companywide training focused on management, marketing, and quality improvement.

Ethyl Corporation
330 South 4th Street
Richmond, VA 23219-4304
(804) 788-5000
Fax: (804) 788-5688

***Federal Express.*** Top-ranking transportation service company.

*Scope.* Award-winning quality training uses classes and computer-based systems to improve employee productivity and performance for its high-tech delivery systems.

Federal Express
2005 Corporate Avenue
Memphis, TN 38132-1796
(901) 369-3600
Fax: (901) 398-1111

***General Tire, Inc.*** Major manufacturer of tires and rubber goods.

*Scope.* Supplements its in-house sales, management, and technical training programs with outside providers of education in company-related specialties.

General Tire, Inc.
1 General Street
Akron, OH 44329
(216) 798-3000
Fax: (216) 798-2103

***Goodyear Tire and Rubber Company.*** Major manufacturing, distribution, and retail company.

*Scope.* Extensive training programs led by full-time professional staff, including courses at fully equipped school facility near headquarters, with company-oriented emphasis on sales, production skills, and staff development.

Goodyear Tire and Rubber Company
1144 East Market Street
Akron, OH 44316
(216) 796-2121
Fax: (216) 796-2222

***Hewlett-Packard Company.*** Innovative manufacturer of computers and electronic equipment.

*Scope.* Extensive orientation into the "HP way" of research, production, distribution, and management through teamwork; specialized training enabling employees to move from one career track to another.

Hewlett-Packard Company
3000 Hanover Street
Palo Alto, CA 94304-1185
(415) 857-1501
Fax: (415) 857-5518

***Intermountain Health Care.*** A major regional health provider.

*Scope.* Direct and indirect training to employees, through nursing education and tuition support for those seeking college degrees in health-related specialties.

Intermountain Health Care
365 State Street
Salt Lake City, UT 84111-1453
(801) 533-8282
Fax: (801) 531-9789

***International Paper.*** International, diversified paper and forest products company.

*Scope.* Broad-based training curriculum, open to all employees, that emphasizes company procedures and technical and engineering programs that offers ongoing training in operations.

International Paper
2 Manhattanville Road
Purchase, NY 10577-2196
(914) 397-1500

***Marriott Corporation.*** Diverse giant in hospitality industry.

*Scope.* Thorough training in all of its specialities: new management training due to company restructuring; programs to develop staff for its life care communities designed for senior citizens.

Marriott Corporation
1 Marriott Drive
Washington, DC 20058
(301) 380-9000

***Martin Marietta.*** Major aerospace company.

*Scope.* Extensive training in TQM mode plus company-specific managerial and technical programs, including mandatory courses that provide expertise in company's processes.

Martin Marietta
6801 Rockledge Drive
Bethesda, MD 20817-1877
(301) 897-6000
Fax: (301) 897-6083

***Micron Technology.*** Major computer and electronics company.

*Scope.* Individualized four-level training and development program for production employees and company- and quality-focused management programs; academic instruction in various fields, including basic skills remediation; on-site associates degree program; graduate engineering program via satellite; 100 percent tuition remission for company-related courses.

Micron Technology
2805 East Columbia Road
Boise, ID 83706-9698
(208) 368-4000
Fax: (208) 343-2536

***PPG Industries.*** Major chemical-products manufacturer and supplier.

*Scope.* Extensive seven-level in-house professionally led training programs for employees from new hires to CEO; elaborate training matrix of courses to develop the eight functional competencies of value to the corporation.

PPG Industries
1 PPG Place
Pittsburgh, PA 15272
(412) 434-3131
Fax: (412) 434-2448

***Reynolds Metals Company.*** Leading metal mining, production, and manufacturing company.

*Scope.* Extensive professionally led management training conducted at corporate headquarters as well as other centers.

Reynolds Metals Company
6601 West Broad Street
Richmond, VA 23230-1701
(804) 281-2000
Fax: (804) 281-3695

***Sheraton Corporation.*** Leader in the hospitality industry.

*Scope.* Welcomes career-changers; offers wide range of company-focused general and job-specific training (e.g., sales, human resources, engineering, guest-service) to all levels—from staff to top management to franchisees—at individual hotels and at regional centers.

Sheraton Corporation
60 State Street
Boston, MA 02109-1815
(617) 367-3600
Fax: (617) 367-5676

***The Travelers Corporation.*** Top-ranking insurance company.

*Scope.* Professionally led training not only for agents but employees at every level in computer, management, and other skills at a headquarters training center.

The Travelers Corporation
1 Tower Square
Hartford, CT 06183
(203) 277-0111
Fax: (203) 277-7979

***Wausau Insurance.*** Widely regarded group of insurance companies.

*Scope.* Broad-based in-house training programs, courses, and workshops for all career paths at training and conference center near headquarters, as well as full support for outside continuing education courses in job-related subjects.

Wausau Insurance
2000 Westwood Drive
Wausau, WI 54401
(715) 845-5211

***Xerox Corporation.*** Leading business products and electronics company.

*Scope.* Extensive technical training and development; sophisticated career redevelopment and management retraining programs geared to company's needs following restructuring.

Xerox Corporation
800 Long Ridge Road
Stamford, CT 06902
(203) 329-8700

**Training for Academic Credit**

Many corporations provide education programs that offer not only training but also academic credit.

ARA Services, Inc.
1101 Market Street
Philadelphia, PA 19107-2988
(215) 238-3000
Fax: (215) 238-3333

*Scope.* Offers a wide range of training to its employees, including some credit-bearing programs. Areas of study include management skills, service management, supervisory skills, and others.

AT&T Center for Systems Education
140 Centennial Avenue
Piscataway, NJ 08854

*Scope.* Provides training and general education to its employees by specialists in their fields. Areas covered include techniques of instruction, analysis and design strategies, basic training development skills, initial designer training, architecture, and consulting skills. Also offered to employees are courses in the areas of telecommunications, computer science, and data processing, such as Assembler language coding, Basic, FORTRAN, COBOL, computer communications system Bisync protocol analysis, data analysis and logic data structuring, modems and facilities, teleprocessing, terminals and line protocol, data gathering for system development, IMS/VS programming, teleprocessing, and many more.

AT&T Corporate Education Center
Management Education Training Division
399 Campus Drive
Room C-131315
Somerset, NJ 08873

*Scope.* Offers training courses to management personnel in areas of marketing principles, theory, and practical application.

Bally's Park Place Casino Hotel
Bally's Park Place and the Boardwalk
Atlantic City, NJ 08401

*Scope.* Provides employees with learning and development opportunities in areas such as human relations and supervision.

Baltimore Gas and Electric Company
Calvert's Cliffs Nuclear Power Plant
Lusby, Maryland 20657

*Scope.* Offers a 10-week program once or twice a year to its employees. The program in nuclear security includes instruction, firearms training, and response force tactical training.

Bell Atlantic Corporation
PONSI Coordinator
Network Services, Inc.
13100 Columbia Pike, D16
Silver Springs, Maryland 20904

*Scope.* Offers employees after-hours courses to sharpen their general skills. Courses offered include math, language, test taking, and thinking.

Bell Communications Research, Inc.
6 Corporate Place
Piscataway, NJ 08854

*Scope.* Offers its employees several computer courses such as Basic and C Language programming.

Bell Communications Research Training and Education Center
6200 Route 53
Lisle, Illinois 60532

*Scope.* Has training programs geared to advancement to executive-level and managerial positions; areas include adult instructional methodology, marketing management and strategy, communications fundamentals, C Language programming, capital cost methodology, capital recovery, central office grounding, competitive analysis, corporate planning, cost studies, data communications (DC-FACT, DC-LAN, DC-PC-FUN, DC-SNA, DS-NTWRK), economic evolution, electrical protection, facilitating groups and meetings, fiber optics, financial management, accounting, managing environmental change, telecommunications, hazards and protection, quantitative forecasting, scientific sampling, strategy analysis for finance and marketing, switch capabilities, transmission theory, and more.

Certified Medical Representatives Institute, Inc.
4316 Brambleton Avenue, S.W.
Roanoke, VA 24018

*Scope.* Offers training to medical representatives in the United States and Canada. Upon satisfactorily completing required scientific and elective courses, the medical representative is awarded the CMR designation, certifying the representative's competence in the field. Courses: anatomy, behavioral pathology and treatment, biochemistry, clinical drug interaction, cardiovascular system, endocrine system, ethics, governmental regulations, health-care community, pharmaceutical industry, immune system, disease states, medical terminology, microbiology, musculoskeletal system, nervous system, physiology, psychology, reproductive system, respiratory system, sensory organs, urinary system, and trends and issues in health care.

Chrysler Corporation Advanced Technical Training
Featherstone Road Engineering Center
2301 Featherstone Road
Auburn Hills, Michigan 48057

*Scope.* Provides technical training to improve skills and productivity of Chrysler employees in areas of production, skilled trades, supervision, and engineering. A sampling of courses in the automotive area: labor, brake systems, electronic transaxle, hydraulic technology, weld controllers, and work standards.

Chrysler Institute Associate Degree Program
Michigan University
Mt. Pleasant, Michigan 48859

*Scope.* Offers a two-year associate degree program with a curriculum which includes subjects in mathematics, communications, interpersonal skills, management, business, manufacturing technology, finance, industrial engineering, manufacturing engineering, personnel, production, production control, and quality control.

Contel Service Corporation
IS Training and Development Department
Contel Service Corporation
245 Parameter Center Parkway
Atlanta, GA 30346

*Scope.* Training provided to employees in areas such as computer literacy, personal computers, programming languages, Digital VAX/VMS, and Honeywell DPS8/SP86 technologies. Facilities include training rooms, computer terminals, personal computers, and audiovisual and network connections.

Control Data
Education and Training
8100 34th Avenue, South
Box O
Minneapolis, Minnesota 55440

*Scope.* Offers its employees and employees from other corporations independent study and computer-based education courses in centers located in most major metropolitan areas. Areas of interest: business and management; CREATE courseware in economics, finance, data processing, accounting, management, mathematics of life insurance, principles of real estate; computer science, mathematics, and mechanical engineering.

Dana Corporation
Dana University Business School
P.O. Box 1000
Toledo, OH 43697

*Scope.* All divisions offer local training and send employees to workshops and seminars at area universities in an effort to promote from within. Dana uses a tuition-refund plan. It also meets the needs for management development education through Dana University. Courses: asset management, effective speaking, business management, manufacturing, problem solving and decision making, sales, and supervisory management.

Del Taco, Inc.
345 Baker Street
Costa Mesa, CA 92626

*Scope.* Offers training to its fast-food restaurant chain employees. All employees receive training in the principles and practices of restaurant operation and sound business management.

Dow Jones and Company, Inc.
Plant Communications Department
Box 300
Princeton, NJ 08543-0300

*Scope.* Offers training for engineering and other technical personnel. Courses taught by trained staff in advanced systems and technology.

Duquesne Light Company
Nuclear Division
P.O. Box 4
Shippingport, PA 15077-0004

*Scope.* Provides nuclear training program to employees responsible for operation of its nuclear facilities.

First Fidelity Bank, N.A., N.J.
Management Training Program
500 Broad Street
Newark, NJ 07192

*Scope.* Has a seven-month classroom training program to identify and train future managers. Participants complete graduate-level courses in managerial accounting, corporate finance, money and banking, and commercial credit and lending.

Ford National Development and Training
UAW
P.O. Box 6002
Dearborn, MI 48121

*Scope.* Offers a UAW-administered training and development program for its employees represented by UAW. Areas include consumer affairs, citizenship and legislative activities, veterans' benefits, time study and engineering, arbitration services, concerns of elderly and retired workers.

### Some Other Corporations That Offer Training

Ace Hardware Corporation
2200 Kensington Court
Oak Brook, IL 60521

ALCOA
425 6th Avenue
Pittsburgh, PA 15219

Alexander and Alexander
Consulting Inc.
125 Chubb Avenue
Lyndhurst, NJ 07071

Allegheny Ludlum Corporation
6 PPG Place, #1000
Pittsburgh, PA 15222

Allstate Insurance Co.
2775 Sanders Road
Northbrook, IL 60062

ALLTEL Corp.
100 Executive Parkway
Hudson, OH 44236

AMAX Inc.
200 Park Avenue
New York, NY 10166

American Cyanamid Co.
1 Cyanamid Plaza
Wayne, NJ 07470

American Electric Co. Inc.
1555 Lynn Field Road
Memphis, TN 38119

American Express Travel Service Co.
World Financial Center
New York, NY 10285

American Greeting Corp.
10500 American Road
Cleveland, OH 44144

American President Co. Ltd.
1800 Harrison Street
Oakland, CA 94612

American Television and
Communications
300 First Stamford Place
Stamford, CT 06902

American Water Works Service Co. Inc.
1025 Laurel Oak Road
Voorhees, NJ 08043

Ameritrust Company
900 Euclid Avenue
Cleveland, OH 44101

Amoco Chemical Co.
300 East Randolph Drive
Chicago, IL 60601

AMP Inc.
470 Friendship Road
Harrisburg, PA 17111

Arby's Inc.
3495 Piedmont Road, Building 10
Atlanta, GA 30305

Arco Chemical Co.
3801 Westchester Pike
Newtown Square, PA 19073

Atlanta Constitution
72 Marietta Street, N.W.
Atlanta, GA 30303

Atlanta Gas Light Co.
235 Peachtree Street N.E.
Atlanta, GA 30303

BankAmerica Corp.
555 California Street
San Francisco, CA 94104

Barclays American Corp.
201 South Tryon Street
Charlotte, NC 28286

Barnett Banks Inc.
100 North Laura Street
Jacksonville, FL 32202

BASF Corp.
8 Campus Drive
Parsippany, NJ 07054

Bell Atlantic Corp.
1600 Market Street, 30th Floor
Philadelphia PA 19103

Boise Cascade Corp.
1000 Third Avenue
New York, NY 10022

Borg-Warner Automotive Inc.
200 South Michigan Avenue
Chicago, IL 60604

Briggs and Stratton Corp.
P.O. Box 702
Milwaukee, WI 53201

Burlington Industries Inc.
1345 Avenue of the Americas
New York, NY 10105

Burnett, Leo, Co. Inc.
35 West Wacker Drive, 21st. Floor
Chicago, IL 60601

Cablevision Systems Corp.
1 Media Crossway Drive
Woodbury, NY 11797

Cargill Inc.
P.O. Box 9300
Minneapolis, MN 55440

Chase Manhattan Bank
1 Chase Manhattan Plaza
New York, NY 10081

Chemical Banking Corp.
277 Park Avenue
New York, NY 10172

CIGNA Company
1600 Arch Street
Philadelphia, PA 19192

Coldwell Banker
27271 Las Ramblas
Mission Viejo, CA 92691

Colgate-Palmolive Co.
300 Park Avenue
New York, NY 10022

Collins and Aikman Corp.
210 Madison Avenue
New York, NY 10016

Comcast Cable Communications Inc.
1414 South Penn Square
Philadelphia, PA 19102

Consolidated Edison Co. NY Inc.
4 Irving Place
New York, NY 10003

Del Monte Foods USA
1 Market Plaza
San Francisco, CA 94105

Domino's Pizza Inc.
P.O. Box 997
Ann Arbor, MI 48106

Dow Chemical Co. USA
2030 Willard H. Dow Center
Midland, MI 48674

Dow Jones & Co. Inc.
200 Liberty Street
New York, NY 10281

Dun & Bradstreet Corp.
299 Park Avenue
New York, NY 10171

Eastman Kodak Co.
343 State Street
Rochester, NY 14650

Eaton Corp.
1111 Superior Avenue East
Cleveland, OH 44114

Esprit de Corp.
900 Minnesota St.
San Francisco, CA 94107

Farmland Foods Inc.
10015 North Executive Hill Boulevard
Kansas City, MO 64153

Farmland Industries Inc.
P.O. Box 7305
Kansas City, MO 64116

Foster Wheeler USA
Peeyville Corporate Park
Clinton, NJ 08809

Gannett News Service
1000 Wilson Boulevard
Arlington, VA 22229

General Dynamics Corp.
7733 Forsyth Boulevard
St. Louis, MO 63105

Georgia Pacific Corp.
P.O. Box 105605
Atlanta, GA 30348

Gerber Products Co.
445 State Street
Freemont, MI 49413

Gillette Company
800 Boylston Street
Boston, MA 02199

Goodyear Tire and Rubber Co.
1144 East Market Street
Akron, OH 44316

Hardee's Food Systems Inc.
1233 Hardees Boulevard
Rocky Mount, NC 27802

Hartford Insurance Group
Hartford Plaza
Hartford, CT 06102

Hershey Foods Corp.
100 Mansion Road
Hershey, PA 17033

Honeywell Inc.
2701 4th Avenue South
Minneapolis, MN 55408

Host International
475 Washington Boulevard
Marina del Rey, CA 90292

Household International Inc.
2700 Sanders Road
Prospect Heights, IL 60070

Humana Inc.
500 West Main Street
Louisville, KY 40202

Ingersoll-Rand Co.
200 Chestnut Ridge Road
Woodcliff Lake, NJ 07675

International Paper Co.
2 Manhattanville Rd.
Purchase, NY 10577

ITT Corp.
320 Park Avenue
New York, NY 10022

K Mart Corp.
3100 W. Big Beaver Road
Troy, MI 48084

Kaiser Permanente
393 East Walnut Street
Pasadena, CA 91188

Kellogg Company
1 Kellogg Square
Battle Creek, MI 49016

Kelly Services, Inc.
999 West Big Beaver Road
Troy, MI 48084

Kimberly Clark Corp.
545 East John W. Carpenter Freeway
Irving, TX 75062

KPMG Peat Marwick
767 5th Avenue
New York, NY 10153

Leviton Manufacturing Company, Inc.
59-25 Little Neck Parkway
Little Neck, NY 11362

Loctite Corp.
10 Columbus Boulevard
Hartford, CT 06106

Lukens Inc.
50 South 1st Avenue
Coatesville, PA 19320

Marriot Corp.
1 Marriot Drive
Charlotte, NC 28202

Medtronic Inc.
7000 Central Avenue NE
Minneapolis, MN 55432

Merck and Co. Inc.
126 East Lincoln Avenue
Rahway, NJ 07065

Metropolitan Life Insurance Co.
1 Madison Avenue
New York, NY 10010

Mobil Corporation
3225 Gallows Road
Fairfax, VA 22037

Monsanto Company
800 North Lindbergh Boulevard
Saint Louis, MO 63167

Morgan Stanley and Co.
1251 6th Avenue
New York, NY 10020

Mutual of Omaha International Shares
10235 Regency Circle
Omaha, NE 68114

Nationwide Insurance Co.
1 Nationwide Plaza
Columbus, OH 43215

Navistar International Transportation Corp.
455 North Cityfront Plaza Drive
Chicago, IL 60611

NCR Corp.
1700 South Patterson Boulevard
Dayton, OH 45479

Norfolk Southern Corp.
3 Commercial Place
Norfolk, VA 23510

North American Philips Corp.
100 East 42d Street
New York, NY 10017

Occidental Petroleum Corp.
10889 Wilshire Boulevard
Los Angeles, CA 90024

Pacific Bell
140 New Montgomery Street
San Francisco, CA 94105

Panhandle Eastern Corp.
5400 Westheimer Court
Houston, TX 77056

JC Penney Co. Inc.
4808 University Drive NW
Huntsville, AL 35816

Peoples Energy Corp.
122 South Michigan Avenue
Chicago, IL 60603

Pizza Huts Inc.
9111 East Douglas Avenue
Wichita, KS 67207

PPG Industries Inc.
1 PPG Place
Pittsburgh, PA 15272

Prentice Hall Simon & Schuster
Prentice Hall Building
Route 9W
Englewood Cliffs, NJ 07632

Procter and Gamble Co.
1 Procter & Gamble Plaza
Cincinnati, OH 45202

Promus Company
1023 Cherry Road
Memphis, TN 38117

Prudential Insurance Co. of America
751 Broad Street
Newark, NJ 07102

Reynolds Metals Company
6601 West Broad Street
Richmond, VA 23230

Rochester Telephone Corp.
180 Clinton Avenue
Rochester, NY 14646

Ryder Truck Rental Inc.
3600 N.W. 82d Avenue
Miami, FL 33166

Sara Lee Bakery Co.
70 West Madison
Chicago, IL 60602

Sea First Bank
1001 4th Avenue
Seattle, WA 98154

Sheraton Hotels
60 State Street
Boston, MA 02109

Society Corp.
800 Superior Avenue East
Cleveland, OH 44114

Sonoco Products Co.
North 2d Street
Hartsville, SC 29550

State Farm Life and Accident Ins. Co.
1 State Farm Plaza
Bloomington, IL 61710

Stouffer Hotel Corp.
29800 Bainbridge Road
Solon, OH 44139

Taco Bell Corp.
17901 Van Karman Avenue
Irvine, CA 92714

Tandy Corporation
1 Tandy Center, #1800
Fort Worth, TX 76102

Texaco Inc.
2000 Westchester Ave.
White Plains, NY 10650

Texas Instruments Inc.
P.O. Box 655474
Dallas, TX 75265

Travelers Corp.
1 Tower Square
Hartford, CT 06183

Upjohn Company
7000 Portage Road
Kalamazoo, MI 49001

USX Corp.
600 Grant Street
Pittsburgh, PA 15219

Wendy's International
4288 West Dublin Granville Road
Dublin, OH 43017

Young and Rubicam Inc.
285 Madison Avenue
New York, NY 10017

## Find Out More

The lists above all provide the names and addresses of specific corporate resources. For more general information, try the following.

### Business Associations

American Management Association
135 West 50th Street
New York, NY 10020
(212) 903-7915

The Conference Board
845 Third Avenue
New York, NY 10022-6601
(212) 759-0900

1755 Massachusetts Avenue, N.W.
Suite 300
Washington, D.C. 20036
(202) 483-0580

360 North Michigan Avenue
Suite 901
Chicago, IL 60601
(312) 609-1302

7 Crow Canyon Court
Suite 104
San Ramon, CA 94583
(415) 820-6399

National Alliance of Business
1201 New York Avenue, N.W.
Washington, DC 20005
(202) 289-2910

National Association of Manufacturers
1331 Pennsylvania Avenue, N.W.
Suite 1500, North Office Lobby
Washington, DC 20004-1703
(202) 637-3000
Fax: (202) 637-3428

### Chambers of Commerce

UNITED STATES

U.S. Chamber of Commerce
1615 H Street NW
Washington, DC 20062-0001

ALABAMA

Alabama Business Council
468 South Perry Street
Montgomery, AL 36104-4236

ALASKA

Alaska State Chamber of Commerce
217 2d Street, No. 201
Juneau, AK 99801

ARIZONA

Arizona Chamber of Commerce
1221 East Osborn Road
Phoenix, AZ 85014

**ARKANSAS**

Arkansas State Chamber of Commerce
410 Cross Street
Little Rock, AR 72201

**CALIFORNIA**

California Chamber of Commerce
1201 K Street, 12th Floor
Sacramento, CA 95814

**COLORADO**

Colorado Association of Commerce and Industry
1776 Lincoln Street, #1200
Denver, CO 80203

**CONNECTICUT**

Connecticut Business and Industry Association
370 Asylum Street, 5th Floor
Hartford, CT 06103

**DELAWARE**

Delaware State Chamber of Commerce
1 Commerce Center, No. 200
Wilmington, DE 19801

**FLORIDA**

Florida State Chamber of Commerce
136 South Bronough Street
Tallahassee, FL 32302

**GEORGIA**

Business Council of Georgia
233 Peachtree Street, No. 200
Atlanta, GA 30303

**HAWAII**

Hawaii Chamber of Commerce
735 Bishop Street, No. 220
Honolulu, HI 96813

**IDAHO**

Boise Area Chamber of Commerce
300 North 6th Street
Boise, ID 83701

**ILLINOIS**

Illinois State Chamber of Commerce
20 North Wacker Drive
Chicago, IL 60606

**INDIANA**

Indiana State Chamber of Commerce
1 North Capitol, No. 200
Indianapolis, IN 46204-2248

**IOWA**

Iowa Department of Economic Development
200 East Grand Avenue
Des Moines, IA 50309

**KANSAS**

Kansas Chamber of Commerce and Industry
500 Bank IB Tower
Topeka, KS 66603

**KENTUCKY**

Kentucky Chamber of Commerce
452 Versailles Road
Frankfort, KY 40602

**LOUISIANA**
Louisiana Association of Business
3113 Valley Creek Drive
Baton Rouge, LA 70898

**MAINE**
Maine Chamber of Commerce
and Industry
126 Sewall Street
Augusta, ME 04330

**MARYLAND**
Maryland Chamber of Commerce
275 West Street, No. 400
Annapolis, MD 21401

**MASSACHUSETTS**
Massachusetts Office of Business
Development
Boston, MA 02202

**MICHIGAN**
Michigan State Chamber of Commerce
600 South Walnut Street
Lansing, MI 48933

**MINNESOTA**
Minnesota Chamber of Commerce
480 Cedar Street, No. 500
Saint Paul, MN 55101

**MISSISSIPPI**
Mississippi Economic Council
P.O. Box 23276
Jackson, MS 39225

**MISSOURI**
Missouri State Chamber of Commerce
428 East Capitol Avenue
Jefferson City, MO 65101

**MONTANA**
Montana Chamber of Commerce
2030 11th Avenue
Helena, MT 59601

**NEBRASKA**
Nebraska Chamber of Commerce
and Industry
1320 Lincoln Mall
Lincoln, NE 68508

**NEVADA**
Nevada State Chamber of Commerce
P.O. Box 3499
Reno, NV 89505

**NEW HAMPSHIRE**
New Hampshire Business and Industry
Association
Concord, NH 03301

**NEW JERSEY**
New Jersey State Chamber
of Commerce
5 Commerce Street
Newark, NJ 07102

**NEW MEXICO**
Association of Commerce and Industry
of New Mexico
Albuquerque, NM 87106

**NORTH CAROLINA**

North Carolina Citizens for Business and Industry
Raleigh, NC 27603

**NORTH DAKOTA**

Greater North Dakota Association
808 3d Avenue South
Fargo, ND 58108

**OHIO**

Ohio State Chamber of Commerce
35 East Gay Street
Columbus, OH 43215

**OKLAHOMA**

Oklahoma State Chamber of Commerce and Industry
Oklahoma City, OK 73105

**PENNSYLVANIA**

Pennsylvania Chamber of Business and Industry
Harrisburg, PA 17101

**RHODE ISLAND**

Greater Providence Chamber of Commerce
30 Exchange Terrace
Providence, RI 02903

**SOUTH CAROLINA**

South Carolina Chamber of Commerce
1201 Main Street, No. 1810
Columbia, SC 29201

**SOUTH DAKOTA**

Industry and Commerce Association of South Dakota
Pierre, SD 57501-2521

**TENNESSEE**

Nashville Area Chamber of Commerce
161 4th Avenue North
Nashville, TN 37219

**TEXAS**

Texas State Chamber of Commerce
900 Congress Avenue, No. 501
Austin, TX 78701

**UTAH**

Provo/Orem Chamber of Commerce
777 South State Street
Orem, UT 84058

**VERMONT**

Vermont Chamber of Commerce
P.O. Box 37
Montpelier, VT 05601

**VIRGINIA**

Virginia Chamber of Commerce
9 South 5th Street
Richmond, VA 23219

**WASHINGTON**

Greater Seattle Chamber of Commerce
600 University Street, No. 1200
Seattle, WA 98101

**WEST VIRGINIA**

West Virginia Chamber of Commerce
300 Capitol Street, No. 1000
Charleston, WV 25301

**WISCONSIN**

Wisconsin Manufacturers
and Commerce Association
501 East Washington
Madison, WI 53701

**WYOMING**

Greater Cheyenne Chamber
of Commerce
301 West 16th Street
Cheyenne, WY 82001

## Making Decisions

From all the companies and other resources listed in this chapter, you *can* find a job that comes with useful training attached. It may not be easy, but it's simple. Here's how:

*Ask.* Call the companies you're interested in directly and ask for information about their training programs. Ask for their annual report. Don't say why you're asking—just that you're interested. Chances are good you'll be able to get this information from many companies in the mail. Or check a good-sized local library, where you're likely to find not only detailed directories of local companies, but files of reports and other corporate information.

Ask what percentage of payroll cost is spent on training: 1 percent is average; 4 percent is great. (If they don't tell you, they're probably not proud of it.)

*Look for a corporate attitude that supports training.* Ask for a printed statement of mission, corporate values, or development philosophy. Whether reading company material or listening to an interviewer, go beyond the words. Every company pays lip service to "employee development." If the words are backed up by such realities as a clear commitment to the TQM mode, a fully staffed human resources department, and/or a generous tuition-reimbursement benefit, chances are good for meaningful training. A thorough orientation program is a good sign, too. And if you can see a catalog of courses offered by the company, look for ones that go beyond the needs of specific jobs.

*Tip:* Find out how much the CEO is paid. If the gap between that salary and others is monstrous, "concern for employees" is an empty phrase. The more equal the pay, the fairer the shake you'll get.

*Be smart.* Don't say, "I want to work for you because I want to take advantage of the training you offer"! You'll find shelves full of books on interviews and other job-seeking techniques. Make use of them. Most advise doing your homework thoroughly before making contact with a potential employer. That's especially good advice when you're seeking not just a job, but training, too. For each employer you consider, be clear about the elements of the formula:

What do I want to do?

\+ What opportunities are available?

\+ What skills are demanded?

− What skills do I have?

= Career training needed to fill gap

*Tip:* Don't settle for "any old job." If you can't find corporate training, there are other resources that you can use while supporting yourself with "any old job."

*Say what it is you have and what it is you want.* Especially if you are at mid-career, be prepared to detail what skills you have to offer an employer in a new field. Remember that even in areas where you have no specific experience, you may have skills: For example, all companies need accountants, and you could "trade" your numbers skills for a new direction.

Present *all* your assets: Check the self-test you did in Chapter 2. And try following scripts like:

"I've been looking for the opportunity to move into a field like yours, because..."

"I want to work for a company forward-looking enough (like yours) to..."

"I think that even though this is a new field for me, my experience fits your needs, because..."

*Tip:* Ask the interviewer or recruiter how he or she has benefited from company training.

*Check for transferable skills*—yours *and* theirs. Rate each possibility against the career-change checklist:

What do I want or need to learn? (What can I learn?)

Where will it get me? (Will it get me where I want to be?)

Is it suited to me? (*Why* is it suited to me?)

How much can I manage? (Can I devote full time? Can I devote part time? Can I live on the stipend or half pay? Can I afford it?)

The job that fits in with your answers to those questions—plus gives you a salary—may be one you want to keep! In any case, on-the-job training is a terrific source for adding to your skills portfolio.

# 6
# Uncle Sam Trains You

## Preview

*Programs:* A vast array of training and educational programs in a wide variety of occupations is provided directly by federal government agencies—including the military—to their civilian and civil service employees *and others.*

*Pros and cons:* Though most require employment by the government, and competition for these jobs may be stiff, some are offered to job candidates and others are offered to nonemployees. Programs available to nonemployees are free; federal workers receive full pay and benefits. Training may require temporary relocation, or you may have to commit to a certain length of employment with the agency that trains you. But, wherever you are in your career, the pro's—in addition to salary and benefits—include outstanding training and a great resume.

*Possibilities:* Here are descriptions of training programs throughout the federal government, with details on gaining access to thousands more. (For federally *sponsored* programs, see Chapter 7.)

Uncle Sam *wants* to train you. You may associate U.S. training with the military's "be all you can be," but you don't have to join up to take advantage of Uncle Sam's career training opportunities. Many government agencies, both military and civilian, provide earn-while-you-learn training for job candidates as well as for employees—and free programs for those outside the government.

While federal employment is competitive, government jobs are open to all. Federal employers don't discriminate by age, gender, or disability. Many recent grads sign on for government service as a way of honing their degrees into something useful. The federal government is also glad to have workers with experience in private industry—just as the private sector looks favorably on those with government experience. Since the end of the draft and the inception of the all-volunteer army, increasing numbers of the career-minded have signed up. Even if you're past draft age, you can take advantage of military training—and without enlisting.

## A Few Facts

The country's biggest employer is also one of the country's leading trainers, with literally thousands of programs available to both employees and the general public. We're not talking workfare programs or make-work projects here, but high-quality professional training that you can receive while working in a steady-paying job.

Military or nonmilitary—the scope of training opportunities is unmatched. Uncle Sam's employees—who work throughout the country and around the world—specialize in

Accounting

Administration

Agricultural science

Arts

Business trade and contracts

Biological and physical sciences

Education

Engineering and electronics

Finance and banking

Health sciences

International relations

Law

Law enforcement

Management

Social services

For some federal jobs—air traffic controller, FBI agent, CIA operative, for instance—you train before you enter the full-time positions. Most federal jobs require expertise for entry, and base acceptance on passing a Civil Service exam. *All* offer continuing education and training. In fact, the Government Employee Training Act *directs* agencies to:

> supplement employee self-education...through programs established to train employees in the performance of their official duties and further develop their knowledge, skills, and abilities....The agency may pay for the training of employees in nongovernmental facilities when such training programs are necessary.

## Some Factors to Consider

The training that accompanies federal employment can be an excellent resource for anyone who can meet the specific eligibility requirements and commit the time required. Don't assume that Uncle Sam's training consists of bureaucratic lectures. Much of it is outstanding and creative. Almost every management seminar or professional workshop you might attend is likely to include at least one federal employee, sent there to learn the same skills that business attendees have been sent to learn. And the Tennessee Valley Authority (TVA) recently initiated the same kind of TQM approach to training as some of the nation's leading corporations, providing, among other types of training, ongoing, mandatory education and development programs in such high-demand management skills as team building, problem solving, and communications skills.

Nor need you be a civil servant to take advantage of federal training. You could, for instance, *join the corps*—Uncle Sam's training and service corps: the Job Corps, the Peace Corps, Teach America, and the Health Service Corps. All provide training or education, plus experience with pay, to those who qualify and are willing to make a commitment.

*The Job Corps.* Formed during the "war on poverty" of the 1960s, the Job Corps is still going strong, though its programs are geared primarily to low-income young people who lack basic skills. For details, call (202) 245-7000.

*The Peace Corps.* The early nineties saw a renewal of interest in the Peace Corps due to a combination of high unemployment rates, heightened idealism, and the opening of new frontiers for service in Asia and eastern Europe. The Peace Corps asks that you bring some skills with you and pass a qualifying training program. Other than that, there are no age or other restrictions, and you can gain training, education, and experience in valuable international skills while being paid (a little) and seeing the world at Uncle Sam's expense. In return, you agree to spend at least two years of your life on a foreign, usually primitive, post. For details, call (202) 606-3886.

*Teach America.* This corps, established in 1991, is a federally funded project that sends teachers into education-poor urban neighborhoods and rural districts. Most who join this corps of teachers are recent college grads—but not all. No teaching experience or education is required: just an interest and enough aptitude to make it through a training period. As a teacher, you're assigned to a district and a job—and some of those assignments can be rugged. But it's a way to get teaching credentials for free if you're willing to commit to a two-year stint. For details, contact (202) 401-3000.

*The National Health Service Corps.* The National Health Service Corps sends health professionals into needy areas of the country, providing them with support and training. For those who qualify, the corps pays medical or nursing school tuition in return for a commitment to serve as assigned for an additional two years. For details, contact the Public Health Service, Department of Health and Human Services, (301) 443-2900.

Is any of this right for you? It is if, as you explore the possibilities, you keep in mind the formula:

What do I want to do?
\+ What opportunities are available?
\+ What skills are demanded?
− What skills do I have?
= Career training needed to fill gap

## How to Find Federal Training Opportunities

The following lists give information about the kinds of training available to civilian employees of the federal government, and, in some cases, to nonemployees. Both civil service and military programs are covered, as well as training that comes with academic credit.

Many of the listings are accompanied by a brief description of the programs and prerequisites, and information about pay and/or credit or certificates received.

### Civil Service Agencies

Agriculture Department
Washington, DC 20250
(202) 447-2791

*Programs:* Career development training in almost all areas managed by the Department of Agriculture, from engineering and conservation through foreign marketing and nutrition, designed to develop specialized skills for department administration, but employment commitment not required.

*Prerequisites:* Must meet government service (GS) requirements for individual jobs. Locate in D.C.

*Pay-Plus:* Trainees receive regular government salaries and benefits.

Central Intelligence Agency
Box 1925
Washington, DC 20013
(202) 482-1100

*Programs:* Career training program; internships for graduate students. Designed to develop specialized skills in a variety of intelligence-gathering activities. Long-term commitment not required.

*Prerequisites:* College degree; candidates are screened; locate in D.C.

*Pay-Plus:* Trainees receive normal pay and benefits.

Drug Enforcement Administration
555 West 57th Street
New York, NY

800 Dirksen Federal Building
Chicago, IL 60604

8400 N.W. 53d Street
Miami, FL 33166

Earl Cabell Federal Building,
Room 4A5
1100 Commerce Street
Dallas, TX 75202

350 South Figuora Street, Suite 800
Los Angeles, CA 90071

*Programs:* Agent training including surveillance, interviewing witnesses, seizure of contraband, raids, and more. Ongoing programs for middle managers, supervisors, and personnel assigned to higher-level positions; in-service programs in areas such as conspiracy investigations and specialized enforcement techniques.

*Prerequisites:* College graduates under the age of 35, excellent physical condition, 1 to 3 years' experience.

*Pay-Plus:* Health and life insurance and pension plan.

Federal Bureau of Investigation
J. Edgar Hoover Building
9th Street and Pennsylvania Avenue, N.W.
Washington, D.C. 20535
(202) 324-3000

*Programs:* Training for special agents and nonagent positions including technical, financial, and management areas.

*Prerequisites:* All applicants must pass a thorough background investigation.

*Pay-Plus:* Special agents and some nonagents are covered by the Civil Service Act. Special agents receive their regular salary while attending training school.

Federal Communications Commission
1919 M Street N.W.
Washington, DC 20544
(202) 632-7000

*Programs:* Career training in law, engineering, accounting, telecommunications, others, toward increasing and focusing expertise in administrative areas.

*Prerequisites:* College, some graduate degrees; locate in D.C.

*Pay-Plus:* Normal pay and benefits for GS level.

Federal Deposit Insurance Corporation
Professional Recruitment Office
550 17th Street N.W.
Washington, DC 20429
(202) 393-6400

*Programs:* Career training supplemented by bank examination school, correspondence courses, resident schools of banking, regional office conferences.

*Prerequisites:* College graduates in business administration, finance, economics, or accounting, or three years of bank or bank examining experience.

*Pay-Plus:* Health and life insurance and retirement plans.

Federal Mine Health and Safety Academy
Administrative Officer
1730 K Street N.W.
Washington, DC 20006
(202) 653-5615

*Programs:* Technical and managerial education and training for coal and metal/nonmetal mine inspectors and other technical specialists required to enforce the provisions of the Federal Mine Safety and Health Act of 1977.

Food and Drug Administration
U.S. Department of Health and Human Services
Public Health Service

5600 Fishers Lane
Rockville, MD 20852
(301) 443-2410

*Programs:* Technical training, training for office and managerial positions, training for chemists, consumer safety officer, and microbiologist.

*Prerequisites:* Vary depending on position—all require bachelor's degree.

*Pay-Plus:* Group health, life insurance, and retirement.

General Accounting Office
Office of Personnel Management
441 G Street N.W.
Washington, DC 20548
(202) 275-6361

*Programs:* Career development, orientation, and technical seminars; on-the-job training.

*Prerequisites:* College graduates.

*Pay-Plus:* Health life insurance, and retirement program.

Interior Department
National Park Service
P.O. Box 37127
Washington, DC 20013-7127
(202) 343-6702

*Programs:* Career development in areas including park rangers, park police, guards, administrative, design and construction, and maintenance; full-time graduate-level work at selected universities.

*Pay-Plus:* Annual and sick leave, retirement, life and health insurance; locations in continental United States, Hawaii, Guam, Puerto Rico, and the Virgin Islands.

Internal Revenue Service
Department of the Treasury
1111 Constitution Avenue N.W.
Washington, D.C. 20224
(202) 566-3617

*Programs:* Career training and development programs—areas include tax law, accounting, auditing standards, and interacting with people as well as policies, procedures, and administrative practices; combination of formal classroom training and on-the-job training.

*Pay-Plus:* Health and life insurance plus annual leaves and retirement plan.

IRS Federal Law Enforcement Training Center

*Programs:* Training programs directly related to IRS operations including a wide range of clerical, secretarial, tax law, technical, and managerial areas.

Justice Department
10th Street and Constitution Avenues N.W.
Washington, D.C. 20530
(202) 514-2000

Immigration and Naturalization Service
Federal Law Enforcement Training Center
Building 20
Glynco, GA 31524

*Programs:* Basic border patrol training through the Border Patrol Academy; training for immigration investigators, examiners, inspectors, and officers through the Immigration Officer Academy.

U.S. Marshals Service
Federal Law Enforcement Training Center

*Programs:* Five-week classroom instruction in basic deputy course; practical exercises; administrative support time.

*Prerequisites:* All students are required to complete a basic course at the Federal Law Enforcement Training Center.

Labor Department
DOL Academy
200 Constitution Avenue N.W.
Washington, D.C. 20210
(202) 523-7316

*Programs:* Training for employees through four institutes—Office Skills Institute, Supervisory Institute, Managerial Institute, and Executive Institute.

National Credit Union Administration
1776 G Street N.W.

Division of Personnel
Washington, DC 20456
(202) 682-9600

*Programs:* Four part training program for examiners—regional orientation, fieldwork, classroom instruction, and follow-up and independent study.

*Prerequisites:* Bachelor's degree or equivalent experience and 24 semester hours of accounting. Willing to train in Washington D.C. and work in one of six locations across the country.

National Cryptologic School
Attention: M322 (AAP)
Ft. Meade, MD 20755

*Programs:* Classes in language and technical and management areas—traditional and self-paced instruction.

*Prerequisites:* College graduates in areas of Asian, Middle Eastern, and Slavic languages; liberal arts; business; and physical science. Personal interviews, background investigation, medical examination. Contact the National Security Agency at least six months prior to date interested. U.S. citizenship is required of all applicants and their immediate family members.

*Pay-Plus:* Part-time with full tuition support at many nearby universities including University of Maryland, Johns Hopkins, and Georgetown. Salaries competitive with private industry and based on qualifications. Health and life insurance, paid holidays and vacation, sick leave.

National Institute of Standards and Technology
Personnel Division, Employment Services
Quince Orchard Road
Gaithersburg, MD 20899
(301) 975-3058

*Programs:* Training in cooperative education; graduate research fellowships; National Research Council postdoctoral research associateship; administrative internship; academic summer program; employee development program.

*Prerequisites:* College graduates in physics, chemistry, mathematics, computer science, metallurgy, and civil, chemical, electronic, electrical, and mechanical engineering.

*Pay-Plus:* Health and life insurance, retirement programs, and educational assistance.

National Labor Relations Board
Personnel Branch
1717 Pennsylvania Avenue N.W.
Washington, DC 20570
(202) 254-9200

*Programs:* Training and career development in varied areas including field examiner, law clerk, and attorney.

*Prerequisites:* Field examiners must have work experience in labor-management relations or related field, or undergraduate study with at least 24 semester hours of related subjects. Attorneys must be a member of the bar. Law graduates accepted for a maximum of 14 months as law clerks—appointment changed to attorney appointment upon admittance to the bar.

National Security Agency
Professional Recruitment
Ft. Meade, MD 20755
(301) 688-6524

*Programs:* Career development and orientations in engineering, computer science, and physics.

*Prerequisites:* College graduate in any area of engineering, physics, mathematics, or computer science.

*Pay-Plus:* Health and life insurance, retirement plans, and educational assistance.

Nuclear Regulatory Commission
Division of Organization and Personnel
Washington, DC 20555
(301) 492-4661

*Programs:* Internships, cooperative education, and summer technical programs.

*Prerequisites:* College graduates or students in technical areas.

*Pay-Plus:* For full-time employees: health and life insurance, disability, credit union, and retirement program.

Office of Personnel Management (OPM)
1900 E Street N.W.
Washington, DC 20415
(202) 606-2424

*Programs:* Training programs through the Training and Investigations Group (TIG).

*Prerequisites:* All permanent staff selected through the civil service merit system; employees nominated by their supervisors.

*Pay-Plus:* TIG centers are located in New York State, Tennessee, Colorado, and Washington, D.C. OPM's five regional centers are located in Atlanta, Chicago, Dallas, Philadelphia, and San Francisco.

Social Security Administration
Division of Personnel
6401 Security Boulevard
Baltimore, MD 21235
(410) 965-2736

*Programs:* Training for social insurance representative and claims authorizer; management intern program; career opportunities and cooperative education program, plus executive development programs, available for employees.

*Prerequisites:* College graduates who have taken the Professional and Administrative Career Examination (PACE).

*Pay-Plus:* Health and life insurance, sick leave, and retirement.

State Department
2201 C Street N.W.
Washington, D.C. 20520
(202) 647-6132

Agency for International Development
Washington, DC 20523

*Programs:* Staff training courses for various government agencies, bureaus, missions, and offices; course catalog can be obtained from AID at above address.

Foreign Service
P.O. Box 9317
Arlington, VA 20009

*Programs:* Career candidate training.

*Prerequisites:* Extensive screening, oral assessment; must be U.S. citizen at least 20 years old, available for worldwide assignment, medical and security clearances.

*Pay-Plus:* Health and retirement benefits, cost-of-living allowances, hardship differentials, educational allowances for children.

International Communications Agency
Professional Recruitment
Washington, DC 20547

*Programs:* Career development including orientation and training in Washington, D.C., comprehensive minority training programs, management intern programs, and international broadcasting program.

*Prerequisites:* College graduates; applicants must take the Foreign Service Officer Examination given each December and an oral examination and evaluation. Application dates are from January 1 to March 31 of each year.

Treasury Department
1500 Pennsylvania Avenue N.W.
Washington, D.C. 20220
(202) 566-2000

Federal Law Enforcement Training Center

*Programs:* Basic and advanced training for law enforcement personnel offered at more than 60 participating federal agencies.

Secret Service
Personnel Office
1800 G Street N.W.
Washington, DC 20233

*Programs:* Secret service training program; uniformed service and special agent training.

*Prerequisites:* Uniformed service applicants must have high school diploma or equivalent or one-year experience as a police officer in a large city. Applicants must pass written test and qualify for top-secret clearance. Special agent applicants must be under 35, have a B.A. or 3 years' experience (two in criminal investigation), or a combination thereof. All applicants must be in good physical condition.

Bureau of Alcohol, Tobacco, and Firearms
1200 Pennsylvania Avenue
Washington, DC 20226

*Programs:* Training for inspectors and special agents.

*Prerequisites:* Inspectors—B.A., 3 years' experience or certificate as CPA. Special agents—B.A. or 1 year's experience plus 2 years of specialized experience including responsibility for criminal investigation.

Must pass the Treasury Enforcement Agent (TEA) examination.

*Pay-Plus:* Civil service employee status.

U.S. Postal Service
Department of Training and Development
475 L'Enfant Plaza S.W.
Washington, DC 20260
(202) 268-3646

*Programs:* Training through the Department of Training and Development within the Human Resources Group located at the U.S. Postal Service Headquarters in Washington, D.C.; programs for postal managers, supervisors, etc., include correspondence programs, an inspection training program, a management academy, a management training series, and technical training; courses are offered at postal employee development centers at major post offices.

Veterans Affairs Department
810 Vermont Avenue N.W.
Washington, DC 20420
(202) 233-4000

*Programs:* Administrative training program in various areas including acquisition and material management, canteen management, accounting, clerical, computers, medical, automotive, air conditioning, industrial, engineering, and nursing.

*Pay-Plus:* Health and life insurance, promotion possibilities.

## Civilian Training from the Military

Defense Department
The Pentagon
Civilian Personnel
Washington, D.C. 20301
(202) 697-9336

Defense Contract Audit Agency
Civilian Personnel Division
Recruitment Branch
Washington, DC 20301

*Programs:* Career development training in intelligence orientation and introduction to military intelligence, management, verbal and written communications, data processing, and technical subjects.

*Prerequisites:* College graduates.

*Pay-Plus:* Health and life insurance, retirement programs, and educational assistance.

Defense Contract Audit Agency
Cameron Station
Alexandria, VA 22314

*Programs:* Professional development with training in specialized technical areas such as advanced accounting; management workshops and seminars; many courses offered by universities and federal agencies.

*Prerequisites:* Bachelor's degree with major in accounting.

*Pay-Plus:* Hospital, surgical, and medical benefits, life insurance, sick leave, annual leave, retirement program.

U.S. Army
Personnel and Employment Service
The Pentagon
Washington, D.C. 20310-6800
(202) 695-0010

Army Corps of Engineers
Chief of Engineers
Department of the Army
Washington, DC 20314

*Programs:* An 18-month graduate engineering program, internships programs; career development programs.

*Prerequisites:* College graduates, willing to relocate as assigned.

U.S. Navy
Civilian Personnel
CCPO-CC, Room 424
Washington, DC 20376
(202) 692-4139

Center for Naval Analyses
2000 North Beauregard Street
P.O. Box 11280
Alexandria, VA 22311

*Programs:* Fellowships, research grants, and scholarships.

*Prerequisites:* College graduate, especially advanced degrees in mathematics, statistics, physical and social sciences, or operations research.

*Pay-Plus:* Health and life insurance, disability coverage, retirement program, credit union, and tuition assistance.

Naval Oceanographic Office
NSTL Station
Bay St. Louis, MO 39522

*Programs:* Varied training programs from secretarial to technical.

*Prerequisites:* Requirements vary according to position.

*Pay-Plus:* Civilian positions for the Navy, 13 to 26 paid vacation days a year plus 10 paid holidays and 13 sick days. Federal retirement plan; locations nationwide; cash incentive awards programs.

Naval Sea Systems Command
Department of the Navy
Washington, DC 20362

*Programs:* On-the-job training, orientation trips, work assignments, meetings and conferences, rotational work assignments, individual counseling.

*Prerequisites:* College graduates in engineering or science with professional experience in appropriate areas.

Naval Ship Weapon Systems Engineering Station
Port Hueneme, CA 93043

*Programs:* Professional development including individual programs, rotational assignment schedules, and on-station seminars.

*Prerequisites:* Bachelor's or master's degree in engineering or equivalent.

*Pay-Plus:* Access to special training and scholarship programs and up to 2080 hours of advanced education in nongovernment facilities during each 10 years of employment.

Naval Surface Weapons Center
College Recruitment Coordinator
Human Resources Division
Silver Spring, MD 20910

*Programs:* Orientation; job-related educational programs; graduate or undergraduate part-time study programs; full-time study and graduate work-study programs; specialized courses and seminars given by universities and industry.

*Prerequisites:* College graduate in science and engineering.

Naval Undersea Center
Employment Office
San Diego, CA 92132

*Programs:* Professional programs, resident day course program, graduate academic program, full-time fellowships.

*Prerequisites:* College graduate in science or engineering.

Navy Acquisitions Management Training Office

*Programs:* Training for civilian employees provided through Department of Defense Civilian Career Program.

*Pay-Plus:* Salary and benefits.

Navy Resale System
3d Avenue and 29th Street
Brooklyn, NY 11232

*Programs:* Management training in the Navy's worldwide retail and service operation, providing food and merchandise to Navy personnel and families. Designed to develop specializations in over a dozen management skills.

*Prerequisites:* College degree and/or experience in business-related fields; willingness to travel and to spend some time employed in Navy retail and service centers.

*Pay-Plus:* Trainees receive regular government salaries and benefits.

Pacific Missile Test Center
Personnel Operations Division
Point Mugu, CA 93042

*Programs:* Training includes engineering, youth opportunity, programs for women, technical and scientific training.

*Prerequisites:* College graduate, especially majors in science, engineering, psychology, and mathematics; willing to work in Point Mugu (one hour north of Los Angeles).

## Programs Offering Academic Credit

Many of the federal government's training and education programs come with academic credit attached. Some examples follow, led by *the* U.S. graduate school, operated by the Department of Agriculture with courses open to the general public as well as to employees:

United States Department of Agriculture
Graduate School
Room 1103, South Agricultural Building
14th and Independence Avenue, N.W.
Washington, DC 20250

*Programs:* Accredited graduate school program designed to improve "government service and self-development through education and training." Program is *not* limited to employees. Classes located in Washington, D.C.; on-site or correspondence. More than 40 subject areas, including accounting, computer science, and editing.

Other programs include:

Department of Defense
Defense Security Institute
c/o Defense General Supply Center
Richmond, VA 23297-5091

*Programs:* Accredited program. Resident, field extension, and correspondence courses relating to the Department of Defense security programs. Courses designed for U.S. government personnel, plus selected employees and representatives of U.S. industry.

*Prerequisites:* Bachelor's or associate degree.

*Pay-Plus:* Course diploma awarded upon demonstration of mastery of course content. Certificates or letter of attendance also given in lieu of diploma depending on individual performance.

Environmental Protection Agency
401 M Street S.W.
Washington, DC 20460
(202) 382-7884

*Programs:* Accredited program. Courses for personnel who respond to emergencies or who investigate and clean up abandoned hazardous waste sites, including hazardous materials, air surveillance, emergency responses to incidents, and personnel protection.

*Pay-Plus:* Certificates are awarded upon completion of program; college credit recommended for those with passing grade of 70 or better and 100 percent class participation.

National Emergency Training Center
The Emergency Management Institute
16825 South Seton Drive
Emmitsburg, MD 21727
(301) 447-1000

*Programs:* Credited courses. Courses, workshops, seminars, and teleconferences in emergency management from earthquakes to hazardous materials to nuclear attack.

*Prerequisite:* Available to emergency workers.

*Pay-Plus:* Off-campus training available.

The National Fire Academy

*Programs:* Credited courses. Training opportunities in fire prevention.

*Prerequisites:* Courses are targeted to middle- and top-level officers and representatives from the allied professions.

*Pay-Plus:* Off-campus training also available through local state fire training officials.

Federal Aviation Administration
800 Independence Avenue S.W.
Washington, DC 20591
(202) 267-3484

*Programs:* Accredited programs for air traffic control specialists, engineers, technicians, and pilots.

Naval Ocean Systems Center
Employment Office
San Diego, CA 92152

*Programs:* One-year professional program, resident day course program, graduate academic program.

*Prerequisites:* Graduates in science and engineering.

*Pay-Plus:* Many courses (especially those on graduate level) can be taken during working hours with a full refund of fees for grades of C or better. Full salary, full tuition, and enrollment expenses while attending a local college or university. Work full time during summers and school vacation and attend classes up to 20 hours a week.

The individual states also provide training for their employees, either through their own staffs or at outside institutions. Budget cutbacks during the early 1990s curtailed many of these programs, and imposed hiring freezes as well—but that doesn't mean they're not worth checking out. See the state single-point-of-contact list at the end of Chapter 7.

## Find Out More

Since virtually every federal agency provides training of some kind, it's advisable to contact your department of choice directly to find out what openings are available and how to apply. You can get federal information assistance through the Federal Job Information Center number under "Office of Personnel Management" in the U.S. government section of your phone book, or you can contact the individual agency or department at the location listed below.

### U.S. Government Departments (Nonmilitary)

U.S. Department of Agriculture
14th Street and Independence Avenue S.W.
Washington, DC 20250
(202) 447-2791

U.S. Department of Commerce
14th Street and Constitution Avenue N.W.
Washington, DC 20230
(202) 377-4807

U.S. Department of Defense
Chief, Staffing and Support Programs
Directorate for Personnel and Security
Washington Headquarters
Services, Room 3E843
The Pentagon
Washington, DC 20301
(202) 695-4436

U.S. Department of Education
400 Maryland Avenue S.W.
Washington, DC 20202
(202) 245-8366

U.S. Department of Energy
Forrestal Building
1000 Independence Avenue S.W.
Washington, DC 20585
(202) 252-8731

U.S. Fish and Wildlife Service
Department of the Interior
Washington, DC 20240
(202) 343-5634

U.S. Department of Health and Human Services
200 Independence Avenue S.W.
Washington, DC 20201
(202) 472-6631

U.S. Department of Housing and Urban Development
451 Seventh Street S.W.
Washington, DC 20410
(202) 755-5500

U.S. Department of Interior
18th and C Streets N.W.
Washington, DC 20240
(202) 343-5065

U.S. Department of Justice
Constitution Avenue and Tenth Street N.W.
Washington, DC 20530
(202) 633-2007

U.S. Department of Labor
200 Constitution Avenue N.W.
Washington, DC 20210
(202) 523-6255

Office of Personnel Management
1900 E Street N.W.
Washington, DC 20415
(202) 606-2424

U.S. Postal Service
Headquarters Personnel Division
475 L'Enfant Plaza
Washington, DC 20260
(202) 245-4263

U.S. Secret Service
1800 G Street N.W.
Washington, DC 20223
(202) 535-5708

U.S. Department of Transportation
400 Seventh Street S.W.
Washington, DC 20590
(202) 426-4000

Or:
Central Employment Training Office
Office of Personnel and Training
U.S. Department of Transportation
Washington, DC 20590
(202) 426-2550

U.S. Department of the Treasury
15th Street and Pennsylvania Avenue N.W.
Washington, DC 20220
(202) 566-5061

Veterans Administration
810 Vermont Avenue
Washington, DC 20420
(202) 233-2741

## U.S. Government Departments (Military)

Department of the Air Force
Civilian Personnel Office
1947 AS/DMPKS Pentagon
Washington, DC 20330
(202) 545-6700

Department of the Army
Personnel and Employment Service
The Pentagon
Washington, DC 20310
(202) 697-0335

Department of the Navy
Navy Civilian Personnel Command
801 North Randolph Street
Arlington, VA 22203
(202) 696-4450

Commandant of the Marine Corps
Code (MPC-30)
Headquarters, U.S. Marine Corps
Washington, DC 20380
(202) 694-2500

## Other Government Organizations

Bureau of the Census
Building 3
Washington, DC 20233
(301) 763-7470

Bureau of Engraving and Printing
Employment and Classification Division
Office of Industrial Relations
14th and C Streets N.W.
Washington, DC 20228
(202) 447-0273

Bureau of Land Management
Personnel Officer
Department of the Interior
Washington, DC 20240
(202) 343-9435

Bureau of Mines
Chief, Division of Personnel
Department of the Interior

2401 E Street N.W.
Washington, DC 20241
(202) 634-4704

Bureau of Reclamation
Call personnel office:
(202) 343-5428

Commodities Futures Trading Commission
Director, Office of Personnel
2033 K Street N.W.
Washington, DC 20581
(202) 254-6387

Congressional Budget Office
Second and D Streets N.W.
Washington, DC 20515
(202) 226-2621

Drug Enforcement Administration
1405 I Street N.W.
Washington, DC 20537
(202) 633-1034

Environmental Protection Agency
401 M Street S.W.
Washington, DC 20460
(202) 382-2973

Equal Employment Opportunity Commission
2401 E Street N.W.
Washington, DC 20507
(202) 634-6922

Export-Import Bank of the U.S.
811 Vermont Avenue N.W.
Washington, DC 20571
(202) 666-8834

Federal Aviation Administration
800 Independence Avenue S.W.
Washington, DC 20590
(202) 426-3383

Federal Bureau of Investigation
Ninth Street and Pennsylvania Avenue N.W.
Washington, DC 20535
(202) 324-3000
or:
Applicant Office
Room 1028
Federal Bureau of Investigation
Ninth and Pennsylvania Avenue N.W.
Washington, DC 20535
(202) 324-4960

Federal Communications Commission
1919 M Street N.W.
Washington, DC 20554
(202) 632-7260

Federal Home Loan Bank Board
1700 G Street N.W.
Washington, DC 20552
(202) 377-6000

Federal Maritime Commission
1100 L Street N.W.
Washington, DC 20573
(202) 523-5707

Federal Reserve System
Board of Governors of the Federal Reserve System
20th Street and Constitution Avenue N.W.
Washington, DC 20551
(202) 452-3204

Federal Trade Commission
Pennsylvania Avenue at Sixth Street N.W.
Washington, DC 20580
(202) 326-2222

Food and Drug Administration
5600 Fishers Lane
Rockville, MD 20857
(301) 443-3220

General Services Administration
General Services Building
18th and F Streets N.W.
Washington, DC 20505
(202) 566-0085

Government Printing Office
North Capitol and H Streets N.W.
Washington, DC 20402
(202) 275-2051

House Office Building
Independence Avenue
Washington, DC 20515

Immigration and Naturalization Service
425 I Street N.W.
Washington, DC 20536
(202) 633-2533

Internal Revenue Service
Contact recruitment coordinator at your regional or district office.

Library of Congress
10 First Street S.E.
Washington, DC 20540
(202) 287-5000

Office of Management and Budget
Personnel Office
Executive Office Building
Washington, DC 20503
(202) 395-7250

National Aeronautics and Space Administration (NASA)
400 Maryland Avenue S.W.
Washington, DC 20456
(202) 453-8480

National Archives and Records Service
Seventh Street and Pennsylvania Avenue N.W.
Washington, DC 20408
(202) 523-5264

National Institutes of Health
Division of Personnel Management
Bethesda, MD 20892
(301) 496-4197

National Oceanic and Atmospheric Association
253 Monticello Avenue
Norfolk, VA 23510
(804) 827-6876

National Park Service
Personnel Office
Washington, DC 20240
(202) 343-7394

Or for seasonal employment:
Division of Personnel Management
National Park Service
P.O. Box 37127
18th and C Streets N.W.
Washington, DC 20013-7127
(202) 343-4885

National Weather Service
Gramax Building
8060 13th Street
Silver Spring, MD 20910

Nuclear Regulatory Commission
1717 H Street N.W.
Washington, DC 20555
(202) 492-8272

Office of Technology Assessment
600 Pennsylvania Avenue S.E.
Washington, DC 20510

Securities and Exchange Commission
450 Fifth Street N.W., Room IC45
Washington, DC
(202) 272-2550

Selective Service System
National Headquarters
Washington, DC 20435
(202) 724-0424

Senate Office Building
First Street and Constitution Avenue
Washington, DC 20515
(202) 224-3121

Small Business Administration
Imperial Building
1441 L Street N.W.
Washington, DC 20416
(202) 653-6832

Smithsonian Institution
1000 Jefferson Drive S.W.
Washington, DC 20560
(202) 357-2465

Social Security Administration
6401 Security Boulevard
Baltimore, MD 21235
(301) 594-3060

U.S. Arms Control and Disarmament Agency
320 21st Street N.W.
Washington, DC 20451
(202) 632-2034

## Making Decisions

To get further information about any of the programs listed here, or to get any information from a government agency, all you have to do is ask: the material is free (rather, you've already paid for it with your tax dollars), and it *must* be made available to anyone who requests it.

That's important to remember, because the nation's richest information source is also its largest bureaucracy. To penetrate it requires patience, persistence, and polite insistence. Here are some tips for avoiding the vertigo that can result from multiple transfers around the federal information lines.

Sit by the phone in a comfortable chair, accompanied by paper, pencil, and a supply of light reading material to keep you calm and entertained during what may be some long waits.

Know what you want. "I would like information on program XYZ" will get a much more effective response than "I'm looking for work..." or "Do you have any training in...?"

Always be polite—even friendly. Chat helps: "You sound busy—hard day?" Treat the clerks like human beings—who are doing a boring and/or high-pressure job.

Never get angry—or at least, never show it. Even try to make the contact laugh.

When you've locked onto the information you want, ask for more: "If there's anything else you can send or tell me about that, I'd really appreciate it." (After all, you've waited long enough—don't waste the opportunity!)

Don't take "no" for a (complete) answer. Persist: "According to this directory, you *do* have...." "If you don't have that, what *do* you have?" "If you can't give me the information, could you tell me who can?" You may even find *yourself* laughing. One clerk adamantly resisted all requests for information, then grudgingly gave in: "Well, I can only send you one copy."

Of course, "one copy" of each of the job and/or training programs is all you need to determine which of Uncle Sam's training resources meets your career goals. Begin by matching them against this modified career-change checklist:

What can I learn? (What do I want or need to learn?)

Where will it get me? (Will it get me where I want to be?)

Is it suited to me? (*Why* is it suited to me?)

How can I get it?

How can I get it? That's the real trick, of course—since for most of these programs, you must be a government employee. To apply for the jobs that carry the training you want, most (but not all) government jobs require a standard procedure, which is detailed later in this chapter.

Although hiring in certain areas is always active, your survey of the job availabilities may be discouraging because the federal government imposes freezes during tight economic times.

Remember, however, that, as with most official procedures, there's usually a loophole, a bypass, or both.

Make yourself eligible for the high-interest openings by shaping your resume and application to fit what *is* available.

Pull strings. Most everyone has at least one string to pull at the capital—so call, write, or visit your congressional representative and see what kind of special help you can persuade yourself into, in order to get the training-plus-job you aim for.

The *Federal Career Directory*, available free from the U.S. Government Printing Office, is a thorough overview. Below are five additional sources:

1. A summary of general information about federal jobs
2. A description of federal jobs that are not part of the competitive civil service
3. A state-by-state listing of OPM Federal Job Information/Testing offices
4. A list of government associations
5. A list of directories containing information about government jobs

If working for Uncle Sam seems impractical—or if it simply doesn't appeal—put him to work for *you:* the next chapter details all the training-related resources provided by the government to any resident of the United States.

## General Information about Federal Jobs*

**Competitive Service.** Most of the jobs you know about, and many you may never have heard of, exist in the Federal civil service. Only about 12 percent of them are in Washington, D.C. Government employees work in offices, shipyards, laboratories, national parks, hospitals, military bases and many other settings across the country and around the world. Most Federal civilian jobs are in the competitive service, which means that people applying for them must be evaluated by the Office of Personnel Management (OPM). The information presented applies only to competitive service jobs.

**Excepted Service.** Some specific occupations (among them lawyers and chaplains) and some agencies (for example, the U.S. Postal Service, the Federal Bureau of Investigation and the Central Intelligence Agency) are excepted from OPM competitive service procedures. *If you are interested in an excepted service job, you should not apply through the Office of Personnel Management, but should contact agencies directly.* [See the next section "Excepted Service Organizations."]

**Federal Job Information Centers.** The Office of Personnel Management maintains Federal Job Information Centers in several major metropolitan areas across the country to provide local job information. They are listed under "U.S. Government" in the white pages of metropolitan area phone directories. In addition, Federal employment opportunities are posted in State Job Service (State Employment Security) offices.

**How Jobs Are Filled.** The Office of Personnel Management accepts applications for Federal employment, based on the number of jobs Government agencies estimate they will fill in various locations over a period of time. After you apply, OPM examiners evaluate your application to see whether you are qualified for the kind of work you want. If you are qualified, your name goes on a list with the names of other people who are qualified for the same kinds of jobs. When Government hiring officials have vacancies, they may ask the Office of Personnel Management for the names of people qualified for the jobs. The best

*The information in this section (pages 157 to 160) is from material published by the U.S. Government Printing Office.

qualified peoples' names are referred from OPM for consideration by the agency.

For some competitive service jobs, usually those which exist in only one agency, the Office of Personnel Management authorizes the hiring agency to examine applicants' qualifications. In that case, you apply directly with the agency. Check with the agency where you want to work to see which procedure is used for the job you're interested in.

**Chances for Employment.** Your chances for being hired depend on your qualifications, how fast vacancies are occurring in the area where you want to work, the number of qualified applicants who want the same kind of job, and the salary level you say you will accept. When there are many qualified applicants on Office of Personnel Management lists, applications are no longer accepted until there is a need for them. Because Government hiring needs vary from time to time and from one location to another, you might be able to apply in one location for a particular kind of job and be unable to apply for the same kind of work in another location.

**Veteran Preference.** Veterans are entitled to certain preferences in obtaining Government jobs and in keeping jobs in the event of a layoff. If you are a veteran, be sure to state that you are when you inquire about a Government job.

If applications were accepted during the time they were on active duty, returning veterans may apply within 120 days after discharge, even if applications are not being accepted from non-veterans. If you are entitled to 10-point Veterans Preference, you may apply for many positions at any time.

**How to Apply.** Contact a Federal Job Information Center to find out whether applications are being accepted in your area for the kind of work you want. If you're not sure what kind of work you are interested in, Job Information Specialists may be able to suggest a type of job for which your education and experience qualify you.

If you call or write a Job Information Center, be sure to state:

1. The level of education you have completed and the amount of paid and unpaid experience you have.
2. The kind of work that interests you.
3. The area or areas where you want to work.
4. The lowest salary you will accept.
5. Dates of your military service, if any, or your child's or spouse's service.

Opportunities to compete for Federal jobs are also posted at all State Job Service (State Employment Security) offices.

**Qualifications Needed.** Government jobs are classified by grade levels based on each job's level of difficulty and responsibility. Salaries correspond to the grades; the higher the grade level, the higher the salary. *A Government employee's pay is determined by the level of the job he or she fills, not necessarily by the employee's qualifications. (For example, if you are qualified for a GS-9, but accept a job at the GS-5 level, you will be paid the GS-5 salary, not the GS-9 salary.)*

There are several pay systems, covering different kinds of jobs. For example, the General Schedule (GS) system covers most white-collar jobs and protective occupations, such as guards. It starts at grade GS-1 and goes up to GS-18. Clerical workers usually start at GS-1, 2 or 3; guards at GS-4 and white-collar workers with experience or education equal to a college degree at GS-5. The grade level for which you qualify depends on your education and experience which is related to the kind of work you want.

**Forms.** You can get the qualifications information and forms you'll need at Federal Job Information Centers. If there is a fairly consistent need for applications for the kind of work you want, you will be asked to submit a complete application. Applications are not accepted when openings are not expected.

**Written Tests.** Written tests are not required for many Government jobs. However, for others—including general administrative and clerical positions—a written test is required. If a written test is required for the kind of job you want, you will receive a notice telling you when and where to take the test, or an information sheet will list the dates and times when the test is given. *It is not necessary to prepare for the test by taking a "Civil Service" course. No school can guarantee that you will be found qualified or that you will be offered a job.*

**Rating.** If you take a written test, you will receive a notice of your score and your name will go on the OPM referral list in the order of your score.

If the job you apply for doesn't require a written test, your rating will be based on the experience, education and training you describe in your application. You will be notified of the status of your application by the office where you applied. For most scientific positions and most jobs at GS-9 and above, you will not receive a notice of your score at the time your application is processed; you will receive a letter acknowledging the receipt of your application and your name will go on the civil service list without a numerical rating. At the time an opening occurs, your qualifications will be reviewed in relation to the requirements of the particular job to be filled. If you are among the best qualified, your name will be referred to the agency along with the names of other best qualified applicants.

**The Rule of Three.** By law, agency hiring officials may choose from among the top three applicants referred to them for a particular job. This explains why a person lower on the list may be hired, while the highest person is not.

When veterans are included in the three names referred, the selecting official generally may not pass over a veteran to hire a nonveteran.

The names of applicants not selected are returned to the Office of Personnel Management for consideration for future vacancies.

**Physical Requirements.** You must be physically able to perform the duties of a job without being a hazard to yourself or others. A physical or mental handicap or a prior emotional problem isn't disqualifying. For information on testing and placement of handicapped persons, contact an OPM regional office or the selective placement coordinator in any agency where you want to work.

Regional offices are located in: Atlanta, GA; Chicago, IL; Dallas, TX; Philadelphia, PA; and San Francisco, CA.

**Age.** Unless you are 16 and a high school graduate, the usual age at which you can be hired is 18.

For some jobs (for example, many law enforcement positions), applicants may not have passed their 35th birthday when they are hired. If this is true for the job you want, the qualifications information will say so.

**Suitability.** At the time they are hired, or shortly thereafter, Federal employees are investigated to ensure their fitness for Government employment. The extent of the investigation depends on how sensitive their jobs are from the viewpoint of national security.

**Citizenship.** With few exceptions, employees in the competitive service must be U.S. citizens. For more information, check with the agency in which you want to work.

**Equal Employment Opportunity.** All applicants for Federal employment receive consideration without regard to race, religion, color, national origin, sex, political affiliation, age (with authorized exceptions), handicapping condition, or any other non-merit factor.

## Excepted Service Organizations*

Most Federal Government jobs are part of the competitive civil service. To get one of these jobs, you must prove yourself qualified by passing an examination administered either by the U.S. Office of Personnel Management (OPM) or by a Federal agency under the direction of OPM. Some Federal organizations, however, are excluded from the competitive civil service. These organizations fill their jobs through their own hiring systems. To get one of those jobs, you do not have to pass an OPM examination.

OPM does not supply application forms or information on the jobs in organizations outside the competitive civil service. If you are interested in a job with one of those organizations, you should contact that organization directly at the address given below.

### U.S. Government Organizations

Defense Intelligence Agency
Civilian Personnel Operations Division
Pentagon
Washington, DC 20301

Federal Bureau of Investigation
10th Street and Pennsylvania Avenue N.W.
Washington, DC 20535

Federal Reserve System, Board of Governors
20th Street and Constitution Avenue N.W.
Washington, DC 20551

General Accounting Office
Room 4650
441 G Street N.W.
Washington, DC 20548

International Development Cooperation Agency*
320 21st Street N.W.
Washington, DC 20523

National Security Agency
Fort Meade, MD 20775

U.S. Nuclear Regulatory Commission*
Division of Organization of Personnel
Personnel Resources and Employment Programs Branch
Washington, DC 20555

Postal Rate Commission
Administrative Office, Room 500
2000 L Street N.W.
Washington, DC 20268

U.S. Postal Service
Contact your local Postmaster

Tennessee Valley Authority
Division of Personnel
Chief, Employment Branch
Knoxville, TN 37902

United States Mission to the United Nations
799 United Nations Plaza
New York, NY 10017

*The information in this section (pages 161 and 162) is from material published by the U.S. Government Printing Office.

Veterans Administration
Department of Medicine and Surgery

Employment Inquiries should be sent to VA Medical Centers nationwide. (Seeking especially physicians, dentists, nurses, nurse anesthetists, physicians' assistants, podiatrists, optometrists, and expanded-function dental auxiliaries. Also seeking licensed practical/vocational nurses, physical therapists, and certified/registered respiratory therapists.)

Judicial Branch of the Government (except the Administrative Office of the United States Courts and the United States Customs Court)

Apply to the individual office with the job you are interested in.

Legislative Branch of the Government (includes Senators' offices, Representatives' offices, the Library of Congress, and the Capitol, but not the Government Printing Office)

Apply to the individual office with the job you are interested in.

**Additional Information**

*Excepted positions:* Even in agencies where most jobs are part of the competitive civil service, there are some jobs excepted by law from civil service examination requirements. Congress has ruled that it is impractical to examine for such positions as Attorney and Chaplain. Policy-making positions and jobs requiring a close and confidential working relationship with someone in a policy-making position are also excepted. No OPM examination is necessary for any excepted position.

*Excepted appointments:* Certain people, such as the severely physically handicapped and Viet Nam era veterans, may obtain positions in the competitive service through special procedures. If you think you may qualify for one of these appointments, please contact your nearest Federal Job Information/Testing Office or the personnel office of the agency in which you wish to work.

## Office of Personnel Management Federal Job Information/Testing Offices

Contact the Federal Job Information/Testing Office which is nearest the location where you would like to work for information on job opportunities in that area and the forms needed to apply.

**ALABAMA**

Hunstville:
Building 600, Suite 341
3322 Memorial Parkway, South, 35801
(205) 544-5802

**ALASKA**

Anchorage:
Federal Building
701 C Street, Box 22, 99513
(907) 271-5821

**ARIZONA**

Phoenix:
U.S. Postal Service Building, Room 120
522 North Central Avenue, 85004
(602) 261-4736

**ARKANSAS**

(See Oklahoma Listing)

**CALIFORNIA**

Los Angeles:
Linder Building, 3d Floor
845 South Figueroa, 90017
(213) 894-3360

Sacramento:
1029 J Street, 2d Floor, 95814
(916) 551-1464

San Diego:
Federal Building, Room 459
880 Front Street, 92118
(619) 557-6165

San Francisco:
211 Main Street, Seventh Floor
Room 235, 94105
(415) 974-9725

**COLORADO**

Denver:
P.O. Box 25167, 80225
(303) 236-4160
Located at: 12345 West Alameda
Parkway
Lakewood, CO
For forms and local supplements dial:
(303) 236-4159

**CONNECTICUT**

Hartford:
Federal Building, Room 613
450 Main Street 06103
(203) 240-3263

**DELAWARE**

(See Philadelphia, PA listing)

**DISTRICT OF COLUMBIA**

Metro Area:
1900 E Street N.W., Room 1416
Washington, DC 20415
(202) 653-8468

**FLORIDA**

Orlando:
Commodore Building, Suite 150
3444 McCrory Place, 32803-3701
(407) 648-6148

**GEORGIA**

Atlanta:
Richard B. Russell Federal Building,
Room 960
75 Spring Street S.W., 30303
(404) 331-4315

**GUAM**

Agana:
Pacific Daily News Building
238 O'Hara Street, Room 902, 96910
472-7451

### HAWAII

Honolulu (and other Hawaiian Islands and overseas):
Federal Building, Room 5316
300 Ala Moana Boulevard, 96850
(808) 541-2791
(808) 541-2784—Overseas Jobs

### IDAHO

(See Washington listing)

### ILLINOIS

Chicago:
175 W. Jackson Boulevard, Room 530, 60604
(312) 353-6192

### INDIANA

Indianapolis:
Minton-Capehart Federal Building
575 North Pennsylvania Street, 46204
(317) 269-7161

### IOWA

(See Kansas City, MO listing)

### KANSAS

Wichita:
One-Twenty Building, Room 101
120 South Market Street, 67202
(316) 426-5702
In Johnson, Leavenworth, and Wyandotte Counties dial (816) 374-5702

### KENTUCKY

(see Ohio listing)

### LOUISIANA

New Orleans:
1515 Pauger Street, Room 608, 70116
(504) 589-2764

### MAINE

(See New Hampshire listing)

### MARYLAND

Baltimore:
Garmatz Federal Building
101 West Lombard Street, 21201
(301) 962-3822

### MASSACHUSETTS

Boston:
Boston Federal Office Building
10 Causeway Street, 02222-1031
(617) 565-5900

### MICHIGAN

Detroit:
477 Michigan Avenue, Room 565, 48226
(313) 226-6950

### MINNESOTA

Twin Cities:
Federal Building
Ft. Snelling, Twin Cities, 55111
(612) 725-3430

### MISSISSIPPI

(See Atlanta, GA listing)

### MISSOURI

Kansas City:
Federal Building, Room 134
601 East 12th Street, 64106
(816) 374-5702

St. Louis:
Old Post Office, Room 400
815 Olive Street, 63101
(314) 425-4285

### MONTANA

(303) 236-4162
For forms and local supplements dial:
(303) 236-4159

### NEBRASKA

(See Kansas listing)

### NEVADA

(See Sacramento, CA listing)

### NEW HAMPSHIRE

Portsmouth:
Thomas J. McIntyre Federal Building,
Room 104
80 Daniel Street, 03801-3879
(603) 431-7115

### NEW JERSEY

Newark:
Peter W. Rodino, Jr. Federal Building
970 Broad Street, 07102
(201) 645-3673
In Camden, dial (215) 597-7440

### NEW MEXICO

Albuquerque:
Federal Building
421 Gold Avenue S.W., 87102
(505) 766-5583

In Dona Ana, Otero, and El Paso Counties, dial (505) 766-1893

### NEW YORK

New York City:
Jacob K. Javits Federal Building
26 Federal Plaza, 10278
(212) 264-0422

Syracuse:
James N. Hanley Federal Building
100 South Clinton Street, 13260
(315) 423-5660

### NORTH CAROLINA

Raleigh:
4505 Fall Neuse Rd.
Suite 4445, 27609
(919) 856-4361

### NORTH DAKOTA

(See Minnesota listing)

### OHIO

Dayton:
Federal Building, Room 506
200 West 2d Street, 45402
(513) 225-2720

### OKLAHOMA

Oklahoma City:
200 N.W. Fifth Street, 2d Floor, 73102
(405) 231-4948

### OREGON

Portland:
Federal Building, Room 376
1220 S.W. Third Street, 97204
(503) 221-3141

### PENNSYLVANIA

Harrisburg:
Federal Building, Room 168
P.O. Box 761, 17108
3d and Walnut Streets
(717) 782-4494

Philadelphia:
Wm. J. Green, Jr., Federal Building
600 Arch Street, Room 1416, 19106
(215) 597-7440

Pittsburgh:
Federal Building
1000 Liberty Avenue, Room 119, 15222
(412) 644-2755

### PUERTO RICO

San Juan:
Federico Degetau Federal Building
Carlos E. Chardon Street
Hato Rey, P.R. 00918
(809) 766-5242

### RHODE ISLAND

Providence:
John O. Pastore Federal Building
Room 310, Kennedy Plaza, 02903
(401) 528-5251

### SOUTH CAROLINA

(See Atlanta, GA listing)

### SOUTH DAKOTA

(See Minnesota listing)

### TENNESSEE

Memphis:
200 Jefferson Avenue
Suite 1312, 38103-2335

### TEXAS

Dallas:
(Mail or phone only)
1100 Commerce Street, Room 6B12, 75242
(214) 767-8035

Houston:
(713) 226-2375

San Antonio:
643 East Durango Boulevard, 78206
(512) 229-6611 or 6600

### UTAH

(303) 236-4165
For forms and local supplements dial:
(303) 236-4159

### VERMONT

(See New Hampshire listing)

### VIRGINIA

Norfolk:
Federal Building, Room 220
200 Granby Mall, 23510-1886
(804) 441-3355

### WASHINGTON

Seattle:
Federal Building
915 Second Avenue, 98174
(206) 442-4365

### WEST VIRGINIA

[See Ohio listing or dial (513) 225-2866]

### WISCONSIN

Residents in Counties of Grant, Iowa, Lafayette, Dane, Green, Rock, Jefferson, Walworth, Waukesha, Racine, Kenosha and Milwaukee should dial (312) 353-6189 for job information.

All other Wisconsin residents should refer to the Minnesota listing for Federal Job Information in their area.

### WYOMING

(303) 236-4165
For forms and local supplements dial:
(303) 236-4159

## Government Associations

American Federation of Government Employees
1325 Massachusetts Avenue N.W.
Washington, DC 20005
(202) 737-8700

American Federation of State, County, and Municipal Employees
1625 L Street N.W.
Washington, DC 20005
(202) 452-4800

American Public Works Association
1313 East 60th Street
Chicago, IL 60637
(312) 667-2200

American Society for Public Administration
1120 G Street N.W., Suite 500
Washington, DC 20005
(202) 393-7878

Civil Service Employees Association
143 Washington Avenue
Albany, NY 12210
(518) 434-0191

Federal Executive and Professional Association
15535 New Hampshire Avenue
Silver Spring, MD 20904
(301) 384-2616

International City Management Association
1120 G Street N.W.
Washington, DC 20005
(202) 626-4600

International Institute of Municipal Clerks
160 North Altadena Drive
Pasadena, CA 91107
(818) 795-6153

National Association of County Training and Employment Professionals
440 First Street, N.W.
Washington, DC 20001
(202) 393-6226

National Association of Government Employees
1313 L Street, N.W.
Washington, DC 20005
(202) 371-6644

National Federation of Federal Employees
1016 16th Street, N.W.
Washington, DC 20005
(202) 862-4400

## Directories

*Capitol Jobs: An Insider's Guide to Finding a Job in Congress*
Congressional Management Foundation
333 Pennsylvania Avenue S.E.
Washington, DC 20003

*Community Jobs* (a listing of opportunities at nonprofit organizations)
1516 P Street, N.W.
Washington, DC 20005

*Congressional Directory*
U.S. Government Printing Office
Washington, DC 20402
(202) 783-3238

*Congressional Staff Directory*
P.O. Box 62
Mount Vernon, VA 22121
(703) 765-3400

*Congressional Yellow Book Directory*
Washington Monitor, Inc.
National Press Building
1301 Pennsylvania Avenue N.W.
Washington, DC 20045
(202) 347-7757

*Federal Career Opportunities*
Federal Research Service, Inc.
370 West Maple Avenue
Vienna, VA 22180
(703) 281-0200

*Federal Jobs Digest*
325 Pennsylvania Avenue S.E.
Washington, DC 20003
(914) 762-5111

*Federal Yellow Book Directory*
Washington Monitor, Inc.
National Press Building
1301 Pennsylvania Avenue N.W.
Washington, DC 20045
(202) 347-7757

*Moody's Municipal and Government Manual*
Moody's Investors Service
99 Church Street
New York, NY 10007
(212) 553-0300

*U.S. Government Manual*
U.S. Government Printing Office
Washington, DC 20402

*Washington Information Directory*
Congressional Quarterly, Inc.
1414 22d Street N.W.
Washington, DC 20037

# 7
# Government-Sponsored Training Resources

## Preview

*Programs:* Huge numbers of job training programs and other career development projects at the local level and through private industry are mandated and funded by the federal government; state and local jurisdictions also sponsor such free programs for those who are eligible; valuable, current information sources and referral services are available, absolutely free, through government agencies nationwide. This chapter provides a list of major types of programs, with a detailed list of all the sources for information on them.

*Pros and cons:* Though you must meet eligibility requirements for supported programs, and the type of training may not be exactly what you're seeking, the scope of these government-sponsored programs may actually expand during tough times. The programs are free to those who qualify, and *all* the information sources are thorough, accessible, and free.

*Possibilities:* Through these resources, you have access to literally millions of career training sources.

*Warning:* make full use of this chapter, and you may never again be able to complain that your government does nothing for you. You needn't completely give up that satisfying activity, of course, but you'll be surprised by the breadth of government-sponsored training opportunities and resource information available. You'll be "surprised," because these sources are, to say the least, poorly publicized—so go ahead and complain about *that* if you must, but first, find out how to take advantage of all the opportunities you've already paid for with your local, state, and federal tax dollars.

## A Few Facts about Public Resources

Federal law mandates, funds, and/or coordinates several very valuable career training resource networks nationwide, through:

The Job Training Partnership Act (JTPA), which provides access to free training in your area if you meet certain eligibility requirements (see Chapter 9).

The National Occupational Information Coordinating Committee (NOICC), established by the same act. Through NOICC's state committees (SOICCs, of course) and their Occupational Information Systems (OISs) and Career Information Delivery Systems (CIDs), you have free and easy access to the entire scope of career and career-training information in your state or locality.

The Federal-State Employment Service, which maintains centers throughout the country for job searches and job-search training.

The Department of Labor has established an Apprenticeship 2000 program to encourage apprenticeship training and a Workforce 2000 program to enhance workplaced-based training. The Department of Education's America 2000 program has begun to establish Skill Clinics designed to guide adults to educational programs for the upgrading of basic and vocational skills. And in January 1992, the President announced the formation of Job Training 2000, not another new program, but an effort to bring together and coordinate all the diverse government training information resources that are administered through over 600 Private Industry Councils (PICs) around the nation.

## Some Factors to Consider

Don't be put off by the federal government's 2000 JTPA, PIC, OICC, CID alphabet soup: it could do more for your career than high-potency vitamins. And don't assume that you're "eligible" for this career boost only if you're down-and-out. When times are hard, a wider spread of people—including you—need publicly sponsored programs. Even when hard times cause program cutbacks, eligibility requirements may be broadened, as they were when the JTPA extended programs to the "dislocated" (read "laid off"; count 10 million? in the early 1990s) as well as the illiterate and poverty-stricken.

Career training resource *information* requires no eligibility at all—just knowledge about how to gain access to it. That's what this chapter provides: details on how to gain access to the thousands of sources for career training and information.

## How to Find Free Career Information

To say that space does not allow a full listing of all the government's career-related operations is to misuse the word "understatement"; requests for information resulted in, literally, crates of material—free material on free programs.

So here you will find examples of the *kinds* of programs that are available to you, no matter what your career training needs, followed by detailed information on how to get free facts and references from listings that are continually updated and easy to get, no matter where you live.

### It's All Free at Your OICC

When you contact *your* OICC, here's what you'll find: *no* questions about your income, job status, or background. This is one Uncle Sam service that's truly for everyone. Instead, you'll be directed to sites near to or even in your home for access to training help and information.

A phone call requesting information (see the state-by-state list below) will get you a fat packet of career guidance and training information, including a summary of how to get more information from the source.

Every state's network has, at a minimum, reference resource sites throughout the state—in community colleges, libraries, or local employment offices. Many are higher tech—offering computer access to resources, information on floppy disks, or even contacts you can reach by modem from your own PC. However you access the system, you'll learn details about every training source (except for corporate employee programs) in your state and gain career planning guidance in print or in person.

On the following pages, you'll find:

Samples of the kind of detailed facts you can gather from your local OICC (Figure 7.1)

An example of career training information based on national OICC guidelines (Figure 7.2)

A list of OICC addresses and telephone numbers (see page 176)

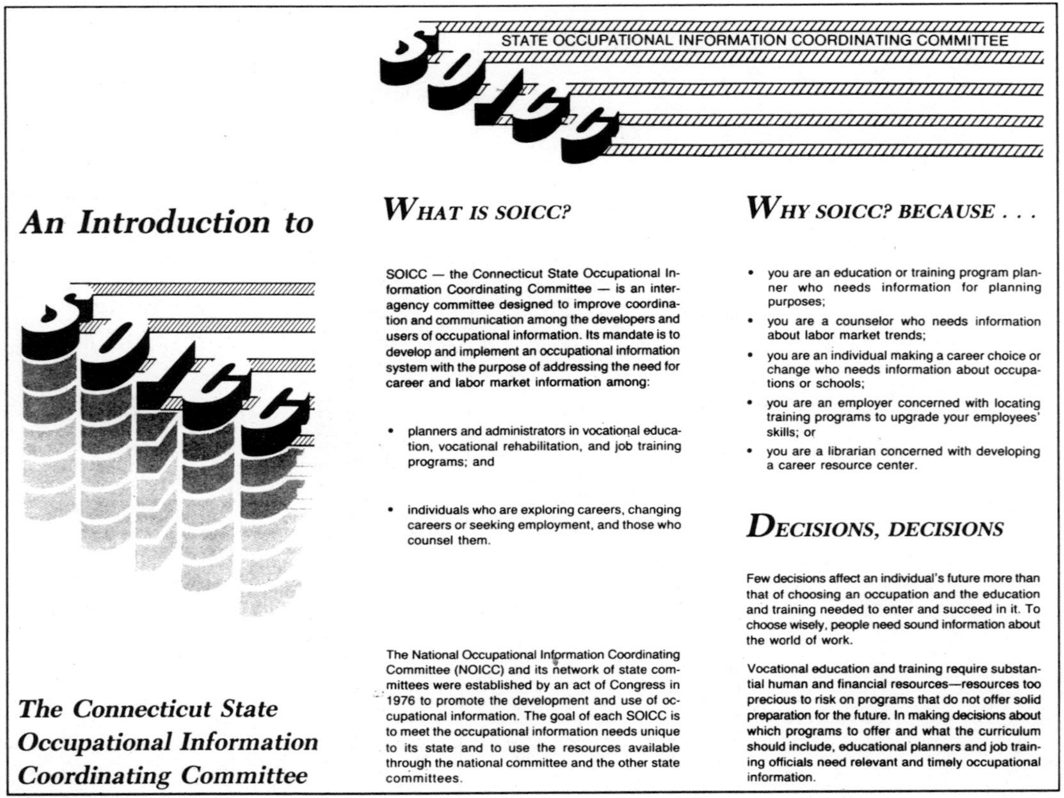

SOICC

STATE OCCUPATIONAL INFORMATION COORDINATING COMMITTEE

## An Introduction to

SOICC

### WHAT IS SOICC?

SOICC — the Connecticut State Occupational Information Coordinating Committee — is an interagency committee designed to improve coordination and communication among the developers and users of occupational information. Its mandate is to develop and implement an occupational information system with the purpose of addressing the need for career and labor market information among:

- planners and administrators in vocational education, vocational rehabilitation, and job training programs; and
- individuals who are exploring careers, changing careers or seeking employment, and those who counsel them.

The National Occupational Information Coordinating Committee (NOICC) and its network of state committees were established by an act of Congress in 1976 to promote the development and use of occupational information. The goal of each SOICC is to meet the occupational information needs unique to its state and to use the resources available through the national committee and the other state committees.

### WHY SOICC? BECAUSE . . .

- you are an education or training program planner who needs information for planning purposes;
- you are a counselor who needs information about labor market trends;
- you are an individual making a career choice or change who needs information about occupations or schools;
- you are an employer concerned with locating training programs to upgrade your employees' skills; or
- you are a librarian concerned with developing a career resource center.

### DECISIONS, DECISIONS

Few decisions affect an individual's future more than that of choosing an occupation and the education and training needed to enter and succeed in it. To choose wisely, people need sound information about the world of work.

Vocational education and training require substantial human and financial resources—resources too precious to risk on programs that do not offer solid preparation for the future. In making decisions about which programs to offer and what the curriculum should include, educational planners and job training officials need relevant and timely occupational information.

*The Connecticut State Occupational Information Coordinating Committee*

**Figure 7.1**

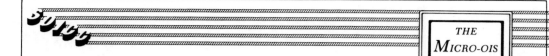

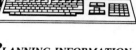

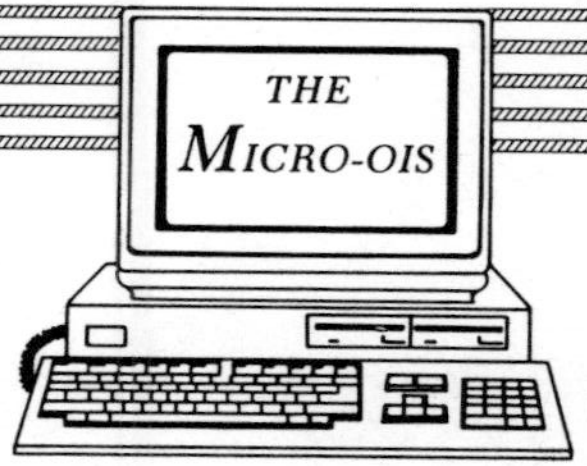


## SERVICES

The SOICC staff collects, systematizes and distributes occupational information produced by various sources, such as the State Departments of Labor, Education and Higher Education. Special attention is given to the labor market information needs of youth.

Activities include the following:

- Providing training workshops and technical assistance in the use of information for program planning and career decision making;
- Responding to individual requests for occupational information;
- Developing training manuals and workshops for teachers on career infusion in the classroom;
- Updating the Micro-OIS files and developing new files; and
- Providing training to vocational rehabilitation counselors in the use of a new software program designed to expand career opportunities for individuals with handicaps.

## CAREER INFORMATION

Effective career decision making requires career information. SOICC facilitates the delivery and use of career information by:

- providing state-specific career information for incorporation into career information delivery systems;
- producing a career tabloid;
- delivering training workshops in the use of career information; and
- publishing newsletters.

### COMPUTERIZED CAREER INFORMATION SYSTEMS

Computerized systems help individuals match personal characteristics with compatible job and career possibilities. Systems generally provide information on occupations; educational institutions and training programs. They are for use in middle schools, high schools, libraries, postsecondary schools and other agencies.

### CONNECTICUT CAREER PATHS

This tabloid presents information about the economic outlook in Connecticut and provides an overview of available careers and educational opportunities. It has a career pullout section highlighting career planning and the job hunting process. *Career Paths* is distributed to high schools, Job Service offices, Service Delivery Areas, community colleges, vocational rehabilitation offices and other agencies.

## PLANNING INFORMATION

The Micro-Occupational Information System (Micro-OIS) is a microcomputer-based system that provides data on current and projected employment, the supply of skilled workers, and sources of vocational training in Connecticut. *It can provide program planners and administrators with documentation to make program decisions and, thus, aid in obtaining approval of plans and funding.*

The occupations and training programs are organized into 136 clusters. These clusters match vocational training programs with the occupations for which they typically provide training.

Being able to sort and select occupational information makes it possible to use the system to identify the following:

- employment areas where there is an unmet need for trained workers; and
- areas where too many people are competing for too few jobs.

The Micro-OIS is available by calling SOICC at 638-4177.

**Figure 7.1** *(Continued)*

### Who should use the SOICC's occupational information products?

The Utah SOICC has found that a diverse group of Utah's citizens are using the informational products it promotes. Users include:

- Planners and administrators in education, rehabilitation, and job training programs who are making decisions about the occupational training programs they will design and support.
- Individuals who are currently seeking employment or who are seeking information to assist them in career transition decisions.
- Students at all educational levels who are exploring careers and making education and career plans.
- Career and guidance counselors in education, job training, and Job Service offices who are helping their clients make informed career decisions.

### How do you learn more about the activities and products of the Utah SOICC?

If you have questions or comments about any SOICC activity or occupational information product, you can contact the Utah SOICC by writing or calling:

Tammy Thorin Stewart, Director
Utah SOICC
140 East 300 South
P. O. Box 11249
Salt Lake City, UT 84147
(801) 536-7806

SOICC
UTAH STATE
OCCUPATIONAL
INFORMATION
COORDINATING
COMMITTEE

In Utah, the following members of the SOICC represent seven agencies that have an interest in seeing that occupational information is accurate, current, locally relevant, and readily available:

Brad T. Barber, Deputy Director
**Office of Planning and Budget**

William R. Horner, Director
Labor Market Information Services
**Utah Department of Employment Security**

Lynn Jensen, Specialist
Guidance and Career Development
Utah State Office of Education
**Utah State Board for Vocational Education**

Douglass T. Jex, Research Analyst
Office of Job Training for Economic Development
**State Job Training Coordinating Council**

Max Lowe, Assistant Commissioner for Vocational Education
Utah System of Higher Education
**Utah State Board of Regents**

Blaine Petersen, Executive Director
**Utah State Office of Rehabilitation**

Randy Rogers, Economist
**Department of Community and Economic Development**

SOICC
UTAH STATE
OCCUPATIONAL
INFORMATION
COORDINATING
COMMITTEE

**Figure 7.2**

## What is the Utah SOICC?

The results of a Gallup Poll released in early 1990 indicated that 65% of adult Americans would try to get more information about their career options if they could plan their worklife again. The survey also indicated that almost 75% of young people ages 18-25 said they would get more information about their job and career options.

The Utah State Occupational Information Coordinating Committee, the SOICC, is dedicated to ensuring that Utah's citizens get the career and labor market information they need to make good decisions for their future and for the future of Utah.

State Occupational Information Coordinating Committees are mandated by acts of Congress -- the Job Training Partnership Act and the Carl Perkins Vocational and Applied Technology Education Act -- to promote the development and use of occupational information. In Utah, the SOICC has been established by an Executive Order of Governor Norman Bangerter, and its membership includes representatives from agencies that have an interest in seeing that occupational information is accurate, current, locally relevant, and readily available.

## How does the SOICC disseminate occupational information in Utah?

The SOICC promotes a variety of activities and products to ensure the citizens of Utah have access to good occupational information:

### Utah's Career Guide

*Utah's Career Guide* is an annual publication containing information regarding career planning, employment trends, job training opportunities, and other timely information for individuals exploring careers and making career plans. Each year, over 50,000 copies of the *Career Guide* are distributed through local schools, Job Service offices, JTPA assessment centers, Rehabilitation Services offices, and other places where people receive career counseling.

### Computer-Based Career Information Systems

The Utah SOICC supports the development and implementation of a comprehensive career information delivery system. In Utah, the delivery system includes using computers to assist individuals in making career choices. Currently, computer-based career information systems are available to students at most secondary schools, Applied Technology Centers, and colleges.

### Improved Career Decision Making Workshops

Improved Career Decision Making (ICDM) Workshops are designed to help career counselors increase their knowledge and use of labor market information. The workshops, organized by the SOICC and conducted by a training team which includes a Labor Market Economist, explore labor market concepts and encourage the use of labor market information in career counseling

### Utah Job Outlook

The *Utah Job Outlook*, published in cooperation with the Utah Department of Employment Security, contains labor supply and demand projections for approximately 150 occupations. Targeted primarily to individuals who plan and operate education and job training programs, the *Outlook* also contains informational articles describing statewide economic conditions and conditions in the state's nine service delivery areas.

### Utah Occupational Information System

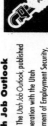

The Utah Occupational Information System (OIS), an automated system to retrieve labor market and occupational information, is an expansion of the *Utah Job Outlook*. The OIS contains projections for over 700 occupations and occupational supply information from most public education and job training programs in the state. Like the *Outlook*, the OIS is targeted primarily to program planners and administrators.

**Figure 7.2** (*Continued*)

A list of Federal Information Centers

A state-by-state single-point-of-contact list, giving your state's source for information on *any* local or federal program

A list of state employment service offices

And it's all *free* (rather, your tax dollars have already paid for it), so you have nothing to lose and everything to gain by using these resources.

### State Occupational Information Coordinating Committee Addresses and Telephone Numbers

Alabama OICC
Bell Building, Suite 400
207 Montgomery Street
Montgomery, AL 36130
(205) 242-2990

Alaska Department of Labor
Research and Analysis Section
Post Office Box 25501
Juneau, AK 99802
(907) 465-4518

American Samoa State OICC
Office of Manpower Resources
American Samoa Government
Pago Pago, AS 96799
(684) 633-4485

Arizona State OICC
Post Office Box 6123, Site Code 897J
1789 West Jefferson Street,
1st Floor North
Phoenix, AZ 85005
(602) 542-3680
Fax: (602) 542-6474

Arkansas OICC/Arkansas
Employment Security Division
Employment and Training Services
Post Office Box 2981
Little Rock, AR 72203
(501) 682-3159
Fax: (501) 682-3713

California OICC
800 Capitol Mall, MIC-67
Sacramento, CA 95814
(916) 323-6544 AVO0630

Colorado OICC
State Board Community College
1391 Speer Boulevard, Suite 600
Denver, CO 80204-2554
(303) 866-4488

Connecticut OICC
Connecticut Department of Education
25 Industrial Park Road
Middletown, CT 06457
(203) 638-4042 AVO0851

Delaware Office of Occupational and
LMI/DOL
University Office Plaza
Post Office Box 9029
Newark, DE 19714-9029
(302) 368-6963 AVO0978
Fax: (302) 368-6748

District of Columbia OICC
Department of Employment Services
500 C Street N.W., Room 215
Washington, D.C. 20001
(202) 639-1090

Florida OICC
Bureau of LMI/DOL, and ES
Suite 200, Hartman Building
2012 Capitol Circle S.E.
Tallahassee, FL 32399-0673
(904) 488-7397 AVO1228
Fax: (904) 488-2558

Georgia OICC/Department of Labor
148 International Boulevard-Sussex Place
Atlanta, GA 30303
(404) 656-9639

Guam OICC/Human Resource Development Agency
Jay Ease Building, 3rd Floor
Post Office Box 2817
Agana, GU 96910
(671) 646-9341, 9342, 9343, 9344 AVO6529

Hawaii State OICC
830 Punchbowl Street
Room 315
Honolulu, HI 96813
(808) 548-3496 AVO1477

Idaho OICC
Len B. Jordan Building, Room 301
650 West State Street
Boise, ID 83720
(208) 334-3705 AVO1611

Illinois OICC
217 East Monroe, Suite 203
Springfield, IL 62706
(217) 785-0789 AVO1737

Indiana OICC
309 West Washington Street, Room 309
Indianapolis, IN 46204
(317) 232-8528
Fax: (317) 232-1815

Iowa OICC
Iowa Department of Economic Development
200 East Grand Avenue
Des Moines, IA 50309
(515) 242-4890 AVO 1977
Fax: (515) 242-4859

Kansas OICC
401 Topeka Avenue
Topeka, KS 66603
(913) 296-1865 AVO2151
Fax: (913) 296-2119

Kentucky OICC
275 East Main Street—2 Center
Frankfort, KY 40621-0001
(502) 564-4258 or 5331

Louisiana OICC
Post Office Box 94094
Baton Rouge, LA 70804-9094
(504) 342-5149 AVO2355

Maine OICC
State House Station 71
Augusta, ME 04333
(207) 289-2331 AVO2477

Maryland SOICC
State Department of Employment and Training
1100 North Eutaw Street, Room 600
Baltimore, MD 21201
(301) 333-5478
Fax: (301) 333-5304

Massachusetts OICC/MA Division of Employment Security
C.F. Hurley Building, 2d Floor
Government Center
Boston, MA 02114
(617) 727-6718 AVO2729
Fax: (617) 727-8014

Michigan OICC
Victor Office Center, 3d Floor
Box 30015
201 North Washington Square—Box 30015
Lansing, MI 48909
(517) 373-0363 AVO2861
Fax: (517) 335-5822

Minnesota OICC/Department of
Economic Security
690 American Center Building
150 East Kellogg Boulevard
St. Paul, MN 55101
(612) 296-2072
Fax: (612) 297-5820

Mississippi Department of Economic
and Community Development
Labor Assistance Division/SOICC
Office
301 West Pearl Street
Jackson, MS 39203-3089
(601) 949-2002 AVO3103
Fax: (601) 949-2291

Missouri OICC
421 East Dunklin Street
Jefferson City, MO 65101
(314) 751-3800 AVO3228
Fax: (314) 751-7973

Montana OICC
1327 Lockey Street, 2d Floor
Post Office Box 1728
Helena, MT 59624
(406) 444-2741 AVO3351
Fax: (406) 444-2638

Nebraska OICC
Post Office Box 94600
State House Station
Lincoln, NE 68509-4600
(402) 471-4845 AVO3477

Nevada OICC
1923 North Carson Street
Suite 211
Carson City, NV 89710
(702) 687-4577 AVO3601
Fax: (702) 883-9158

New Hampshire State OICC
64B Old Suncook Road
Concord, NH 03301
(603) 228-3349
Fax: (603) 228-8557

New Jersey OICC
1008 Labor and Industry Building
CN 056
Trenton, NJ 08625-0056
(609) 292-2682 AVO3856
Fax: (609) 292-6692

New Mexico OICC
401 Broadway, N.E.—Tiwa Building
Post Office Box 1928
Albuquerque, NM 87103
(505) 841-8455 AVO3982

New York State OICC/DOL
Research and Statistics Division
State Campus, Building 12—Room 400
Albany, NY 12240
(518) 457-6182 AVO4101
Fax: (518) 457-0620

North Carolina OICC
1311 St. Mary's Street, Suite 250
Post Office Box 27625
Raleigh, NC 27611
(919) 733-6700 AVO4227

North Dakota OICC
1600 East Interstate, Suite 14
Post Office Box 1537
Bismarck, ND 58502-1537
(701) 224-2197 AVO4353
Fax: (701) 224-3420

Northern Mariana Islands OICC
Post Office Box 149
Saipan, CM 96950
(671) 234-7394

Ohio OICC/Division of LMI
Ohio Bureau of Employment Services
1160 Dublin Road, Building A
Columbus, OH 43215
(614) 644-2689 AVO4477
Fax: (614) 481-8543

Oklahoma OICC
Department of Voc/Tech Education
1500 West Seventh Avenue
Stillwater, OK 74074
(405) 743-5198 AVO4603

Oregon OICC
875 Union Street, N.E.
Salem, OR 97311
(503) 378-8146 AVO4740
Fax: (503) 373-7515

Pennsylvania OICC
Pennsylvania Department of Labor and Industry
1224 Labor and Industry Building
Harrisburg, PA 17120
(717) 787-8646 or 8647 AVO4858
Fax: (717) 772-2168

Puerto Rico OICC
202 Del Cristo Street
Post Office Box 6212
San Juan, PR 00936-6212
(809) 723-7110
Fax: (809) 724-6374

Rhode Island OICC
22 Hayes Street—Room 133
Providence, RI 02908
(401) 272-0830 AVO4977

South Carolina OICC
1550 Gadsden Street
Post Office Box 995
Columbia, SC 29202
(803) 737-2733
Fax: (803) 737-2642

South Dakota Occupational Information Coordinating Committee
South Dakota Department of Labor
420 South Roosevelt Street
Post Office Box 4730
Aberdeen, SD 57402-4730
(605) 622-2314 AVO5227

Tennessee OICC
11th Floor Volunteer Plaza
500 James Robertson Parkway
Nashville, TN 37219
(615) 741-6451

Texas OICC
Texas Employment Commission Building
15th and Congress, Room 526T
Austin, TX 78778
(512) 463-2399

Utah OICC
Utah Department of Employment Security
Post Office Box 11249
174 Social Hall Avenue
Salt Lake City, UT 84147-0249
(801) 533-2274 AVO5602
Fax: (801) 533-2466

Vermont OICC
Green Mountain Drive
Post Office Box 488
Montpelier, VT 05601-0488
(802) 229-0311 AVO5730

Virginia OICC/VA Employment Commission
703 East Main Street
Post Office Box 1358
Richmond, VA 23211
(804) 786-7496
Fax: (804) 786-7844

Virgin Islands OICC
Post Office Box 3359
St. Thomas, US VI 00801
(809) 776-3700

Washington OICC
212 Maple Park, MS KG-11
Olympia, WA 98504-5311
(206) 438-4803 AVO5983
Fax: (206) 438-3215

West Virginia OICC
One Dunbar Plaza, Suite E
Dunbar, WV 25064
(304) 293-5314 AVO6104
Fax: (304) 766-7846

Wyoming OICC
Post Office Box 2760
100 West Midwest
Casper, WY 82602
(307) 235-3642

The Wisconsin OICCouncil/Division of
E&T Policy
201 East Washington Avenue
Post Office Box 7972
Madison, WI 53707
(608) 266-8012
Fax: (608) 267-0330

**The Federal Information Centers Program.** The Federal Information Centers Program (FIC) is a focal point for information about the federal government. The FIC assists people who have questions about federal services, programs, and regulations, but do not know where to turn for an answer. FIC information specialists either answer an inquirer's questions directly, or perform the necessary research to locate and refer the inquirer to the expert best able to help. Residents of 72 key metropolitan areas reach the FIC through locally listed, toll-free telephone numbers; statewide toll-free "800" service is available to the residents of four states: Iowa, Kansas, Missouri, and Nebraska. The FIC telephone numbers are listed below. If you are not in one of the metropolitan areas listed below, you may call the FIC on (301) 722-9098 or write to Federal Information Center, P.O. Box 600, Cumberland, MD 21501-600. TDD users may reach the FIC by dialing a toll-free number: (800) 326-2996.

Alabama
Birmingham—(800) 366-2998
Mobile—(800) 366-2998

Alaska
Anchorage—(800) 729-8003

Arizona
Phoenix—(800) 359-3997

Arkansas
Little Rock—(800) 366-2998

California
Los Angeles—(800) 726-4995
Sacramento—(916) 973-1695
San Diego—(800) 726-4995
San Francisco—(800) 726-4995
Santa Ana—(800) 726-4995

Colorado
Colorado Springs—(800) 359-3997
Denver—(800) 359-3997
Pueblo—(800) 359-3997

Connecticut
Hartford—(800) 347-1997
New Haven—(800) 347-1997

Florida
Ft. Lauderdale—(800) 347-1997
Jacksonville—(800) 347-1997
Miami—(800) 347-1997
Orlando—(800) 347-1997
St. Petersburg—(800) 347-1997
Tampa—(800) 347-1997
West Palm Beach—(800) 347-1997

Georgia
Atlanta—(800) 347-1997

Hawaii
Honolulu—(800) 733-5996

Illinois
Chicago—(800) 366-2998

Indiana
Gary—(800) 366-2998
Indianapolis—(800) 347-1997

Iowa
From all points in Iowa—(800) 735-8004

Kansas
From all points in Kansas—
(800) 735-8004

Kentucky
Louisville—(800) 347-1997

Louisiana
New Orleans—(800) 366-2998

Maryland
Baltimore—(800) 347-1997

Massachusetts
Boston—(800) 347-1997

Michigan
Detroit—(800) 347-1997
Grand Rapids—(800) 347-1997

Minnesota
Minneapolis—(800) 366-2998

Missouri
St. Louis—(800) 366-2998
From elsewhere in Missouri—
(800) 735-8004

Nebraska
Omaha—(800) 366-2998
From Elsewhere in Nebraska—
(800) 735-8004

New Jersey
Newark—(800) 347-1997
Trenton—(800) 347-1997

New Mexico
Albuquerque—(800) 359-3997

New York
Albany—(800) 347-1997
Buffalo—(800) 347-1997
New York—(800) 347-1997
Rochester—(800) 347-1997
Syracuse—(800) 347-1997

North Carolina
Charlotte—(800) 347-1997

Ohio
Akron—(800) 347-1997
Cincinnati—(800) 347-1997
Cleveland—(800) 347-1997
Columbus—(800) 347-1997
Dayton—(800) 347-1997
Toledo—(800) 347-1997

Oklahoma
Oklahoma City—(800) 366-2998
Tulsa—(800) 366-2998

Oregon
Portland—(800) 726-4995

Pennsylvania
Philadelphia—(800) 347-1997
Pittsburgh—(800) 347-1997

Rhode Island
Providence—(800) 347-1997

Tennessee
Chattanooga—(800) 347-1997
Memphis—(800) 366-2998
Nashville—(800) 366-2998

Texas
Austin—(800) 366-2998
Dallas—(800) 366-2998
Forth Worth—(800) 366-2998
Houston—(800) 366-2998
San Antonio—(800) 366-2998

Utah
Salt Lake City—(800) 359-3997

Virginia
Norfolk—(800) 347-1997
Richmond—(800) 347-1997
Roanoke—(800) 347-1997

Washington
Seattle—(800) 726-4995
Tacoma—(800) 726-4995

Wisconsin
Milwaukee—(800) 366-2998

## Find Out More

To find out about other programs in your state, call the offices of the state employment service, or call a *very* useful source for any information about state services—the *single point of contact.*

### State Single Point of Contacts

**ALABAMA**

State Single Point of Contact
Alabama Department of Economic and Community Affairs
3465 Norman Bridge Road
P.O. Box 250347
Montgomery, AL 36125-0347
(205) 284-8905

**ARIZONA**

Arizona State Clearinghouse
3800 North Central Avenue
Fourteenth Floor
Phoenix, AZ 85012
(602) 280-1315

**ARKANSAS**

State Clearinghouse
Office of Intergovernmental Service
Department of Finance and Administration
P.O. Box 3278
Little Rock, AK 72203
(501) 371-1074

**CALIFORNIA**

Grants Coordinator
Office of Planning and Research
1400 Tenth Street
Sacramento, CA 95814
(916) 323-7480

**COLORADO**

State Single Point of Contact
State Clearinghouse
Division of Local Government
1313 Sherman Street
Room 520
Denver, CO 80203
(303) 866-2156

**CONNECTICUT**

Under Secretary
Attn: Intergovernmental Review Coordinator
Comprehensive Planning Division
Office of Policy and Management
80 Washington Street
Hartford, CT 06106-4459
(203) 566-3410

**DELAWARE**

State Single Point of Contact
Executive Department
Thomas Collins Building
Dover, DE 19903
(302) 736-3326

**DISTRICT OF COLUMBIA**

State Single Point of Contact
Executive Office of the Mayor
Office of Intergovernmental Relations
Room 416, District Building
1350 Pennsylvania Avenue, N.W.
Washington, DC 20004
(202) 727-9111

### FLORIDA

Florida State Clearinghouse
Executive Office of the Governor
Office of Planning and Budgeting
The Capitol
Tallahassee, FL 32399-0001
(904) 488-8114

### GEORGIA

Georgia State Clearinghouse
270 Washington Street, S.W.
Atlanta, GA 30334
(404) 656-3855

### HAWAII

Office of State Planning
Department of Planning and Economic Development
Office of the Governor
State Capitol—Room 406
Honolulu, HI 96813
(808) 548-5893 FAX (808) 548-8172

### ILLINOIS

State Single Point of Contact
Office of the Governor
State of Illinois
Springfield, IL 62706
(217) 782-8639

### INDIANA

Budget Director
State Budget Agency
212 State House
Indianapolis, IN 46204
(317) 232-5610

### IOWA

Division for Community Progress
Iowa Department of Economic Development
200 East Grand Avenue
Des Moines, IA 50309
(515) 281-3725

### KENTUCKY

State Single Point of Contact
Kentucky State Clearinghouse
2d Floor, Capital Plaza Tower
Frankfort, KY 40601
(502) 564-2382

### MAINE

State Single Point of Contact
State Planning Office
State House Station No. 38
Augusta, ME 04333
(207) 289-3261

### MARYLAND

Maryland State Clearinghouse
Department of State Planning
301 West Preston Street
Baltimore, MD 21201-2365
(301) 225-4490

### MASSACHUSETTS

State Single Point of Contact
Executive Office of Communities and Development
100 Cambridge Street
Room 1803
Boston, MA 02202
(617) 727-7001

### MICHIGAN

Michigan Neighborhood Builders Alliance
Michigan Department of Commerce
(517) 373-7111
Attn: Manager, Federal Project Review
Michigan Department of Commerce
Michigan Neighborhood Builders Alliance
P.O. Box 30242
Lansing, MI 48909
(517) 373-6223

**MISSISSIPPI**

Clearinghouse Officer
Department of Finance and Administration
Office of Policy Development
421 West Pascagoula Street
Jackson, MS 39203
(601) 960-4280

**MISSOURI**

Federal Assistance Clearinghouse
Office of Administration
Division of General Services
P.O. Box 809
Room 430, Truman Building
Jefferson City, MO 65102
(314) 751-4834

**MONTANA**

State Single Point of Contact
Intergovernmental Review Clearinghouse
c/o Office of Budget and Program Planning
Capitol Station
Room 202—State Capitol
Helena, MT 59620
(406) 444-5522

**NEVADA**

Department of Administration
State Clearinghouse
Capitol Complex
Carson City, NV 89710

**NEW HAMPSHIRE**

New Hampshire Office of State Planning
Attn: Intergovernmental Review Process
2 1/2 Beacon Street
Concord, NH 03301
(603) 271-2155

**NEW JERSEY**

Division of Community Resources
Department of Community Affairs
CN 803
Trenton, NJ 08625-0814
(609) 292-6613
Note: Please direct correspondence and questions to:
State Review Process
Division of Community Resources
CN 814, Room 609
Trenton,NJ 08625-0814
(609) 292-9025

**NEW MEXICO**

State Budget Division
Department of Finance and Administration
Room 190, Bataan Memorial Building
Santa Fe, NM 87503
(505) 827-3640
Fax: (505) 827-3006

**NEW YORK**

New York State Clearinghouse
Division of the Budget
State Capitol
Albany, NY 12224
(518) 474-1605

**NORTH CAROLINA**

Intergovernmental Relations
North Carolina Department of Administration
116 West Jones Street
Raleigh, NC 27611
(919) 733-0499

**NORTH DAKOTA**

State Single Point of Contact
Office of Intergovernmental Affairs
Office of Management and Budget
14th Floor, State Capitol
Bismarck, ND 58505
(701) 224-2094

### OHIO

State Single Point of Contact
State/Federal Funds Coordinator
State Clearinghouse
Office of Budget and Management
30 East Broad Street, 34th Floor
Columbus, OH 43266-0411
(614) 466-0698

### OKLAHOMA

State Single Point of Contact
Oklahoma Department of Commerce
Office of Federal Assistance Management
6601 Broadway Extension
Oklahoma City, OK 73116
(405) 843-9770

### OREGON

State Single Point of Contact
Intergovernmental Relations Division
State Clearinghouse
155 Cottage Street, N.E.
Salem, OR 97310
(503) 373-1998

### PENNSYLVANIA

State Single Point of Contact
Pennsylvania Intergovernmental Council
P.O. Box 11880
Harrisburg, PA 17108
(717) 783-3700

### RHODE ISLAND

Statewide Planning Program
Department of Administration
Division of Planning
265 Melrose Street
Providence, RI 02907
(401) 277-2656
Note: Please direct correspondence and questions to:
Review Coordinator
Office of Strategic Planning

### SOUTH CAROLINA

State Single Point of Contact
Grant Services
Office of the Governor
1205 Pendleton Street, Room 477
Columbia, SC 29201
(803) 734-0493

### SOUTH DAKOTA

State Clearinghouse Coordinator
Office of the Governor
500 East Capitol
Pierre, SD 57501
(605) 773-3212

### TENNESSEE

State Single Point of Contact
State Planning Office
500 Charlotte Avenue
309 John Sevier Building
Nashville, TN 37219
(615) 741-1676

### TEXAS

Governor's Office of Budget and Planning
P.O. Box 12428
Austin, TX 78711
(512) 463-1778

### UTAH

Utah State Clearinghouse
Office of Planning and Budget
116 State Capitol Building
Salt Lake City, UT 84114
(801) 538-1535

### VERMONT

Office of Policy Research and Coordination
Pavilion Office Building
109 State Street
Montpelier, VT 05602
(802) 828-3326

### WASHINGTON

Washington Intergovernmental
Review Process
Department of Community
Development
9th and Columbia Building
Mail Stop GH-51
Olympia, WA 98504-4151
(206) 753-4978

### WEST VIRGINIA

Community Development Division
Governor's Office of Community and
Industrial Development
Building No. 6, Room 553
Charleston, WV 25305
(304) 348-4010

### WISCONSIN

Federal/State Relations
IGA Relations
101 South Webster Street
P.O. Box 7864
Madison, WI 53707-7864
(608) 266-1741
Attn: Section Chief
Federal/State Relations Office
Wisconsin Department of
Administration
(608) 266-0267

### WYOMING

State Single Point of Contact
Wyoming State Clearinghouse
State Planning Coordinator's Office
Capitol Building
Cheyenne, WY 82002
(307) 777-7574

### GUAM

Director of Budget and Management
Research
Office of the Governor
P.O. Box 2950
Agana, GU 96910
(671) 472-2285

### NORTHERN MARIANA ISLANDS

State Single Point of Contact
Planning and Budget Office
Office of the Governor
Saipan, CM
Northern Mariana Islands 96950

### PUERTO RICO

Director
Puerto Rico Planning Board
Minillas Government Center
P.O. Box 41119
San Juan, PR 00940-9985
(809) 727-4444

### VIRGIN ISLANDS

Director
Office of Management and Budget
No. 32 and 33 Kongens Gade
Charlotte Amalie, VI 00802

To unearth private and local career training programs and resources, try your local chamber of commerce (listed in Chapter 5), or your state's Employment Service office:

## State Employment Service Offices

### ALABAMA

Employment Service Department of Industry Relations
649 Monroe Street
Montgomery, AL 36130
(205) 261-5364

### ALASKA

Employment Service
Employment Security Division
P.O. Box 3-7000
Juneau, AK 99802
(907) 465-2712

### ARIZONA

Department of Economic Security
P.O. Box 6123
Site Code 730A
Phoenix, AZ 85005
(602) 542-4016

### ARKANSAS

Employment Security Division
P.O. Box 2981
Little Rock, AR 72203
(501) 371-1683

### CALIFORNIA

Job Service Division
Employment Development Department
800 Capitol Mall
Sacramento, CA 95814
(916) 322-7318

### COLORADO

Employment Programs
Division of Employment and Training
251 East 12th Avenue
Denver, CO 80203
(303) 866-6180

### CONNECTICUT

Job Service
CT Labor Department
200 Folly Brook Boulevard
Wethersfield, CT 06109
(203) 566-8818

### DELAWARE

Employment and Training Division
DE Department of Labor
P.O. Box 9029
Newark, DE 19711
(302) 368-6911

### DISTRICT OF COLUMBIA

Office of Job Service
Department of Employment Services
500 C Street N.W., Room 317
Washington, DC 20001
(202) 639-1115

### FLORIDA

Department of Labor and Employment Security
1320 Executive Center Circle
300 Atkins Building
Tallahassee, FL 32301
(904) 488-7228

### GEORGIA

Employment Service
148 International Boulevard North, Room 400
Atlanta, GA 30303
(404) 656-0380

### HAWAII

Employment Service Division
Department of Labor and Industry Relations
1347 Kapiolani Blvd.
Honolulu, HI 96814
(808) 548-6468

### IDAHO

Operations Division of Employment Services
Department of Employment
317 Main Street
Boise, ID 83735
(208) 334-3977

### ILLINOIS

Employment Services
Employment Security Division
910 South Michigan Avenue
Chicago, IL 60605
(312) 793-6074

### INDIANA

Employment Services Employment Security Division
10 North Senate Avenue
Indianapolis, IN 46204
(317) 232-7680

### IOWA

Job Service Program Bureau
Department of Job Service
1000 East Grand Avenue
Des Moines, IA 50319
(515) 281-5134

### KANSAS

Division of Employment and Training
Department of Human Resources
401 Topeka Avenue
Topeka, KS 66603
(913) 296-5317

### KENTUCKY

Department for Employment Services
275 East Main Street, 2d Floor
Frankfort, KY 40621
(502) 564-5331

### LOUISIANA

Employment Service
Office of Employment Security
P.O. Box 94094
Baton Rouge, LA 70804-9094
(504) 342-3016

### MAINE

Job Service Division
Bureau of Employment Security
P.O. Box 309
Augusta, ME 04330
(207) 289-3431

### MARYLAND

MD Department of Employment and Economics Development
1100 North Eutaw Street, Room 701
Baltimore, MD 21201
(301) 383-5353

### MASSACHUSETTS

Division of Employment Security
Charles F. Hurley Building
Government Center
Boston, MA 02114
(617) 727-6810

### MICHIGAN

Bureau of Employment Service
Employment Security Commission
7310 Woodward Avenue
Detroit, MI 48202
(313) 876-5309

### MINNESOTA

Job Service and UI Operations
690 American Center Building
150 East Kellogg
St. Paul, MN 55101
(612) 296-3627

### MISSISSIPPI

Employment Service Division
Employment Service Commission
P.O. Box 1699
Jackson, MS 39215-1699
(601) 354-8711

### MISSOURI

Employment Service
Division of Employment Security
P.O. Box 59
Jefferson City, MO 65104
(314) 751-3790

**MONTANA**

Job Service/Employment and Training Division
P.O. Box 1728
Helena, MT 59624
(406) 444-4524

**NEBRASKA**

Job Service
NE Department of Labor
P.O. Box 94600
Lincoln, NE 68509
(402) 475-8451

**NEVADA**

Employment Service
Employment Security Department
500 East Third Street
Carson City, NV 89713
(702) 885-4510

**NEW HAMPSHIRE**

Employment Service Bureau
Department of Employment Security
32 South Main Street
Concord, NH 03301
(603) 224-3311

**NEW JERSEY**

NJ Department of Labor
Labor and Industry Building
CN 058
Trenton, NJ 08625
(609) 292-2400

**NEW MEXICO**

Employment Service Employment Security Department
P.O. Box 1928
Albuquerque, NM 87103
(305) 841-8437

**NEW YORK**

Job Service Division
NY State Department of Labor
State Campus
Building 12g
Albany, NY 12240
(518) 457-2612

**NORTH CAROLINA**

Employment Security Commission of North Carolina
P.O. Box 27625
Raleigh, NC 27611
(919) 733-7522

**NORTH DAKOTA**

Employment and Training Division
North Dakota Job Service
P.O. Box 1537
Bismarck, ND 58502
(701) 224-2842

**OHIO**

Employment Service Division
Bureau of Employment Services
145 South Front Street, Room 640
Columbus, OH 43215
(614) 466-2421

**OKLAHOMA**

Employment Service
Employment Security Commission
Will Rogers Memorial Office Building
Oklahoma City, OK 73105
(405) 521-3652

**OREGON**

Employment Service
OR Employment Division
875 Union Street N.E.
Salem, OR 97311
(503) 378-3212

### PENNSYLVANIA

Bureau of Job Service
Labor 7 Industry Building
Seventh and Forster Streets
Harrisburg, PA 17121
(717) 787-3354

### PUERTO RICO

Employment Service Division
Bureau of Employment Security
505 Munoz Rivera Avenue
Hato Rey, PR 00918
(809) 754-5326

### RHODE ISLAND

Job Service Division
Department of Employment Security
24 Mason Street
Providence, RI 02903
(401) 277-3722

### SOUTH CAROLINA

Employment Service
P.O. Box 995
Columbia, SC 29202
(803) 737-2400

### SOUTH DAKOTA

SD Department of Labor
700 Governors Drive
Pierre, SD 57501
(605) 773-3101

### TENNESSEE

Employment Service
Department of Employment Security
503 Cordell Hull Building
Nashville, TN 37219
(615) 741-0922

### TEXAS

Employment Service
Texas Employment Commission
12th and Trinity, 504BT
Austin, TX 78778
(512) 463-2820

### UTAH

Employment Services/Field Operations
Department of Employment Security
174 Social Hall Avenue
Salt Lake City, UT 84147
(801) 533-2201

### VERMONT

Employment Service
Department of Employment and Training
P.O. Box 488
Montpelier, VT 05602
(802) 229-0311

### VIRGINIA

Employment Service
VA Employment Commission
P.O. Box 1258
Richmond, VA 23211
(804) 786-7097

### VIRGIN ISLANDS

Employment Service
Employment Security Agency
P.O. Box 1090
Charlotte Amalie, VI 00801
(809) 776-3700

### WASHINGTON

Employment Security Department
212 Maple Park
Olympia, WA 98504
(206) 753-0747

### WEST VIRGINIA

Employment Service Division
Department of Employment Security
112 California Avenue
Charleston, WV 25305
(304) 348-9180

WISCONSIN

Job Service
P.O. Box 7905
Madison, WI 53707
(608) 266-8561

WYOMING

Employment Service
Employment Security Commission
P.O. Box 2760
Casper, WY 82602
(307) 235-3611

NATIONAL OFFICE

United States Employment Service
200 Constitution Avenue N.W.
Washington, DC 20210
(202) 539-0188

## Making Decisions

Though sources at the PICs and SOICCs are generally friendly and receptive to requests for information, you may want to review the "patience, persistence, and polite insistence" tips that were given at the end of Chapter 6.

Though the training programs you find through local OICCs are not necessarily free, the information is, as is the professional guidance that can help you fill in the blanks on the four-point formula.

Prepare by having this chapter handy: using the alphabet jargon—PIC, CID, OICC, and the like—lets your source know that *you* know what's available. And don't forget—it's available, free, to you: you're entitled!

# 8 Success by Association

## Preview

*Programs:* Professional societies, trade unions, and managerial associations either provide or sponsor training programs for their own members or would-be members, and, in some cases, for the general public.

*Pros and cons:* High-quality, focused training at low or no cost is available, though often in highly specific fields. Though membership, usually based on professional experience, may be required to get the best deals, it's possible to gain access or at least referrals to programs through the organizations listed here.

*Possibilities:* Here are lists of associations by type that offer specialized training, including for-credit programs—as well as those that can provide referrals to high-quality training programs.

Chances are good that you either belong to or are eligible to join associations that provide, manage, or fund training and education programs. Examples? Trade associations, professional societies, unions, service clubs, alumni associations, and even hobby clubs. Since these are likely to be related in some way not only to your areas of expertise but also to new career interests you may want to develop, why not look into what they have to offer besides a membership card? You'll also want to take advantage of programs these groups offer to *non*members.

## A Few Facts

Over 25,000 major voluntary associations exist in the United States. A primary purpose of many of the professional and trade-related groups is to control entry into the field and regulate the professional behavior of members. But they also work to maintain and enhance the status of their work by providing development programs in areas of value to their members. According to a 1991 survey by the American Society of Association Executives, 90 percent of all U.S. associations offer educational courses to members, 71 percent to nonmembers. Not all of these courses are directly related to the organization's primary purpose—and many use training as a way of attracting new members, both to the group and to the trade or profession.

The *Direct Marketing Association*, for instance, not only sponsors its own training Institutes, but also provides funds for direct marketing programs in educational institutions and offers grants and scholarships to those who wish to study the subject. The *National Association of Printers and Lithographers* offers courses leading to a certificate in management.

The United Auto Workers offers not only work-related skills training through its National Education, Development, and Training Center, but liberal arts courses as well.

The American Association of Retired Persons (AARP), which provides many direct services to its members (50 and over), also offers job training and guidance and even places older workers into jobs and internships.

And *many* small and large associations—even religious and community groups—provide free or low-cost training in such areas as computer literacy or financial planning.

## Some Factors to Consider

Career development programs offered by associations may be free (except, of course, for the fee you pay for membership), or there may be a small fee. Even when these private groups contract with an outside training organization to provide services, members are likely to get a discount on the going rate.

Some other pluses: Associations that don't provide training themselves can serve as a formal or informal clearinghouse to programs that members have found valuable, just as unions may either provide or direct you to apprenticeships.

And if you aren't eligible for membership in a given association, but would like to enter or advance in a trade or profession it represents, it can be a valuable source of facts for your four-point formula:

What do I want to do?
+ What opportunities are available?
+ What skills are demanded?
− What skills do I have?
= Career training needed to fill gap

The association's staff, or its publications and summary of membership requirements, can provide a clear idea of career opportunities in the field and of the education and training possessed by most of its members. Absorb this information, ask questions, and ask for suggestions on training resources within the association itself or the field in general.

## Find Association Training

### The AMA

Some associations *specialize* in providing training—in addition to the other services they offer members. The American Management Association (AMA), a nonprofit educational organization, is such an organization. In fact, the AMA has received a "top trainer" award from *Training* magazine. While it's known for the presentation of upscale seminars for major corporations, it can also be a valuable resource for adding finance, communications, foreign-language, or computer skills as well as management expertise to an individual's skills portfolio. The AMA's Extension Institute provides self-study kits of audio, visual, and printed materials (at an average cost of $100), as well as on-line computer-access programs for home study of a wide range of management-related subjects. Or you can participate as an individual in AMA seminars (for a considerably higher fee).

If you qualify as a "practicing manager" in any field, for under $200 a year you can join the association and get discounts on all of its training services, as well as other potentially valuable resource and guidance material. (*Tip:* If the company you work for is an AMA member, you may have access to these resources even if your employer doesn't have an AMA training contract—it's worth checking out.)

*Plus:* The association offers a money-back guarantee on its education programs, and many of them lead to continuing education credits—evidence of the quality of the training.

The AMA has centers around the country and the world. For information, contact headquarters at:

135 West 50th Street
New York, NY 10020
(212) 586-8100

## Other Association Training

The following examples of association-sponsored training should give you an idea of the scope and variety of programs you can find from associations other than the AMA, in a wide variety of fields. Remember that using an association as a training source also provides you with networking contacts in your career of choice. So learning from "the company you keep" can bring multiple rewards.

American Newspaper Publishers Association
Box 17407
Dulles Airport
Washington, DC 20041
(703) 648-1069

*Programs:* Training sessions available for members and nonmembers in a variety of areas including building and managing the human resource function, compensation and benefits, management skills, marketing, telecommunications, and others.

American Vocational Association
1410 King Street
Alexandria, VA 22314
(703) 683-3111

*Programs:* Books, videos, software, cassettes for teaching and job search; AVA publishes two job market newsletters a year.

Association for Systems Management
P.O. Box 38370
Cleveland, OH 44138
(216) 243-6900
Fax: (216) 234-2930

*Programs:* Over a dozen seminars on information systems and management—in-house and public nationwide; annual information systems conference; publications program, including monthly magazine *Journal of Systems Management*. ASM's network of 100 chapters across North America offers monthly local educational meetings and forums.

*Pay-Plus:* Seminars and conference available to all, but members receive substantial discounts.

Center for International Trade Development
Oklahoma State University
Hall of Fame and Washington
Stillwater, OK 74078-0390
(405) 755-0228

*Programs:* Seminars with a global perspective—Eastern Europe, Middle East, the Pacific Rim.

*Prerequisites:* Willing to participate in seminars held in Stillwater, Oklahoma.

*Pay-Plus:* These seminars are offered through Oklahoma State University. Seminar fees are $95 per person per seminar, $85 per seminar for two or more enrolled together from the same firm, or $85 for any individual enrolling for more than one seminar at the same time. Fees include instruction materials, lunch, and refreshments.

Direct Marketing Educational Foundation
6 East 43d Street
New York, NY 10017
(212) 768-7277
Fax: (212) 599-1268

*Programs:* The Collegiate Institute offers three or four 4-day seminars in direct marketing basics; summer internships in direct marketing—8–10 weeks, paid.

The Folio Show
911 Hope Street, Box 4232
Stamford, CT 06907-0232

*Programs:* Seminars in many areas of magazine publishing—management, editorial, sales and marketing, production, design, and circulation; special events.

*Prerequisites:* Membership and registration fees.

*Pay-Plus:* Continuing education units for seminars.

Human Resources Development Institute
AFL-CIO
815 16th Street N.W.
Washington, DC 20006
(202) 638-3912

*Programs:* Joint training programs and apprenticeships involving unions and major corporations: United Auto Workers and Ford Motor Company, UAW and General Motors, UAW and Chrysler Corporation, United Steelworkers of America and Bethlehem Steel, United Mine Workers of America and Bituminous Coal Operators Association, International Union of Electrical Workers and Packard Electrical, Aerospace Machinists Industrial District Lodge 751 and the Boeing Company, and more.

*Prerequisites:* Union membership.

Institute of Real Estate Management (IREM) of the National Association of Realtors
430 North Michigan Avenue
P.O. Box 109025
Chicago, IL 60610-9025
(312) 661-0004

*Programs:* Training for managers of all types of income-producing properties: courses, seminars, and publications. Subjects covered include real estate financing, computers, budgets, marketing, insurance, ethics, maintenance, management, and more.

*Prerequisites:* Courses for executive-level property managers and asset managers, mid-level professionals, on-site managers, bankers, property owners, or newcomers.

National Association of Printers and Lithographers (NAPL)
780 Palisades Avenue
Teaneck, NJ 07666
(201) 342-0700

*Programs:* The Carl Didde Workplace Program: a comprehensive training program designed for improving skills in math, reading, and writing; critical thinking and problem solving; and the graphic arts process in the printing and publishing industry. Also, seminars and workshops for managers.

National Farmworker Service Center
P.O. Box 62
Keene, CA 93531
(805) 822-5571

*Programs:* Instituto Campesino para Educacion y Desarrollo—a job skills vocational training for unskilled low-income people. Training opportunities for executive secretaries, accountants, painters, and apartment managers.

*Prerequisites:* Anyone interested and willing to work along the guidelines of the center. Programs are geared to low-income people.

*Pay-Plus:* Grants available to cover cost of training. No salary, but residence, food, basic needs, and small cash stipend provided.

Society of Actuaries
475 North Martingale Road
Schaumburg, IL 60173
(708) 706-3500
Fax: (708) 706-3599

*Programs:* Training programs available nationwide and in Canada.

*Prerequisites:* Programs are available for actuaries and those entering the actuarial field.

Society for Human Resource Management
606 North Washington Street
Alexandria, VA 22314
(703) 548-3440

*Programs:* Seminars in human resources management including benefits plans, American Disabilities Act, recruiting strategies for Workforce 2000, compensation management, and more.

*Prerequisites:* Registration and fees.

*Pay-Plus:* Attending SHRM programs carries recertification credit. Each seminary is awarded 0.6 continuing education units upon completion.

Telecommunications Industry Association
150 North Michigan Avenue, Suite 600
Chicago, IL 60601
(312) 782-8597

*Programs:* Annual Expo. Over 50 free telecommunication seminars.

*Prerequisites:* Telecommunications employees.

Vocational Foundation, Inc.
902 Broadway, 15th Floor
New York, NY 10010
(212) 777-0760

*Programs:* Training in various areas, including: clerical, clothing pattern grading, drafting, and construction inspection; services for young fathers; GED classes; job placement.

*Prerequisites:* Anyone under 18 must be officially discharged from school. Participants must be 16 to 21 years old and out of school, and must meet income or other need-based standards. All interested must attend a two-hour group orientation and an individual meeting with a counselor.

*Pay-Plus:* All services are free—No fees, no loans.

## Association Training Offering Academic Credit

Many associations provide training programs of quality and scope strong enough to qualify for academic credit. Among them:

American Bankers Association
1120 Connecticut Avenue N.W.
Washington, DC 20036
(202) 663-5000

The ABA offers one of the largest adult education programs in the world and is part of the Education Policy and Development Council. Programs include consumer credit and real estate finance; commercial lending; bank operations and accounting; general banking.

American Institute for Property and Liability
Underwriters Insurance Institute of America
720 Providence Road
Malverne, PA 19355
(215) 644-2100

The institute administers the Chartered Casualty Underwriter Program, with offerings in general insurance and insurance claims, loss control, insurance production, accounting and finance, marine insurance, automation management, loss control, risk management, underwriting, and reinsurance. Courses are held nationwide in three formats—formal classes, informal study groups, and independent study.

Credit Union National Association
Certified Credit Union Executive Program
P.O. Box 431
Madison, WI 53701
(608) 231-4600

This program is primarily an independent study program with some courses offered on site at colleges in conventional classroom style. Participants must be actively engaged in the credit union industry. Areas of study include: accounting, business law, credit collections, financial counseling, management, marketing, personnel administration, risk management, and insurance.

Health Insurance Association of America
Insurance Education Program
1025 Connecticut Avenue N.W.
Washington, DC 20036
(202) 223-7780

Offers a two-part individual health insurance course and a three-part group life/health insurance course. HIAA also provides self-study materials and allows for independent study to help candidates prepare for final examinations.

Institute of Certified Professional Managers
James Madison University
Harrisonburg, VA 22807
(703) 568-6211

Offers three examinations to earn the designation Certified Manager. Areas covered by the exams are administrative skills, interpersonal skills, and personal skills of managers. Preparatory courses are available.

Institute of Financial Education
111 East Wacker Drive
Chicago, IL 60601
(312) 644-3100

Provides professional education and training programs for savings association personnel in both operations and management areas. Programs include correspondence courses, in-house programs, resident schools, and networking through 220 local chapters. Courses offered include accounting principles, business math, commercial banking, commercial law, communications skills, economics, consumer lending, office writing and speaking, housing construction, human relations, financial statement analysis, human resources management, income property lending, electronic data processing, savings institution business, marketing for financial institutions, mortgage loan servicing, personal investments, personal money management, principles of management, real estate law, real estate principles, residential appraisal, residential mortgage lending, savings institution operations, and customer counseling.

Insurance Data Management Association
85 John Street
New York, NY 10038
(212) 669-0496

Offers seminars, meetings, and forums on related topics and a seven-course curriculum leading to designation as Certified Data Manager. Courses offered include data administration, insurance accounting and data quality, insurance collection, and statistical reporting.

Insurance Educational Association
Insurance Institute of America
720 Providence Road
Malvern, PA 19355
(215) 644-2142

Provides training leading to certification for careers in insurance, risk management, and employee benefits, and provides continuing education for employees in these fields. Certificate program areas: commercial multiple line insurance and workers' compensation claims. Courses include commercial liability insurance coverages, commercial property insurance coverage, law of torts, surety bonding, workers' compensation, and tax auditing.

National Association of Realtors(r)
430 North Michigan Avenue
Chicago, IL 60611
(312) 329-8200

Provides facilities for education, research, and information exchange for those in recognized branches of the real estate business. Through local associations and institutes, the association offers programs nationally leading to designations recognized nationwide. Programs and courses are offered through American Institute of Real Estate Appraisers; Realtors(r) National Marketing Institute; Society of Industrial and Office Realtors(r), Realtors(r) Land Institute; Institute of Real Estate Management; and Realtors(r) Institute.

Professional Insurance Agents
Director of Education
Education Department
National Association of Professional
Insurance Agents
400 North Washington Street
Alexandria, VA 22314
(703) 836-9430

Offers a three-week residential program at Drake University in Des Moines, Iowa, to familiarize students with fundamentals of business and personal risk and the basic principles of insurance contacts and casualty and liability insurance.

Seafarers Harry Lundeberg School of
Seamanship
Piney Point, MD 20674
(301) 899-0675

Prepares young people to pursue careers on the seas or on America's network of inland and coastal waterways. The school also provides opportunities to seafarers to upgrade their skills. Courses include able seaman; deck—inland and ocean; assistant cook and baker; basic engine; basic steward; navigation and piloting; conveyer; fueler; watertender; hydraulics; lifeboat; liquid cargo operations; marine electrical maintenance; master/mate freight and towing; and others.

## Find Out More

The following groups offer training to a greater or lesser extent. Contact the ones in your areas of interest; general printed information should be yours for the asking.

ACME Inc. Association Management
Consulting Firm
230 Park Avenue, Suite 544
New York, NY 10169

Advertising Research Foundation
3 East 54th Street, 15th Floor
New York, NY 10022

Aerospace Industries Association of
America
1250 First Street N.W., Suite 1100
Washington, DC 20005

Allied Printing Trades Council
3606 Gravois
Saint Louis, MO 60004

Amalgamated Clothing and TWU
15 Union Square West
New York, NY 10003

American Advertising Federation
1400 K Street N.W., Suite 1000
Washington, DC 20005

American Angus Association
3201 Frederick Avenue
Saint Joseph, MO 64506

American Association of Advertising Agencies
666 3d Avenue, 13th Floor
New York, NY 10017

American Association of Medical Assistants
20 North Wacker Drive, No. 1575
Chicago, IL 60606

American Association of Museums
1225 I Street N.W., No. 200
Washington, DC 20005-3943

American Association of Nurserymen
1250 I Street N.W., No. 500
Washington, DC 20005

American Bankers Association
1120 Connecticut Avenue N.W.
Washington, DC 20036

American Cancer Society
1599 Clifton Road N.E.
Atlanta, GA 30329-4251

American Council of Life Insurance
1001 Pennsylvania Avenue N.W.
Washington, DC 20006-3704

American Electronics Association
5201 Great American Parkway
Santa Clara, CA 95054

American Farm Bureau Federation
225 West Touhy Avenue
Park Ridge, IL 60068-5874

American Federation of Government Employees
80 F Street N.W.
Washington, DC 20001

American Federation of Small Businesses
407 South Dearborn Street, No. 500
Chicago, IL 60606

American Federation of State Coun. and M.E.
1625 L Street N.W.
Washington, DC 20036

American Forest Council
1250 Connecticut Avenue N.W., Suite 320
Washington, DC 20036

American Gas Association
1515 Wilson Boulevard
Arlington, VA 22209

American Health Care Association
1201 L Street N.W.
Washington, DC 20005-4046

American Hotel and Motel Association
1201 New York Avenue N.W., Suite 600
Washington, DC 20005

American Industrial Health Council
1330 Connecticut Avenue N.W., Suite 300
Washington, DC 20036-1790

American Industrial Hygiene Association
345 White Pond Drive
Akron, OH 44320-1155

American Institute of CPAs
1211 Avenue of Americas
New York, NY 10036-8703

American Institute of Real Estate Appraisers
430 North Michigan Avenue, 9th Floor
Chicago, IL 60611

American Iron and Steel Institute
1133 15th Street N.W.
Washington, DC 20005

American Newspaper Publishers Association
11600 Sunrise Valley Drive
Reston, VA 22091-1499

American Paper Institute
260 Madison Avenue
New York, NY 10016

American Public Health Association
1015 15th Street N.W., Suite 300
Washington, DC 20005

American Public Power Association
2301 M Street N.W.
Washington, DC 20037-1484

American Red Cross
430 17th Street N.W.
Washington, DC 20005

American Society of Appraisers
535 Herndon Parkway, No. 150
Herndon, VA 22070-5226

American Society of Public Administration
1120 G Street N.W., No. 500
Washington, DC 20005

Association of Builders and Contractors Inc.
729 15th Street N.W.
Washington, DC 20005-2100

Association of General Contractors of America
1957 E Street N.W.
Washington, DC 20006-5107

Building Owners and Manufacturing Association International
1201 New York Avenue N.W., Suite 300
Washington, DC 20005

Business Conference for International Understanding
420 Lexington Avenue, Suite 1620
New York, NY 10170

Business and Institutional Furniture Manufacturers Association
2335 Burton Street S.E.
Grand Rapids, MI 49506-4669

College and University Personnel Association
1233 20th Street N.W., No. 503
Washington, DC 20036-2344

Computer and Business Equipment Manufacturers Association
311 1st Street N.W., No. 500
Washington, DC 20001-2145

Computer Communication Industry Association
666 11 Street N.W., No. 600
Washington, DC 20001-4542

Computer Software and Services Industry Association/ADAPSO
1300 17th Street North, No. 300
Arlington, VA 22209-3801

Data Processing Management Association
505 Busse Highway
Park Ridge, IL 60068

Direct Marketing Association
11 West 42d Street, 25th Floor
New York, NY 10036

Electronic Industries Association
2001 Pennsylvania Avenue N.W.
Washington, DC 20006-1807

Environmental Industry Council
1825 K Street N.W., Suite 210
Washington, DC 20006

Federation of American Health Systems
1111 19th Street N.W., Suite 402
Washington, DC 20036

Grocery Manufacturers of America
1019 Wisconsin Avenue N.W., Suite 510
Washington, DC 20007-3603

Health Industry Distributors Association
225 Reinekers Lane, Suite 650
Alexandria, VA 22314

Health Insurance Association of America
1025 Connecticut Avenue N.W., Suite 1200
Washington, DC 20036

Independent Insurance Agents of America Inc.
127 South Peyton Street
Alexandria, VA 22201

Industrial Research Institute
1550 M Street N.W., 11th Floor
Washington, DC 20005

Information Industry Association
555 New Jersey Avenue N.W., Suite 800
Washington, DC 20001-2082

Institute of Food Technologists
221 North La Salle Street, No. 300
Chicago, IL 60601-1207

Institute of Management Consultants
230 Park Avenue, No. 544
New York, NY 10169

Institute of Management Sciences
290 Westminster Street
Providence, RI 02903

Insurance Information Institute
110 William Street, 4th Floor
New York, NY 10038

International Association of Business Communicators
1 Hallidie Plaza, No. 600
San Francisco, CA 94102-2818

International Chiropractors Association
1110 North Glebe Road, Suite 1000
Arlington, VA 22201

Manufacturers Agents National Association
230 16 Mill Creek Road
Laguna Hills, CA 92653-1277

Mortgage Bankers Association of America
1125 15th Street N.W.
Washington, DC 20005

Motion Pictures Association of America
1133 Avenue of the Americas, 18th Floor
New York, NY 10036

Motor Vehicle Manufacturers Association of the United States
7430 2d Avenue, Suite 300
Detroit, MI 48202-2705

National Association Bank Loan and Credit Office
1 Liberty Place, Suite 2300
Philadelphia, PA 19103

National Association of Counties
440 1st Street N.W., 8th Floor
Washington, DC 20001-2080

National Association of Credit Management
8815 Centre Park Drive, No. 200
Columbia, MD 21045

National Association of Industrial and Office Park
1215 Jefferson Davis Highway, Suite 100
Arlington, VA 22202

National Association of Professional Insurance Agents
400 North Washington Street
Alexandria, VA 22314

National Association of Purchasing Management
2055 East Centennial Circle
Tempe, AZ 85284

National Association of Realtors
430 North Michigan Avenue, Suite 500
Chicago, IL 60611

National Automobile Dealers Association
8400 Westpark Drive
McLean, VA 22102-3591

National Farmers Organization
2505 Elwood Drive
Ames, IA 50010-8288

National Federation of Business and Professional Women's Club Inc.
2012 Massachusetts Avenue N.W.
Washington, DC 20024

National Forest Products Association
1250 Connecticut Avenue N.W., Suite 200
Washington, DC 20036

National League of Cities
1301 Pennsylvania Avenue N.W., Suite 600
Washington, DC 20004-1763

National Petroleum Refiners Association
1899 Street N.W., Suite 1000
Washington, DC 20036

National Society of Public Accountants
1010 North Fairfax Street
Alexandria, VA 22314-1574

Pharmaceutical Manufacturers Association
1100 15th Street N.W., Suite 900
Washington, DC 20005

Recording Industry Association of America
1020 19th Street N.W., No. 200
Washington, DC 20036

Sales and Marketing Executives International
1127 Euclid Avenue, Statler Office Tower, No. 458
Cleveland, OH 44115

Society of Actuaries
475 North Martingale Road, Suite 800
Schaumburg, IL 60173-2252

Society of the Plastics Industry Inc.
1275 K Street N.W., Suite 400
Washington, DC 20005

Telecommunications Industry Association
150 North Michigan Avenue, Suite 600
Chicago, IL 60601

United States League of Savings Institutions
111 East Wacker Drive, 24th Floor
Chicago, IL 60601

If you want more details or a more personal approach, here are some suggestions:

Associations proliferate in such abundance that a relatively new specialty has arisen: the "association management" firm, which promotes the activities of groups of groups and can provide information about any training programs they offer. For example, *Smith, Bucklin and Associates* (111 East Wacker Drive, Chicago, IL 60601), one of the largest, can provide details on the activities of over 100 associations, specializing in anything from battery manufacture to nuclear medicine. For a list of these firms, including the associations they represent, contact:

The Foundation Center
75 Fifth Avenue
New York, NY 10011
(212) 620-4230

The Foundation Center, which has branches around the country, is also an outstanding resource for information on grants, scholarships, and other supported training.

*The Encyclopedia of Associations*, an annual published by Gale Research Company of Detroit, consists of three large volumes of fine-print descriptive listings of associations, so if you haven't found a likely source of training from the groups listed in this small space, don't be discouraged. Instead, go to the reference room of your library to find that directory, as well as others that the librarian might suggest to meet your specific needs.

You may also find useful referrals from these groups:

American Association for the
Advancement of Science
1333 H Street N.W.
Washington, DC 20005

World's largest federation of scientific and engineering societies.

American Association of Engineering
Societies
415 2d Street N.E., Suite 200
Washington, DC 20002

A federation of 43 engineering societies, AAES is a wealth of information on all aspects of engineering careers and practice. It publishes annual surveys of engineering salaries in industry and education, studies of supply and demand, and special reports on careers and employment.

Commission on Professionals in
Science and Technology
1500 Massachusetts Avenue N.W., Suite 831
Washington, DC 20005

This group provides information on human resources, education and training, and salaries in the fields of science, engineering, etc.

The National Health Council, Inc.
350 Fifth Avenue
New York, NY 10118
(212) 268-8900

An umbrella group for all associations in health-related fields, many of which provide training referrals.

National Society of Professional Engineers
1420 King Street
Alexandria, VA 22314-2715

A membership organization for practicing engineers, it provides information on professional issues such as ethics, registration, professional development, salaries, and legislative developments.

## Making Decisions

Don't assume that you're ineligible for membership in associations that may be the best training source for you. Instead, jot down *all* of your work and leisure activities. Compare that list with categories here or in the *Encyclopedia of Associations.* You're likely to find more than a couple that would be happy to have you join. How about the American Automobile Association? The Triple-A offers some training programs. And don't forget alumni associations from your school, or organizations in which your employer may hold a company membership that entitles you to benefits.

What if your groups don't provide training? Ask them to. If enough members are interested, you'll get access to some skills training (in computers, for example, or communications) at a cut rate.

In choosing any program, from these lists or from other sources, remember not to waste your time with training that's not right for you, even if it's cheap or free. Instead, look at the answers to your career-change checklist:

What can I learn?

Where will it get me?

Is it suited to me?

How much can I manage?

*Some final tips:*

Your association's membership fee—as well as any course costs—may be deductible from your income tax. Check to see what qualifies.

Be sure the course costs from an association are *less* than that for similar training from other possible sources. Some "nonprofit" associations make their profits from tuition.

Remember that using an association as a training source also provides you with networking contacts in your career of choice. So learning from "the company you keep" can bring multiple rewards.

# 9 Exceptional Opportunities

## Preview

*Programs:* Tens of thousands of training opportunities are offered to exceptional people—veterans, minorities, women, the elderly, the disabled, and the unemployed—not only by public and private organizations, but now, by law or good sense, by virtually every employer.

*Pros and cons:* Free and specially designed programs for special needs, available in every community for those who have specific required qualifications. Training may not match interests, but persistence can result in satisfaction—and you can *make* yourself special, too.

*Possibilities:* Here are the types of training you can qualify for, along with lists of agencies and groups that either train or refer to training for "special" people.

If you're "officially" special, you have special opportunities. Veterans, minorities, the disabled, the displaced: Take advantage!

For decades, armed forces veterans have been entitled to free training, low-cost education, and jobs priority. The equal opportunities legislation begun in the 1960s made women and minorities eligible for special training opportunities. During the 1980s, not only was it illegal to discriminate in employment on account of age, but a number of federally sponsored or mandated programs for older workers came into effect. With the passage of the Job Training Partnership Act (JTPA) in 1982, especially as amended, all it takes to be eligible for free training programs is unemployment—something that millions of Americans experienced during the early 1990s. And when the Americans With Disabilities Act (ADA) came into force in 1992, people faced with physical challenges of almost any sort began to be entitled to special training and accommodation on the job.

## A Few Facts

Government and industry are gearing up to provide training, not out of the goodness of their hearts or even a sense of justice. The fact is that qualified workers of all kinds are *needed:* economic dips may reduce demand for employees, but the overall demographic picture means a shrinking pool of well-trained workers.

That predicted 8 million gap between the 24 million new job openings and the 16 million new workers in 2010 A.D. has to be filled somehow. According to the International Foundation of Employee Benefit Plans, most employers plan to fill it with (in this order) women, minorities, the elderly, immigrants, and the disabled. This means that people who once had two strikes against them now find the count turning in their favor, since training is becoming increasingly available at little or no cost to meet the growing need.

An estimated 10 million of the new openings will be in jobs that don't even exist now—most of them high-tech occupations. This is good news for the disabled, since many of these high tech jobs—for example, those involving computer-based skills—don't demand full physical capabilities. More good news: new technologies make it possible to train and employ even those with the most daunting physical challenges. The blind, for example, can learn and perform complex computer processes on the job, thanks to recently developed hardware and programs.

## How to Find Exceptional Training

### Job Training Partnerships and PICs

Every state and many localities maintain a JTPA program with federal funds. JTPA legislation was designed to help the poor and "at-risk" populations, and JTPA's Title III amendment expanded program eligibility to include "dislocated" workers—meaning those who had been put out of work by plant closings and other business shutdowns during the recession of the early 1990s.

JTPA training, provided by a partnership of public agencies and local businesses, is officially available to virtually everyone out of work and in financial trouble because of job cutbacks. Though actual programs are limited by available funding, some 600,000 workers were trained during fiscal year 1991–92. Training, which ranges from basic to sophisticated, is offered through state agencies, private training firms, or on-the-job corporate programs, and much of it is followed by a permanent job. Many laid-off managers and production workers are among those who found JTPA projects a way of learning new skills, gaining career guidance, and finding at least some kinds of work. Some examples:

- In Delaware, a private training agency under contract with the local Private Industry Council (PIC) provides, to those who qualify under federal guidelines, training for entry-level employment in the general business and banking fields. The 8-week program includes instruction in typing, computers, word processing, operation of the 10-key calculator by touch, customer service techniques, resume preparation, and job placement assistance. The placement rate for graduates of the program is 85 percent.
- Austin, Texas, where the PIC provides training and/or jobs for over 600 county residents a year, sends potential employer-trainers a detailed brochure describing the program and its advantages in "saving you the time and expense involved in screening skilled employees to meet the demands of your growing business." Austin's PIC provides short-term, on-the-job, and readiness training, as well as vocational evaluation, job-search training, and employment counseling. It also offers support groups and maintains a local job bank.

Over 600 PIC centers exist around the country, each offering essentially the same programs within their local service delivery centers. Youths, welfare recipients, and low-income elderly may get priority, depending on the jobs and training available, but to qualify under Title III, you may just have to provide proof of citizenship and proof of layoff.

Sound worth looking into? For the addresses and phone numbers of the Private Industry Councils (there are 678 of them) closest to you, contact:

The National Association of Private Industry Councils (NAPIC)
1201 New York Avenue N.W.
Washington, DC 20005
(202) 289-2950

Or call your local Chamber of Commerce (see pages 125 to 129) or your state employment service offices (pages 187 to 191).

## Meeting the Challenge

Over 12 million working-age Americans with disabilities are in the country's potential labor pool. This figure is growing at the rate of one-half million a year, yet only one-third who want jobs have them. This should change dramatically during the 1990s as ADA legislation continues to add force to earlier "hire the handicapped" and antidiscrimination laws. Already, many private and public agencies are active in helping employers reach out to the disabled. Examples are:

The Dole Foundation (220 I Street N.E., Washington, DC 20002, (202) 543-6303

The National Alliance of Business (1015 15th Street N.W., Washington, DC 20005, (202) 457-0010)

The AFL-CIO's Human Resources Development Institute

IAM CARES—the International Association of Machinists Center for Administering Rehabilitation and Employment Services

How wide has the door been opened to training for physically challenged people? While the ADA doesn't specifically mandate training, it does forbid discrimination. Since employers need workers, and are required to make the workplace accessible to all, programs are multiplying rapidly.

And do you qualify? (You may, even if you have only a minor disability.) Here are some organizations that will guide you to the optimum resource.

Federation Employment and Guidance Service
114 Fifth Avenue
New York, NY 10011
(212) 366-8400

Serves persons with economic, educational, physical, developmental, emotional, and social disabilities, as well as individuals in need of career planning and employment assistance, by providing comprehensive and individualized services.

Federation of the Handicapped, Inc.
154 West 14 Street
New York, NY 10011
(212) 727-4200

Its purpose is the vocational rehabilitation of the disabled.

Goodwill Industries of America, Inc.
9200 Wisconsin Avenue
Bethesda, MD 20814
(301) 530-6500

A leading nonprofit provider of vocational rehabilitation and employment services for disabled adults.

Human Resources Center
201 Willets Road
Albertson, NY 11507
(516) 747-5400

A nonprofit organization composed of five coordinated units: Vocational Rehabilitation, Human Resources School, The Employment Research and Training Center, Abilities, Inc., and Industry-Labor Council.

International Center for the Disabled (ICD)
340 East 24th Street
New York, NY 10010
(212) 679-0100

An international organization dedicated to the rehabilitation of disabled persons; the provision of job-skill education, training, and placement services; and research and professional education.

Job Opportunities for the Blind (JOB)
National Federation of the Blind
1800 Johnson Street
Baltimore, MD 21230
(800) 638-7518

The nationwide job listing and job referral system of the NFB.

National Rehabilitation Information Center (NARIC)
8455 Colesville Road, No. 935
Silver Spring, MD 20910
(800) 34-NARIC

An outstanding resource: a clearinghouse for information and referrals for vocational and other rehabilitation including ABLEDATA, a national computerized databank giving information about commercially available rehabilitation aids and equipment. Plus—regional information-exchange offices around the country.

Governments at the federal, state, and local levels sponsor training activities for people with disabilities, including JTPA and PIC programs, state Job Training Coordinating Council programs, and Council on Disabilities programs. Details on such resources are available from the President's Committee on Employment of People with Disabilities, Washington, DC 20036, (202) 635-5044. And if you feel you're not being treated fairly under the ADA, contact the ADA Office of the U.S. Department of Justice, (202) 514-0301; TDD: (202) 514-0381.

**A Few Tips.** Surveys show that people with disabilities are most likely to find work (with concomitant training) from larger companies. McDonalds, AT&T, Sears, Federal Express, and Dupont are a few of the major U.S. corporations with a history of actively reaching out for workers with disabilities.

And the federal government for many years has had a policy of hiring and training workers with disabilities. Contact the U.S. Office of Personnel Management or the personnel office of the federal agency you aim for (see Chapter 6).

Computer-related careers—in every industry—offer the most opportunities for the disabled, as well as the widest opportunities for training. For information:

AbleData
Adaptive Equipment Department
Newington Children's Hospital
181 East Cedar Street
Newington, CT 06111
(800) 346-2742 or (203) 667-5405

Accent on Information
P.O. Box 700
Bloomington, IL 61702
(309) 378-2961

CompuServe
Disabilities Forum
P.O. Box 20212
5000 Arlington Centre Boulevard
Columbus, OH 43220
(800) 848-8199 or (614) 457-8600

Direct Link for the Disabled
P.O. Box 1036
Solkvang, CA 93463
(805) 688-1603

IBM National Support Center for
People with Disabilities
P.O. Box 2150
Atlanta, GA 30055
(800) 426-2133

Choosing training programs carefully is perhaps especially important for people with disabilities. Such programs abound, but the *ideal* program will provide:

In-depth, broad-ranging, personalized inventory of abilities and interests

Facilities and equipment that adapt to individual disabilities

Training and/or education in fields that *you* want or need counseling toward adapting to the "world of work," from work ethics and office etiquette to resume advisement and internships

Job placement assistance and follow-up

## Major Possibilities?

While it may be true that "minorities" will soon be a majority in the work force, minority group members are still entitled to a wide variety of special training and other programs. For example:

Inroads, a national nonprofit organization, places Hispanic, Black, and Native American students (of any age) in internships with corporations.

Inroads
1221 Locust Street, No. 800
St. Louis, MO 63103
(314) 241-7488

The Business and Professional Women's Foundation awards training-program scholarships to black women over the age of 25. Write 2012 Massachusetts Avenue N.W., Washington, DC 20036

The American Association of Advertising Agencies offers paid internships to minority students in agencies around the country. Contact AAAA, 666 Third Avenue, New York, NY 10017.

And there are many, many more, as is indicated by the extensiveness of the following list of resources for information and referral on minority career and training.

### ASSOCIATIONS AND ORGANIZATIONS

American Indian Science and Engineering Society
1085 14th Street, Suite 1506
Boulder, CO 80302
(303) 492-8658

Asian-American Journalists Association
1765 Sutter Street
San Francisco, CA 94115
(415) 346-2051

Association of Black CPA Firms
1101 Connecticut Avenue N.W.
Washington, DC 20036
(202) 857-1100

Black Women in Publishing
P.O. Box 6275
FDR Station
New York, NY 10150
(212) 772-5951

Council of Asian-American Business Associations
1670 Pine Street
San Francisco, CA 94109

Interracial Council for Business Opportunity
51 Madison Avenue
New York, NY 10010
(212) 779-4360

Latin Business Association
5400 East Olympic Boulevard, Suite 237
Los Angeles, CA 90022
(213) 721-4000

National Association of Black Accountants
900 Second Street N.E.
Washington, DC 20002
(202) 682-0222

National Association of Hispanic Journalists
National Press Building, Suite 634
Washington, DC 20045
(202) 662-7145

National Association of Minority Entrepreneurs
322 West Jefferson, Suite 301
Dallas, TX 75208
(214) 943-7198

National Association of Minority Women in Business
2705 Garfield
Kansas City, MO 64109
(816) 421-3335

National Association of Negro Business and Professional Women's Clubs
1806 New Hampshire Avenue N.W.
Washington, DC 20009
(202) 483-4206

National Bankers Association
127 C Street N.W., Suite 240
Washington, DC 20001
(202) 783-3200

National Black M.B.A. Association
111 East Wacker Drive, Suite 600
Chicago, IL 60601
(312) 644-6610

National Black Police Association
1100 17th Street N.W., Suite 1000
Washington, DC 20036
(202) 457-0564

National Conference of Black Lawyers
2 West 125th Street
New York, NY 10026
(212) 864-4000

National Council for Equal Business Opportunity
1221 Connecticut Avenue N.W., 4th Floor
Washington, DC 20036
(202) 293-3960

National Hispanic Business Group
730 Fifth Avenue
New York, NY 10459
(212) 333-8738

National Organization of Black Law Enforcement Executives
1221 Pennsylvania Avenue S.E.
Washington, DC 20003
(202) 546-8811

National Society of Black Engineers
344 Commerce Street
Alexandria, VA 22314
(703) 549-2207

Native American Communication and Career Development
P.O. Box 1281
Scottsdale, AZ 85252-1281
(602) 483-8212

Society of Hispanic Professional Engineers
5400 East Olympic Boulevard, Suite 120
Los Angeles, CA 90022
(213) 725-3970

Society of Spanish Engineers, Planners and Architects
P.O. Box 75
Church Street Station
New York, NY 10017
(212) 292-0970

Trade Union Women of African Heritage
530 West 23rd Street
New York, NY 10011
(212) 929-6449

United Indian Development Association
9650 Flair Drive
El Monte, CA 91731
(818) 442-3701

**DIRECTORIES**

*Affirmative Action Register*
Affirmative Action, Inc.
8356 Olive Boulevard
St. Louis, MO 63132
(314) 991-1335

*Directory of Career Resources for Minorities*
Ready Reference Press
P.O. Box 5169
Santa Monica, CA 90405
(310) 474-5175

*Directory of Minority Public Relations Professionals*
Public Relations Society of America
33 Irving Place
New York, NY 10003
(212) 228-7228

*Directory of Special Programs for Minority Group Members*
Garrett Park Press
P.O. Box 190F
Garrett Park, MD 20896
(301) 946-2553

*Guide to Obtaining Minority Business Directories*
National Minority Business Campaign
65 22d Avenue N.E.
Minneapolis, MN 55418
(612) 781-6819

The federal government, in addition to its equal-opportunity and affirmative-action statutes and the upgrade and support programs it provides or mandates for the disadvantaged, provides practical support to minority members in business careers. For example:

**Minority Business Development Centers (MBDC).** Part of the Minority Business Development Agency (MBDA) of the U.S. Department of Commerce, these centers provide business development services for a minimal fee to minority firms and individuals interested in entering, expanding, or improving their efforts in the marketplace. Minority business development center operators provide a wide range of services to clients, from initial consultations to the identification and resolution of specific business problems. The assistance is given through Project Grants (Cooperative Agreements).

The MBDA competitively selects and funds approximately 100 MBDCs to provide management and technical assistance to minority clients located in designated metropolitan statistical areas (MSAs) throughout the country.

**American Indian Program (AIP).** The American Indian Program provides business development service to American Indians interested in entering, expanding, or improving their efforts in the marketplace. The goal is to help American Indian business development centers and American Indian business consultants to provide a wide range of services to American Indian clients, from initial consultation to the identification and resolution of specific business problems. The assistance is given through Project Grants (Cooperative Agreements).

It's not only public agencies and private groups that provide career training and support: these days, many corporations make a special outreach effort to African Americans and other racial and ethnic groups, since they're aware of their potential value in the work force.

For example, most companies considered "The Best Places for Blacks to Work" in 1992 by *Black Enterprise* magazine qualified for the honor because of their special training programs. They are:

Ameritech

AT&T

Avon

Chrysler

Coca-Cola

Corning

DuPont

Equitable

Federal Express

Ford

Gannett

General Mills

General Motors

Johnson & Johnson

IBM

Kellogg's

Marriott

McDonald's

Merck

Nynex

Pepsi-Cola

Philip Morris

Teachers Insurance Annuity Association–College Retirement Equities Fund (TIAA-CREF)

United Air Lines

Xerox

All branches of the U.S. armed services also qualified for this honor.

It's worth noting how many of those organizations are listed elsewhere in this book as having a positive training-focused attitude and outstanding development programs—which offers a clue to success in finding training as a minority member. Not only should you take advantage of all the special programs available, but you should seek out employers who actively recruit minorities, rather than ones who hire only the minimum to meet legal requirements. The first group will be much more likely to train you into a good career.

## Women's Place

Most women work. Most working women still work in lower-paying jobs. Yet a vast array of special training and support is available to women, for the same legal and practical reasons that these resources are available to minorities and the disabled.

The best source for information about training programs specifically for women is:

The Women's Bureau of the U.S. Department
of Labor
200 Constitution Avenue N.W.
Washington, DC 20210
(202) 523-6665 or (800) 827-5335

Among its many information and referral services, the Women's Bureau operates the Displaced Homemakers Job Network, which helps women to enter or reenter the job market.

Many of the for-women-only programs are offered through organizations of women who have led the way into higher-status careers. For information and referrals, contact:

**Women's Trade and Professional Associations**

American Association of Black Women Entrepreneurs
1326 Missouri Avenue, Suite 4
Washington DC 20011
(202) 231-3751

American Business Women's Association
9100 Ward Parkway
Kansas City, MO 64114
(816) 361-6621

American Medical Women's Association
801 North Fairfax Street
Alexandria, VA 22314
(703) 838-0500

American Society of Professional and Executive Women
1511 Walnut Street
Philadelphia, PA 19102
(215) 563-4415

American Society of Women Accountants
35 East Wacker Drive, Suite 1036
Chicago, IL 60601
(312) 726-9030

American Women's Economic Development Corp.
60 East 42nd Street
New York, NY 10165
(212) 692-9100

American Woman's Society of Certified Public Accountants
401 North Michigan Avenue, Suite 1400
Chicago, IL 60611
(312) 644-6610

American Women in Radio and Television
1101 Connecticut Avenue NW, Suite 700
Washington, DC 20036
(202) 429-5102

Association for Professional Insurance Women
c/o St. Paul Fire and Marine
456 Montgomery Street
San Francisco, CA 94104
(415) 774-4391

Association for Women in Mathematics
P.O. Box 178
Wellesley College
Wellesley, MA 02181
(617) 235-0320

Association for Women in Science
1522 K Street
Washington, DC 20037
(202) 408-0742

Association of Professional Mortgage Women
P.O. Box 8613
Walnut Creek, CA 94596
(510) 932-6690

Association of Women in Architecture
7440 University Drive
St. Louis, MO 63130
(314) 621-3484

Black Women in Publishing
P.O. Box 6275
FDR Station
New York, NY 10150
(212) 772-5951

The National Federation of Business
and Professional Women's Clubs, Inc.
2012 Massachusetts Avenue NW
Washington, DC 20036
(202) 293-1100

Catalyst
250 Park Avenue South
New York, NY 10022
(212) 777-8900

Coalition of Labor Union Women
15 Union Square West
New York, NY 10003
(212) 242-0700

Federally Employed Women
1010 Vermont Avenue, NW
Washington, DC 20005
(202) 638-4404

Financial Women's Association
of New York
P.O. Box 1605
New York, NY 10185
(212) 764-6476

International Association
of Women Police
P.O. Box 15207
Wedgewood Station
Seattle, WA 98115
(206) 625-4465

International Federation of Women
Lawyers
186 Fifth Avenue
New York, NY 10010
(212) 206-1666

National Association for Female
Executives
120 East 56th Street
New York, NY 10021
(212) 371-0740

National Association for Professional
Sales Women
P.O. Box 255708
Sacramento, CA 25865
(916) 484-1234

National Association of Bank Women
500 North Michigan Avenue, Suite 1400
Chicago, IL 60601
(312) 661-1700

National Association of Black Women
Attorneys
508 Fifth Street NW
Washington, DC 20001
(202) 638-5715

National Association of Black Women
Entrepreneurs
P.O. Box 1375
Detroit, MI 48231
(313) 341-7400

National Association of Insurance
Women
P.O. Box 4410
1847 East 15th
Tulsa, OK 74159
(918) 744-5195

National Association of Media Women
1185 Niskey Lake Road S.W.
Atlanta, GA 30331
(404) 344-3862

National Association of Minority
Women in Business
2705 Garfield
Kansas City, MO 64109
(816) 421-3335

National Association of Women Artists
41 Union Square West
New York, NY 10003
(212) 675-1616

National Association of Women in
Construction
327 South Adams Street
Ft. Worth, TX 76104
(817) 877-5551

National Association of Women
Lawyers
750 North Lake Shore Drive
Chicago, IL 60611
(312) 988-6186

National Conference of Women's Bar Associations
P.O. Box 77
Edentown, NC 27932-0077
(919) 482-8202

National Federation of Press Women
P.O. Box 99
Blue Springs, MO 64015
(816) 229-1666

National Forum for Executive Women
1101 15th Street N.W., Suite 400
Washington, DC 20005
(202) 857-3100

National League of American Pen Women
1300 17th Street N.W.
Washington, DC 20036
(202) 785-1997

National Network of Women in Sales
P.O. Box 578442
Chicago, IL 60657
(312) 577-1944

National Women's Economic Alliance
605 14th Street N.W., Suite 900
Washington, DC 20005
(202) 393-5257

National Women's Employment and Education
8781 Rockefeller Center Station
New York, NY 10175
(212) 842-1200

9 to 5—National Association of Working Women
614 Superior Avenue NW, Suite 852
Cleveland, OH 44113
(216) 566-9308 or (800) 245-9TO5

Older Women's League
1325 G Street N.W.
Washington, DC 20005
(202) 783-6686

Professional Women Photographers
c/o Photographers Unlimited
17 West 17th Street, No. 14
New York, NY 10011
(212) 255-9676

Section for Women in Public Administration
c/o Georgia Lyn Brown
6865 Newland Street
Arvada, CO 80003
(303) 825-7141

Society of Women Engineers
P.O. Box 411
Larkspur, CA 94939
(415) 924-8084

Wider Opportunities for Women
1325 G Street N.W., Lower Level
Washington, DC 20005
(202) 638-3143

Women Construction Owners and Executives
P.O. Box 883034
San Francisco, CA 94118
(415) 468-1920

Women Entrepreneurs
1275 Market Street
San Francisco, CA 94103
(415) 929-0129

Women Executives International Tourism Association
136 East 56th Street
New York, NY 10022
(212) 759-5268

Women in Data Processing
P.O. Box 22818
San Diego, CA 92122
(619) 569-5615

Women in Sales Association
8 Madison Avenue
P.O. Box M
Valhalla, NY 10595
(914) 946-3802

Women Life Underwriters Conference
1922 F Street N.W.
Washington, DC 20006
(202) 331-6008

Women's National Book Association
160 Fifth Avenue
New York, NY 10010
(212) 675-7804

Women's Direct Response Group
224 Seventh Street
Garden City, NY 11530
(212) 503-4938

*Tip:* Experts suggest that women train for careers in "nontraditional" jobs—areas not thought of as "woman's work," for example, air traffic controller, auto mechanic, dentist, police officer, veterinarian. The U.S. Women's Bureau can provide detailed suggestions.

## Veterans Affairs

Although the oldest and widest in scope of special training programs are those designed for military veterans, a surprisingly small number of vets take advantage of the variety of possibilities. If you've ever served in the armed forces, don't overlook the opportunities available to you. For example:

All honorably discharged veterans receive a "five-point preference" in being hired for federal jobs (see below, under "Federal Employment Assistance for Veterans").

Disabled vets are entitled to the training or on-the-job experience to make them qualified for federal openings.

Vets on a VA pension are entitled to free vocational training.

Post-Vietnam era vets are entitled to grants to pay for educational, professional, or vocational training programs.

The Veterans Employment and Training Service (VETS) of the Department of Labor [(202) 523-9116] administers counseling and skills training programs, among other services, for vets around the country.

The Department of Veterans Affairs [(202) 233-2044] provides information and assistance in education and training.

And there's much more. Contact your regional office of the U.S. Department of Veterans Affairs (the number is in your phone book) or call (800) 669-8477 for the nearest office that can provide information about these training-related areas:

For education and training:

Montgomery GI Bill (active duty)

Montgomery GI Bill (selected reserve)

Veterans' educational assistance program

Limited loan program

Vocational rehabilitation

- Subsistence allowance
- Special program for veterans rated unemployable
- Special program for veterans receiving pension

For employment assistance:

Reemployment rights

Unemployment compensation

Affirmative action

Job training partnership act

Disabled veterans outreach

Employment in the federal government

The following sections provide more detailed information about two of these areas: (1) employment assistance and (2) the Montgomery GI Bill, active duty.

## Federal Employment Assistance for Veterans

*Uses and Use Restrictions*

1. All veterans are entitled to employment information from Office of Personnel Management (OPM) offices.
2. Veterans separated from the armed forces under honorable conditions before October 15, 1976, receive five points added to earned eligible ratings in Civil Service examination. Disabled veterans and certain wives or husbands, widows or widowers, and mothers of veterans receive ten points. As of October 15, 1976, veterans preference is awarded only under very limited conditions.
3. Under the Veterans Readjustment Appointment (VRA) Program, noncompetitive appointments of certain eligible Vietnam era veterans and post-Vietnam era veterans may be made to established positions in the competitive service in certain grades in accordance with

regulations issued by OPM. Veterans must meet minimum qualification requirements for the positions. Written tests, if required, may be waived for veterans readjustment appointees by an agency. Eligible veterans must have other than a dishonorable discharge from military service.

4. Under the special appointing authority for 30 percent or more disabled veterans, veterans with service-connected disability ratings of 30 percent or more may be appointed noncompetitively to any grade level in the competitive service.
5. OPM assumed responsibility for planning, implementing and overseeing the Disabled Veterans Affirmative Action Program (DVAAP) in the Federal service on October 1, 1982. Agencies must have current DVAAP plans for the employment and advancement of disabled veterans.

*Eligibility*

1. Five-point preference is given to veterans separated under honorable conditions, and to those whose dishonorable DD-214 military discharge documentation has been upgraded to honorable conditions and who served on active duty in the armed forces of the United States during certain periods of time. Ten-point preference is given to disabled veterans and certain wives or husbands, widows or widowers, and mothers of veterans.
2. Certain veterans who served in the armed forces during the period August 5, 1964 through May 7, 1975, and post-Vietnam era veterans, are eligible for a veterans readjustment appointment.
3. Public Law 94-502 authorizes federal agencies to provide unpaid training or work experience, as a part of the Department of Veterans Affairs vocational rehabilitation for a disabled veteran. Such training may be designed to provide noncompetitive appointment.

**All-Volunteer Force Educational Assistance (Montgomery GI Bill Active Duty)**

*Objectives.* The objectives of the Montgomery GI Bill, active duty, are to help servicepersons readjust to civilian life after their separation from military service; to assist in the recruitment and retention of highly qualified personnel in the active and reserve components in the Armed Forces; to extend the benefits of a higher education to those who may not otherwise be able to afford it; to restore lost educational opportunities to those who served on active duty, and to enhance the nation's competitiveness through a more highly educated work force.

*Uses and Use Restrictions.* The veteran may select a program of education to assist him or her in attaining an educational, professional, or vocational objective at any approved educational institution he or she chooses which will accept him or her as a student. The Chief Benefits Director will not approve enrollment in certain courses, such as those he or she finds avocational or recreational in character. An individual must have met the requirements of a secondary school diploma or the equivalent before completing the initial obligated period of active duty.

Assistance is given through a system of direct payments.

## Never Too Old

Today, fewer people are retiring at ages 60 or 65, and many don't expect to retire at all. With the average life span extending, discrimination laws in effect, and a need for employing older workers, a variety of programs are in place for training and retraining older workers. For instance:

### Senior Community Service Employment Program (SCSEP), Older Worker Program

Office of Special Targeted Programs
Employment and Training Administration
Department of Labor, Room N4641
200 Constitution Avenue N.W.
Washington, DC 20210

*Objectives:* To provide, foster, and promote part-time work opportunities (usually 20 hours per week) in community service activities for low-income persons who are 55 years old and older. To the extent feasible the program assists and promotes the transition of program enrollees into unsubsidized employment.

*Types of assistance:* Formula grants; project grants.

*Uses and use restrictions:* Organizations which receive project grants may use the funds to create and pay for part-time community service job positions for persons 55 and above whose income is at or below 125 percent of the poverty level. The individuals who are employed may be placed in work assignments at local service agencies (e.g., schools, hospitals, day-care centers, park systems, etc.), or may be given work assignments in connection with community service projects. A portion of project funds may be used to provide participants with training, counseling, and other supportive services. No more than 13.5 percent of the federal share of the project costs may be spent for administration. Participants may not be employed in projects involving political activities, sectarian activities, or involving work which would ordinarily be performed by the private sector; nor may participants displace any employed worker or perform work which impairs existing contracts for service.

*Eligibility requirements:* The following types of organizations are eligible to receive project grants: (1) states, (2) national public and private nonprofit agencies and organizations other than political parties and (3) U.S. territories.

**Senior Environmental Employment Program (SEE)**

*Federal agency:* Office of Research and Development, Environmental Protection Agency

*Authorization:* Environmental Programs Assistance Act of 1984, Public Law 98-313, 42 U.S.C. 4368a.

*Objectives:* To use the talents of older Americans to provide technical assistance to federal, state, and local environmental agencies for projects of pollution prevention, abatement, and control.

*Types of assistance:* Project grants (cooperative agreements).

*Uses and use restrictions:* The SEE program is to be used only in two situations: (1) for projects of direct benefit to EPA; or (2) for projects of mutual benefit to EPA and another federal agency which is funded by EPA.

*Eligibility requirements:* Applicants must be private, nonprofit organizations designated by the Secretary of Labor under Title V of the Older Americans Act of 1965. Eligible beneficiaries are federal, state, and local environmental agencies and individuals 55 years old or older.

*Examples of funded projects:* Provide senior citizens to do national nonagricultural pesticide surveys; monitor for asbestos compliance in schools; provide support to the agency to review and monitor in the import car program; use senior citizens to monitor for the antifuel switching program; provide senior citizens to EPA to do research and general administrative and clerical tasks.

If you're over 40 and looking for a new job or career, check your phone book for the 40+ Club.

If you're 50 or over, find out about training for your second (or third or fourth) career through the American Association of Retired Persons (AARP), which offers counseling, education, training, and job placement services for economically disadvantaged older persons. For the location of the nearest of AARP's 4000 chapters, call (202) 728-4300.

Your state's Office of the Aging is an outstanding resource for information on all of the special programs you're entitled to as an "older" person. Every state has one. Some are located in the state government department related to human services, but in many states there is a separate listing under "Aging."

## *Make* Yourself Special

Even if you don't qualify as "special" by reason of gender, age, race, ethnic background, or military service, it's likely that you belong to some category that sets you apart from others. Jot down every characteristic of yourself you can think of: residence, national background, religion, schools attended, hobbies. *Some* group—possibly one you already belong to—thinks you're special enough to qualify for a scholarship or training program. If you can't think of any, contact the Foundation Center, 79 Fifth Avenue, New York, NY 10003, (212) 620-4230.

The center's library and its data banks in New York and at sites around the country list foundations and other charitable organizations that provide grants, scholarships, and other incentives to study in some often unexpected areas of learning for people in very special—even odd—categories. For example, over 120 foundations maintain or sponsor internship programs. More than five times that many offer scholarships and other student aid in a variety of fields to members of special groups:

The Olin Charitable Trust gives scholarships to children of employees.

The Pew Charitable Trust supports Pennsylvanians seeking education.

If you live in Muskegon, Michigan, you can apply to the Muskegon Foundation for a scholarship.

If you or a next-of-kin works for UPS, you may get scholarship help from the UPS Foundation.

If you belong to certain Christian churches, the Donald Foundation will consider you for a scholarship.

And so forth. Get details from the Foundation Center—and don't sell yourself short. Chances are good that *somebody* considers you special.

## Making Decisions

The exceptional opportunities listed here aren't for other people—they're for you if you qualify. Don't assume you don't: check out *all* the possibilities offered by corporations, nonprofit groups, and federal, state, and local governments. (To give you an idea of the scope available, the final listing in this chapter, starting on the next page, outlines the "special" career training programs provided by just one state—New York.)

But even if you're entitled to special treatment and it's free, don't take just *any* training. Apply the four-point formula as you investigate the available programs.

What do I want to do?

\+ What opportunities are available?

\+ What skills are demanded?

− What skills do I have?

= Career training needed

Evaluating training programs may be even trickier just because you *are* special, since providers may think you're a captive market. So answer the checklist questions:

What do I want or need to learn? (What can I learn?)

Where will it get me? (Will it get me where I want to be?)

Is it suited to me? (*Why* is it suited to me?)

How much can I manage?

Then be sure to ask about accreditation or licensing, accessibility, success rates, and financial aid. You want to take advantage, not be taken.

*A final tip:* In seeking inclusion into special training programs, you may find it necessary to *insist* that you have a right to the training because of...(have your facts organized and handy), and then *persist* in getting the information and support that you know is available.

**Index of New York State "Special" Programs by Agency**

City University of New York
  Community College Contract Course Program
  Structural Unemployment Retraining Programs (SURP)
  Youth Internship Program
Green Thumb Environmental Beautification, Inc.
  Green Thumb Environmental Beautification Program
New York State Government
  Department of Correctional Services
    Academic Education Program
    Occupational Training Program
  Department of Economic Development, Economic Development Skills Training Program
  Department of Health, Emergency Medical Services Training
  Department of Labor (DOL)
    Adolescent Vocational Exploration Program (AVE)
    Affirmative Action Grants
    Apprenticeship Training Program
    Capital Abatement Program
    Career and Education Expo
    Chamber of Commerce On The Job (OJT) Training Program
    Department of Economic Development On-the-Job Training
    Displaced Homemaker Program
    Employment and Training Services for Dislocated Workers
    Employment Services for Homeless Youth
    Health Care Worker Upgrade Training Program
    Job Service-Labor Exchange
      Community Service Centers
      Disabled Veterans Outreach Program
      Federal Bonding Program
      Hotline Trabajo
      Joint High School Program
      Local Veterans Employment Representative
      Migrant and Seasonal Farm Workers
      New York City Job and Career Center
      New York City Youth Opportunity Center
      Occupational Analysis Industrial Services
      Placement Program for Developmentally Disabled Persons
      Senior Citizen Employment Opportunities Program (SCEOP)
      Targeted Jobs Tax Credit (TJTC)
      Test Research Project
      Test Utilization

        - Trade Adjustment Assistance (TAA)
        - Work Rules Program
    - Job Training Services for Youth and Adults (JTPA IIA)
    - Job Training Services to Older Individuals (JTPA IIA 3%)
    - JTPA IIB Summer Youth Employment and Training Program
    - JTPA IV-C Veterans Employment and Training Grant
    - Labor Market Information Program: Local Area Unemployment Statistics
    - Mentoring Program
    - Model Youth Fund
    - Occupational Projections
    - Occupational Safety and Health Training and Education
    - School to Employment Program (STEP)
    - Shared Work
    - State Occupational Information Coordinating Committee (SOICC)
    - State/Local Planning Information
    - Structured Educational Support Program (SESP)
    - Unemployment Insurance Section 599.2
    - Youth Work Skills (YWS) Program
- Department of Social Services (DSS)
    - Commission for the Blind and Visually Handicapped
        - Supported Employment (SE) for Legally Blind Persons
        - Vocational Rehabilitation for the Blind and Visually Handicapped
    - Comprehensive Employment Opportunity Support Centers (CEOSC)
    - Comprehensive Employment Program (CEP)
    - Food Stamp Employment and Training Program (FSET)
    - Work Incentive Demonstration (WIN-DEMO) Program
- Department of State, Community Services Block Grant (CSBG) Program
- Division of Substance Abuse Services, Vocational Services for Ex-Substance Abusers
- Division for Youth
    - Division for Youth Local Services Program
    - Job Development Program
    - Maintenance Team Programs
    - Residential Employability Development Program
    - Residential Transitional Occupational Education Service
- Education Department (SED)
    - Adult Education Program
    - Adult Literacy Education (ALE)
    - Apprenticeship Related and Supplemental Instruction Program
    - College Work Study Reimbursement Program

COPREP
Education Information Centers (EIC)
Employer Specific Skills Training Program
Employment Preparation Education Program (see Adult Education Program)
Equivalent Attendance State Aid
Independent Living Centers
JTPA State Education Coordination and Grants (8%)
Office of Vocational and Educational Services to Individuals with Disabilities (VESID)
Supported Employment Program
Vocational Rehabilitation Program
Science and Technology Entry Program (STEP) and College Science and Technology Entry Program (CSTEP)
Vocational Education Program (Carl Perkins)
Welfare Education Program (WEP) (see Adult Education Program)
Workplace Literacy Program
Higher Education Services Corporation, Tuition Assistance Program and Aid for Part-Time Study
Office of Advocate for the Disabled, Employment, Affirmative Action, Sections 503 and 504, Rehabilitation Act, Technical Assistance and Information and Referral
Office for the Aging, Senior Community Service Employment Program (SCSEP)
Office of Mental Health (OMH)
Office of Mental Health Sheltered Workshop Program
Office of Mental Health Special Employment Programs
Office of Mental Retardation and Developmental Disabilities (OMRDD)
Habilitation Assistant Training
Letchworth Plan for Employing Public Assistance Recipients
OMRDD Employment Training Program
State Office for the Aging (SOFA) Project
Supported Work/Transitional Employment
Youth Opportunity Program (YOP)
Office of Parks, Recreation and Historic Preservation, New York State Conservation Corps
Urban Development Corporation, The Governor's School and Business Alliance
State University of New York (SUNY)
Community College Contract Course Program
State University of New York Educational Opportunity Centers
Structural Unemployment Retraining Program
Youth Internship Program

# 10
# Doing Well by Doing Good

## Preview

*Programs:* Many voluntary and nonprofit organizations provide formalized, organized training for their unpaid workers—and of course you can volunteer almost anywhere and gain benefits that equal free training, so that you can turn service into success in a field where you have no previous experience.

*Pros and cons:* Though this kind of training is free, looks good on your resume, and makes you feel good, too, you'll need to find the time and insist on participating in the programs that will benefit you, while avoiding well-intentioned abuse.

*Possibilities:* Given here are narrative descriptions of the kinds of work you can learn to do as a volunteer, with examples from a few groups and lists of umbrella organizations that serve as clearinghouses for volunteer groups by type and can put you in contact with groups that interest you and that offer expertise and training to volunteers.

*Volunteer your way to a new career?* Sound too good to be true? It's not. *Any work you do, paid or unpaid, belongs on your resume.* For years, that's been standard advice for young people planning careers, who may not realize that their sports, club, or youth group activities count as credible experience for an otherwise empty resume. It's also good advice for job-seeking housewives who may forget that long hours laboring for the PTA or the community center are, indeed, "working."

The same advice applies to you. No matter how long your career or how dense your resume, you can use volunteering to advance your career or shift its direction. You'll find plenty of valuable opportunities to choose from now and through the 1990s, because public agencies and nonprofit organizations are in great need of volunteers, since the outflow of women from volunteer work to the job market has drained the supply of helpers and budget cutbacks have drained the funds for paid workers.

## A Few Facts

Well over half of all American adults perform volunteer work of some kind, according to a survey by Independent Sector, an umbrella group of nonprofit organizations. The popularity of voluntarism is growing especially rapidly among young professionals. It's in. It's chic. In the 1990s, it's pitched as patriotic, too.

Increasingly, too, major corporations are also getting involved. Some 750 large corporations have formal volunteer programs: adopting company "projects"; working with their surrounding communities to address specific local problems; even lending employees to service organizations. Many more encourage voluntarism through measures ranging from allowing employees time off to perform service to incorporating service work into their corporate training programs. Businesses consider this kind of activity an important investment in the communities that support them. It's also great PR.

What this means for you is that an inclusion of significant volunteer activity on your resume can itself help you advance your career, especially since businesses make use of voluntarism in training.

In a more specific "career resource" sense, the fact is that volunteering is an outstanding, absolutely free (and often tax-deductible) resource for training that will advance your career or prepare you for a completely new one. Here are some cases in point:

- Soon after an office manager began volunteering as a youth group leader in her parish, she was treated as an apprentice by professional youth educators in the church, which also sent her to seminars and training workshops. Continuing her studies and expanding her volunteer activities, she'll be ready for a new, paid, social-work career by the time she's eligible for early retirement.
- A telephone sales rep in a dying industry devoted his off hours to helping to raise money first for his town's ailing community center,

and then, as his reputation spread, for other nonprofits in his county. In not long, he had valuable credentials as a fundraiser and has entered a new career in that more lucrative field.

- The retired comptroller of a small company began to help out at a neighborhood hospital and within a short time had been hired into a "retirement" career as an accountant.

Are you a computer buff who would like to enter the systems management field? A marketer who'd like to break into the hot-track health care industry? Volunteering in the right place can provide the practice and the experience credits to help you get to where you want to go.

## Some Factors to Consider

The trick is, of course, to find the volunteer service that meets *your* career goals. This may require some maneuvering and/or tact, because, understandably, volunteer groups want to make use of the skills you have rather than point you in a new direction. If you write advertising copy for a living, you'll have to be firm about wanting to be, say, an events organizer for a local theater. Sometimes the best move is to find a volunteer group in the field you want to move toward and offer the skills you have: writing brochures for a medical center can get you out of the advertising game and into the health-care field.

Whatever you do, if you want to come away from a charitable stint with more than the warm glow for "doing good," don't take volunteering casually. Use the four-point formula as a guideline for careful choice:

What do I want to do?

\+ What opportunities are available?

\+ What skills are demanded?

− What skills do I have?

= Career training needed to fill gap

## How to Find Volunteer Training

Anything you can do, you like to do, or you'd like to learn to do better, you can do as a volunteer.

Anywhere you look, from your neighborhood to the White House, you'll find organizations that will appreciate your help—and help you to learn new skills. These can be as simple and close to home as organizing a Little League team (evidence of those sought-after communications, leadership, and teamwork competencies), as committed and long-term as two years in the jungle as a missionary for your church, or as formal and elaborate as these government-sponsored activities:

*RSVP (Retired Senior Volunteer Program):* RSVP is a network that taps the skills of older people in a wide variety of volunteer service activities, which can form a network of new career opportunities for you if you're not ready to retire. *Contact:*

RSVP
1100 Vermont Avenue N.W.
Washington, DC 20525
(202) 606-4855

*SCORE (Service Corps of Retired Executives):* Affiliated with the Small Business Administration, SCORE is a national network of people with managerial experience who provide advice and assistance to new or growing businesses in their communities. Participation in SCORE is a good way to make contacts for your "retirement" career. *Contact:* SBA, (202) 523-9148.

*VISTA (Volunteers in Service to America):* VISTA is a federally sponsored program that provides full-time volunteers for a year of service to live and work in poverty-stricken or troubled communities that request help. Volunteers receive a week-long orientation, and during their service, are given a training program concentrating on planning, strategy, and team organization. VISTA volunteers receive a small monthly stipend and full medical coverage. *Contact:* ACTION, (202) 634-9108.

To find groups whose work will give you experience that you can use on your career-change resume, you might begin by simply looking in the yellow pages of your phone book and in the community organizations' file at your local library. Find those that provide service in your areas of interest and possible training options toward your career goals.

As you consider your options from among groups in your community, or from among the 30 organizations listed below which *do* provide significant training to volunteers, keep in mind the items on the checklist:

What do I want or need to learn?
(What can I learn?)

Where will it get me?
(Will it get me where I want to be?)

Is it suited to me?
(*Why* is it suited to me?)

How much can I manage?

**National Volunteer Groups Offering Training**

American Cancer Society
1599 Clifton Road N.E.
Atlanta, GA 30329
(404) 320-3333

American Foundation for the Blind
15 West 16th Street
New York, NY 10011
(212) 620-2000

American Heart Association
7320 Greenville Avenue
Dallas, TX 75231
(214) 373-6300

American Humane Association
623 Inverness Drive East
Englewood, CO 80112
(303) 695-0811

The American ORT Federation
817 Broadway
New York, NY 10003
(212) 677-4400

American Red Cross
430 17th Street N.W.
Washington, DC 20006
(202) 737-8300

Amnesty International USA
322 Eighth Avenue
New York, NY 10001
(212) 807-8400

Arthritis Foundation
1314 Spring St. N.W.
Atlanta, GA 30309
(404) 872-7100

ASPCA
441 East 92d Street
New York, NY 10128
(212) 876-7700

Big Brothers/Sisters of America
230 North 13th Street
Philadelphia, PA 19107
(215) 567-7700

Camp Fire Inc.
4601 Madison Avenue
Kansas, MO 64112
(816) 756-1950

Cancer Care Inc.
1180 Avenue of the Americas
New York, NY 10036
(212) 221-3300

CARE
660 First Avenue
New York, NY 10016
(212) 686-3110

Catholic Relief Services
209 West Fayette Street
Baltimore, MD 21201
(410) 625-2220

Child Welfare League of America
440 1st Street N.W., Suite 310
Washington, DC 20001
(202) 638-2952

Defenders of Wildlife
1244 19th Street N.W.
Washington, DC 20036
(202) 659-9510

Environmental Defense Fund
257 Park Avenue South
New York, NY 10010
(212) 505-2100

Friends of the Earth
1841 Broadway
New York, NY 10023
(212) 247-8077

Girl Scouts of the USA
830 3d Avenue
New York, NY 10022
(212) 940-7500

Izaak Walton League of America
1401 Wilson Boulevard, Level B
Arlington, VA 22209
(703) 528-1818

National Audubon Society
950 Third Avenue
New York, NY 10022
(212) 832-3200

National Wildlife Federation
1400 16th Street N.W.
Washington, DC 20036
(202) 797-6800

Natural Resources Defense Council
40 West 20th Street
New York, NY 10011
(212) 727-2700

Open Lands Project
220 South State Street
One Quincy Court, No. 1880
Chicago, IL 60604
(312) 427-4256

OXFAM-America
115 Broadway
Boston, MA 02118
(617) 482-1211

The Salvation Army
799 Bloomfield Avenue
Verona NJ 07044
(201) 239-0606

Second Harvest
116 South Michigan, Suite 4
Chicago, IL 60603
(312) 263-2303

Sierra Club
730 Polk Street
San Francisco, CA 94109
(415) 776-2211

United Way of America
701 North Fairfax Street
Alexandria, VA 22314
(703) 836-7100

Volunteers of America
340 West 86th Street
New York, NY 10024
(212) 873-2600

## Find Out More

For detailed information and referrals on volunteering possibilities, contact these professional coordinating agencies:

ACTION
1100 Vermont Avenue N.W.
Washington, DC 20525
(202) 634-9282

A government agency that administers nationwide federally sponsored volunteer activities.

Independent Sector
1828 L Street N.W.
Washington, DC 20036
(202) 223-8100

A private coalition of 650 nonprofit organizations in need of volunteers.

Points of Light Foundation
766 Jackson Place, N.W.
Washington, D.C. 20503
(202) 408-5162

Private nonprofit coordinating organization that provides information on volunteer action centers nationwide.

VOLUNTEER—The National Center
766 Jackson Place N.W.
Washington, DC 20503
(202) 408-5162

Private nonprofit coordinating organization that provides information on volunteer action centers nationwide.

## Follow-up

To make the most of volunteering as a training experience and career resource, you'll need to put in extra effort—finding the right source, using the training effectively, and keeping a record of your experience. Here are some suggestions.

After deciding on the kind of work you want to do and why, focus in on a few of the groups that seem most valuable and arrange to go in for an interview. When you talk with the person who will "hire" you as a volunteer, you can expect to be asked

Why you want to perform this service

What you are capable of doing and why

Why you have chosen this particular outlet for your skills and interests

*You'll* need to be up-front about the training you hope to gain, or you may not get what you need.

In many organizations, the interview may be conducted just as though you were seeking paid work, so you'll also need to *get* a lot of information:

What services are available for me to perform?

What is actually asked of me?

Exactly what training is provided?

How much time is asked of me? How much can I give?

What will it cost me?

The last question applies to more than time. In most volunteer work, you can expect respect—but sometimes "free" service is misused or even abused, and you may find yourself putting out a lot more than you get back. So, make only a tentative commitment. The organization counts on you to show up, but it's OK for you to say that you'd like to try it out for a while "to be sure that I can do what you ask." There's no point in spending your free time unpleasantly, or in wasting it on training you were promised but aren't getting.

During your tryout period, check your experiences against your training goals. But if your "doing good" isn't going well, don't just yield to your temptation to simply disappear. Treat it like a "real" job. Talk about the difficulty to someone in charge—because the rewards you can gain from a happy ending to a volunteer experience can add up to more than any specific training you get.

Always ask for a letter of recommendation. Many well-organized groups will provide one automatically, but if yours doesn't, ask for one from someone in charge. References like these can do wonders for your resume:

> Responsible, hardworking and quick to learn....Reorganized our filing system, learned our computer system, and helped with numerous mailings....One of the finest volunteers I have had the pleasure to work with....Involved in computerizing statistics...Boundless creativity and energy....Efforts of volunteer largely responsible for us meeting our deadline.

Not bad! But be sure the supervisor itemizes in the letter the specific skills you used or received training in—because you want to walk away with benefits more practical than the good feeling you gain from doing good.

# 11
# Inspect the Unexpected

## Preview

*Programs:* Temporary agencies, real estate chains, and franchisers offer training—some of it quite comprehensive—to their agents or franchisees, and an extensive network exists for training and supporting the self-employed and entrepreneurs.

*Pros and cons:* While training programs are specifically designed to meet the agency's or franchise's business aims, the training can be put to your more generalized use. Although, depending on the sponsoring organization, you may or may not need to invest money and/or time to get the most training possible, if you choose carefully, you can find the kind of short-term training best suited to your long-term plans, be paid (if only a little) to train, and even work another job while preparing for a new career. And if starting your own business seems only a dream, free training and advice can help you begin without giving up your current job.

*Possibilities:* Given here are descriptions of some of the most comprehensive training programs, plus listings of further information resources.

- Henry Randall, in his thirties, had gone back to college while working as an office administrator. Needing more time for his studies, he left the job and signed on with a temporary agency, just as a way of maintaining the cash flow with time flexibility. But the agency taught him word processing, and by the time he'd gotten his B.A. he had acquired valuable, sophisticated computer skills, which he now uses in a high-paying career as a systems analyst, a job he loves.

- Jody Caswell was a teacher near burnout. A career counselor had told her that she (like many teachers) had excellent aptitude for sales, but she didn't want to just quit her job and embark on a new career. Instead, she went to the local office of a real estate chain and found training she could do in nonschool hours. She found she enjoyed the work, and now she sells real estate full time. Will she keep that up? Maybe not, she says—but she has a whole new set of skills to take wherever else she wants to go.
- John Lin had always dreamed of owning his own business but couldn't take the risk, until, close to retirement, he invested in a franchise operation which gave him the training and support he needed.
- Maritza Lopez had been running her own business, almost without realizing it: a typing service she provided nights and weekends to supplement her income. When one of her clients suggested expansion, she found advice and financing through a small business group and was eventually able to quit her "regular" job.

Do those success stories strike an "I wish..." chord in you? Well, training and support are available to turn wish into reality.

## A Few Facts

It's in the best interests of the national temporary and real estate agencies and nationally known franchisers to provide quality training, since their "good name" rests with the millions of people they employ or contract with. Though not all of them provide it, the ones that do are well worth looking to as a resource.

You may not expect to get sophisticated training with long-term value from temporary agencies or franchisers—but you can, for free and even for pay. You may not expect that the skills you can gain from these sources are ones you would want—but they are. It's not just office skills or real estate you learn from an agency, but computer techniques and sales skills; not just storekeeping from a franchiser, but management and finance.

Likewise, you may not think of "going out on your own" as a way to get training. After all, learning on the job when you've got your own investment at stake can be stupid and dangerous. But entrepreneurship needn't be risky if you get ready for it before you leave your salaried job and lean on all the support that's available from small business agencies, organizations, and networks.

Here's how to inspect the unexpected.

## Some Factors to Consider

Is this kind of training for you? It is if you apply the four-point formula:

What do I want to do?

\+ What opportunities are available?

\+ What skills are demanded?

− What skills do I have?

= Career training needed to fill gap

and come up with the right answer to the question, "Does this training fill that gap?"

Take H&R Block as an example. This leading tax-preparation service is actually a chain of franchises—but it stands out in the franchising field because it requires *no* initial cash investment and provides thorough, in-depth, ongoing training and support for its franchise operators. It's also exemplary as a source for temporary employment because although the heaviest demand is seasonal (at "tax time") tax preparation skills are always in demand and the company provides excellent training in these highly transferable, marketable skills. (It makes its tax-prep training available at low cost to the general public, as well, because it uses the training program as an initial screening for likely permanent employees or franchisees.)

H&R Block is an outstanding training source—maybe the best around—if you want temporary work or are aiming for franchise dealership. But it's not a good bet unless you have a talent for figures and a knack for dealing with people. So no matter how good the opportunity looks, you'll know if it's right for *you* only when you match it against the checklist:

What do I want or need to learn?
(What can I learn?)

Where will it get me?
(Will it get me where I want to be?)

Is it suited to me?
(Why is it suited to me?)

How much can I manage?

Finally, a big plus in the "unexpected" resources for training listed in this chapter—whether a temp agency, a franchiser, or a group that offers advice to would-be entrepreneurs—is that you *can* "try them on for size" without making a major commitment.

## Train as a Temp for Permanent Career Skills

Once upon a time there was the "Kelly Girl." She wore white gloves and came in to type when the boss's "girl" was on vacation. That was in the days of carbon paper. Today, temping is a vital year-round fact of American business life, and temporary employees (of both sexes, and in every kind of job) make up a rapidly growing percentage of the nation's regular work force. This flexible work force is good for employers, who needn't pay for expensive benefits or maintain an underworked staff during slow periods. Is it for you?

It is, if like Henry Randall you need to support another full-time activity and/or need some specific skills to back up a general, liberal arts education. It is if you're reentering the work force or out of a job and want to use temp work to get pay and training—*and* get the chance to see a lot of different businesses. The drawbacks are schedules you can't count on and the need for great adaptability as you move from site to site.

Whether you want to make a career of office work or not, you can benefit from the high-tech training many office temp agencies offer, all while earning an hourly wage. At some agencies, if you're a "regular," you also become entitled to benefits.

Two of the more training-rich agencies are Kelly Services and Manpower Temporary Services.

Kelly Services
999 West Big Beaver Road
Troy, Michigan 48084
(313) 244-4305
Fax: (313) 244-4154

Kelly Services, which has locations nationwide, provides temp employees to franchises and businesses in the areas of office, marketing, light industrial, and technical services. Kelly provides training in word processing and spreadsheet programs to short-term employees, and offers benefits to longer-term employees.

Manpower Temporary Services
5301 North Ironwood Road
Milwaukee, WI 53201
(414) 961-1000

Manpower is the world's largest temporary service agency, employing over a million workers around the world and offering training in office techniques and high-tech skills via its "Skillware" system in automated office equipment. Manpower also offers follow-up support for new employees on the job. Benefits are available for longer-term temps.

To find long-term training from temp services in your area, check the phone book. You're most likely to find a solid training program with one of the national or regional agencies (Olsten or Norrell, for example, as well as Manpower and Kelly), but even those may vary depending on local management: Uniforce, for instance, has an elaborate training system for its franchises (see below), but training of temps varies from agency to agency. So ask.

Figure out what you want to gain from temp employment: the training you need, how much time you can give, and how much you have to earn. Then interview the agencies. What kind of services do their temps (you) perform? Where? And what kind of training do they offer?

## Real Estate for Real Training in Sales

In the 1980s, it seemed like everyone was selling real estate, at least in their spare time. Maybe you want to go into it. More likely, especially if you're reading this in the context of the real estate market of the 1990s, you may wonder why *anyone* would want to enter this field. But if real estate itself doesn't appeal to you, how about sales? Or small business management? Some real estate chains provide outstanding training to their agents.

Coldwell Banker Residential Group [4000 MacArthur Boulevard, Newport Beach, CA 92660, (714) 955-6500], for example, trains its personnel at Coldwell Banker University in California, offering courses for certification in a sales institute *or* a management institute, so that even if you didn't stick with real estate as a permanent career, you'd come away with some valuable skills under your belt.

Century 21 [(714) 553-2100] and ERA Real Estate [(913) 491-1000] have similar, if less formal-sounding, programs.

Good news/bad news about Coldwell: You must be "currently associated" with an office of the agency and "be engaged in residential sales as your primary job activity," as Coldwell Banker puts it. Good news: You have a job while you receive training. Bad news: You can't just be a "Sunday sales rep," but must at least give the impression of having a major interest in real estate work. Still, the hours are flexible, and if the training meets your goals, it's worth your while to check it out. Call (a phone call is more anonymous than a visit) any large agencies in your area or any agency that is part of a national chain and ask about training programs. If you get positive feedback, find out about joining the team.

## Franchises: All the Training You Need to Be a Retailer?

Maybe you've always dreamed of going into business for yourself but felt your skills weren't up to snuff—or didn't want to take the major risks of entrepreneurship. Franchising could be the answer. Franchising grew in boom proportions in the early 1990s, perhaps in part capitalizing on the interest in self-employment. Because of the boom, information networks, support organizations, and satellite industries like franchise brokerages proliferated—a plus factor in entering the field now. But a minus is that, with so many possibilities, you need to choose very carefully—especially if what you seek is a kind of on-the-job training without too much risk.

You have to finance the acquisition of the franchise—the license to do business under another's name—and you'll have to be accepted by the licenser and be willing to make a commitment to the operation. Because costs for these operations can range from nothing (H&R Block) to literally millions of dollars, a good idea is to go in with someone else to share the work and the financing—and to get sound advice before you sign on. In general, the smaller the initial outlay, the greater a percentage of profit you pay into the parent company, but this is *not* always true.

You might think, too, that the greater your investment, the more training and other support you receive—but this isn't the case either. Some franchisers take your cash and give you a paper packet of suggestions. Others present you not only with in-depth training but with a fully set up "turnkey" operation to start with.

As a spokesman for MAACO [381 Brooks Road, King of Prussia, PA 19406 (215) 265-6606] explained, "If the franchisees don't succeed, we're in trouble. Our business is franchisees, not painting cars. Our job at headquarters is to see that they succeed in the car-painting business, so we hold their hands as much as they need." MAACO's hand holding includes a month's intensive mandatory training at headquarters, followed by continuing on-site training before and after the franchise opening, followed by steady visits and phone calls as needed.

As a franchiser with an operation like that, you can learn how to be in business for yourself without being out on your own. Here are some examples of "hand-holding," training-oriented franchisers:

H&R Block, Inc.
Corporate Headquarters
4410 Main Street
Kansas City, MO 64111
(816) 753-6900

No licensing fee. Start-up assistance with advertising and supplies provided. Management training and procedural training program, plus advanced training in tax-preparation techniques.

Martin Franchises Inc.
2005 Ross Avenue
Cincinnati, OH 45212
(513) 351-6211

Dry cleaning franchises. One Hour Martinizing training program consisting of 3 weeks of hands-on training at One Hour Martinizing International Headquarters in Cincinnati and on-site training.

7-Eleven/The Southland Corporation
2711 North Haskell Avenue
Dallas, TX 75204
(214) 828-7345

A turnkey operation, with store in place. Initial training programs in store operation and management, followed by ongoing training.

Sir Speedy
The Business Printers
23131 Verdugo Drive
Laguna Hills, CA 92653-1342
(714) 472-0330; (800) 854-3321

Franchise with training available: 2 weeks at Sir Speedy University in Laguna Hills, California, travel and lodging included, plus on-the-job training at business site and training in electronic publishing. Financing available (up to 100 percent if you qualify, of investment cost of $180,000, which includes equipment and location rental).

Thrifty Rent-A-Car System, Inc.
P.O. Box 352
Tulsa, OK 74153-0250
(918) 665-9379

Franchise training for all new licensees; financing to assist in the purchase of the franchise; programs available to assist licensees, such as insurance and counter automation software; ongoing training for all levels of employees.

Uniforce Temporary Personnel, Inc.
1335 Jericho Turnpike
New Hyde Park, NY 11040
(516) 437-3300

All new franchisees attend Temp University for marketing and management skills, followed by ongoing videotaped training programs. Headquarters office handles payroll and other paperwork management for agencies.

Following are other major franchisers. If the area of business interests you, contact them, but be sure they offer the kind of deal—and training—you need:

Burger King Corporation
17777 Old Cutler Road
Miami, FL 33157
(305) 378-7011

Coverall North America, Inc.
Cleaning Concepts
3111 Camino Del Rio North, Suite 1200
San Diego, CA 92108
(619) 584-1911; (800) 537-3371

Gymboree Corporation
577 Airport Boulevard, Suite 400
Burlingame, CA 94010-2000
(415) 579-0600

Tandy Corporation—Radio Shack
1800 One Tandy Center
Fort Worth, TX 76102-9876
(817) 390-3700

Among the *many* other U.S. franchise operations:

AAMCO Industries Inc.
1 President Blvd.
Bala-Cynwyd, PA 19004-1034
(215) 668-2900

ACW Management DBA "A Cleaner World" Dry Cleaners
2334 English Road
High Point, NC 27262-8056
(919) 841-4188

All-V's Submarine Sandwiches
26 West Dry Creek Circle, Suite 390
Littleton, CO 80120-4475
(303) 795-3400

American Advertising Distributors Inc.
234 South Extension Road
Mesa, AZ 85210-8427
(602) 964-9393

American Franchise Association
2730 Wilshire Boulevard, Suite 400
Santa Monica, CA 90403
(213) 829-0841

ARCO
515 South Flower Street
Los Angeles, CA 90071-2202
(213) 486-3511

Art Management Services, Inc.
265 Old Gate Lane
Milford, CT 06460-3652
(203) 877-4541

Autospa Corp.
343 Great Neck Road
Great Neck, NY 11021-4220
(516) 829-7800

Barbizone International Inc.
950 3d Avenue
New York, NY 10022-2705
(212) 371-4300

Bathtique International Ltd.
247 Goodman Street North
Rochester, NY 14607-1195
(716) 442-9190

B-Dry System Inc.
1341 Copley Road
Akron, OH 44320-2653
(216) 867-2576

Blockbuster Entert. Corp.
901 East Las Olas Boulevard
Fort Lauderdale, FL 33301
(305) 524-8200

Boz Hot Dogs Inc.
14207 Chicago Road
Dolton, IL 60419-1203
(708) 841-3747

Budget Printing Center
4133 Presidential Drive
Lafayette Hill, PA 19444
(215) 836-5215

Business Cards Overnight
19 6th Road
Woburn, MA 01801-1757
(617) 935-1153

Business Cards Tomorrow Inc.
3000 N.E. 30th Place
Fort Lauderdale, FL 33306-1900
(305) 563-1224

C&P Enterprises Inc.
DBA New Waldo's Pizza
14 5th Avenue South
Saint Cloud, MN 56301-0001
(612) 253-7170

Conroy's Inc.
6621 Pacific Coast Highway
Long Beach, CA 90803-4200
(213) 594-4484

Cottman Transmission Systems Inc.
240 New York Drive
Fort Washington, PA 19034-2598
(215) 643-5885

Coverall North America Inc.
3111 Camino Del Rio N.
San Diego, CA 92108
(619) 584-1911

Culligan International Co.
1 Culligan Parkway
Northbrook, IL 60062-6287
(708) 205-6000

Cutco Industries Inc.
DBA "Haircraft"
125 South Service Road
Jericho, NY 11753-1008
(903) 586-3648

Dairy Queen
605 East Brusk Street
Jacksonville, TX 75766
(903) 586-3648

Dennis and Dennis Personal Service
1600 North Broadway, Suite 110
Santa Ana, CA 92706
(714) 835-1185

Dollar Rent A Car Systems Inc.
6141 West Century Boulevard
Los Angeles, CA 90045
(213) 776-8100

Domino's Pizza, Inc.
P.O. Box 997
Ann Arbor, MI 48106
(313) 930-3030

Dr. Nick's Transmissions
64 Hollow Road. Hollow Road
Hauppauge, NY 11788
(516) 232-1919

Druther's International Inc.
2440 Grinstead Drive
Louisville, KY 40204
(502) 458-0040

Elmer's Pancake and Steak House
11802 S.E. Stark Street
Portland, OR 97216
(503) 252-1485

Empress Auto Appearance Center
1725 Washington Road, Suite 205
Pittsburgh, PA 15241
(412) 831-1255

Endust Auto Appearance Center
1725 Washington Road, Suite 205
Pittsburgh, PA 15241
(412) 831-1255

Engineering Corp. of America
2705 California Avenue S.W.
Seattle, WA 98116
(206) 932-0654

Ernie's Wine and Liquor
P.O. Box 525
Rutherford, CA 94573
(707) 963-9573

Floor To Ceiling Store
40909 Highway 52 North
Rochester, MN 55901
(507) 285-1918

Foremost Sales Promotion Inc.
5252 North Broadway
Chicago, IL 60640
(312) 334-0077

F-O-R-T-U-N-E Franchise Corp.
655 3d Avenue, Room 1805
New York, NY 10017
(212) 697-4314

Foster's Donuts Inc.
4685 Industrial Street, Suite 3-J
Simi Valley, CA 93063-3468
(805) 522-2144

Frame and Save
3126 Dixie Highway
Erlanger, KY 41018
(606) 341-1210

Franchise Consultants International
5147 South Angela Road
Memphis, TN 38117
(901) 761-3085

Friedmans Franchisers
2301 Broadway
Oakland, CA 94612-2487
(415) 444-1139

Friendship Inns
6135 Park Road, Suite 304
Charlotte, NC 28210
(704) 552-9131

Gelet Enterprises
8214 Van Nuys Boulevard
Panorama City, CA 91402
(818) 716-0600

Gibraltar Transmissions Corp.
5 Delaware Drive
Lake Success, NY 11042
(516) 358-5500

Hallmark Cards Inc.
2501 McGee Trafficway
Kansas City, MO 64108
(816) 274-5111

Hardee's Food Systems Inc.
1233 Hardees Boulevard
Rocky Mount, NC 27802
(919) 977-2000

Hickory Farms of Ohio, Inc.
1505 Holland Road
Maumee, OH 43537
(419) 893-7611

Hilton Hotels Corp.
9336 Civic Center Drive
Beverly Hills, CA 90209
(213) 278-4321

International Franchise Association
1350 New York Avenue N.W., Suite 900
Washington, DC 20005
(202) 628-8000

Jack in the Box
9330 Balboa Avenue
San Diego, CA 92123
(619) 571-2121

Jolly Pirate Enterprises, Inc.
3923 East Broad Street
Columbus, OH 43213
(614) 235-4501

Judith Sans Internationale Inc.
3853 Oakcliff Industrial Ct.
Atlanta, GA 30340
(404) 449-7196

K-Bob's Inc.
5307 East Mockingbird Lane
Dallas, TX 75206
(214) 824-9898

Kentucky Fried Chicken Corp.
1441 Gardiner Lane
Louisville, KY 40213
(612) 830-0200

Kwik-Kopy Corp.
1 Kwik-Kopy Lane
Cypress, TX 77429
(713) 373-3535

La Quinta Motor Inns
10010 San Pedro Avenue
San Antonio, TX 78216
(512) 366-6000

Lawn Doctor Inc.
142 Highway 34
Matawan, NJ 07747
(908) 583-4700

Little Big Men Inc.
220 South First Avenue
Laurel, MT 59044
(406) 628-8241

Long John Silver's Inc.
101 Jerrico Drive
Lexington, KY 40511
(606) 263-6000

Machinery Wholesalers Corp.
3510 Biscayne Boulevard
Miami, FL 33137
(305) 576-2000

Manpower Temporary Services
5301 North Ironwood Lane
Milwaukee, WI 53217
(414) 961-1000

Midas International Corp.
225 North Michigan Avenue
Chicago, IL 60601
(312) 565-7500

Miracle Auto Painting Inc.
1065 East Hillsdale Boulevard
Foster City, CA 94404
(415) 570-2211

Naked Furniture Inc.
1099 Jay Street, Building 3
Rochester, NY 14611
(716) 436-4191

National Auto Service Center
1605 South Missouri Avenue
Clearwater, FL 34616
(813) 581-4061

1 Potato 2 Inc.
5640 International Parkway
New Hope, MN 55428-5409
(612) 537-3833

Physicians Weight Loss Center of America Inc.
395 Springside Drive
Akron, OH 44333
(216) 666-7952

Pizza Hut Inc.
9111 East Douglas Avenue
Wichita, KS 67207
(316) 681-9000

Powers, John Robert Finishing Modeling and Career School
175 Andover Street
Danvers, MA 01923
(508) 777-8677

Printmasters Inc.
370 South Crenshaw Boulevard
Torrance, CA 90503
(213) 328-0303

Quality Inns International, Inc.
10750 Columbia Pike
Silver Spring, MD 20901
(301) 593-5600

Quik Stop Markets Inc.
P.O. Box 5745
Fremond, CA 94537
(415) 657-8500

Rax Restaurants Inc.
1266 Dublin Road
Columbus, OH 43215
(614) 486-3669

Rent-a-Wreck
6053 West Sentry, Suite 550
Los Angeles, CA 90045
(213) 641-4000

Sales Consultants International
1127 Euclid Avenue, Suite 1400
Cleveland, OH 44115
(216) 696-1122

Software City
111 Galway Place
Teaneck, NJ 07666
(201) 833-8510

Sterling Sports
450 Oak Brook Parkway, Suite 106
Saint Paul, MN 55127
(612) 482-1137

Subway World Headquarters
325 Bic Drive
Milford, CT 06460
(203) 877-4221

Taco Bell Corp.
17901 Von Karman Avenue
Irvin, CA 92714
(714) 863-4500

Tastee Donuts Inc.
5600 Mounes Street
Harahan, LA 70123
(504) 734-5333

Thrifty Rent-a-Car System
5350 East 31st Street, Suite 900
Tulsa, OK 74135

Tubby's Sub Shops, Inc.
34500 Doreka Drive
Fraser, MI 48026

U-Save Auto Rental of America
7525 Connelley Drive, Suite A
Hanover, MD 21075
(301) 760-8733

Video Data Services
24 Grove Street
Pittsford, NY 14534
(716) 835-4773

Weight Watchers International
500 North Broadway
Jericho, NY 11753
(516) 939-0400

Western Sizzlin' Inc.
17090 Dallas Parkway
Dallas,TX 75248
(214) 407-9700

Yogi Bear's Jellystone Park
6201 Kellogg Avenue
Cincinnati, OH 45228
(513) 232-6800

## On Your Own—Almost

Entrepreneurship—small business and self-employment—was the fastest growing area of U.S. business in the early 1990s, with 1.3 million new businesses opening in 1991 alone. In part, experts thought, this was due to the recession, with millions of jobless people falling back on moonlighting or cottage operations or simply calling themselves "consultants" or "self-employed" in preference to "out of work." In part, it may have been due to the same discontent with "big businesses" that pushed people toward mid-sized employers. Whatever the explanation, the phenomenon encouraged the formation and growth of small business networks and support services that provided, among other benefits, training. Plenty of new entrepreneurship guidebooks have hit the shelves recently—and low-cost educational institutions have added to their small business how-to courses to meet the demand.

So if you've ever considered opening your own business, now would be a good time to get serious. But, though there's plenty of free or cheap help available, don't be fooled into thinking that entrepreneurship itself isn't hard, costly work. On the other hand, don't assume that it's impossible for you—too costly or too risky. Instead, check it out first-hand, without leaving your current job. Volunteer to help a friend running her business; even talk with shopkeepers in your neighborhood about their experiences.

You can build a small business or free-lance service on the side, based on special skills or interests that you may or may not use in your salaried job. This "on your own" work can provide extra income (or at least tax deductions) if you're careful—and will be there when you "retire." Or you may be able to use your side business as a personal training program, the basis for switching careers.

Get all the information you can from the groups listed below, and try on some of their training for size. If it feels comfortable, pursue entrepreneurship while earning other pay and taking advantage of all the training the groups offer. Join associations that relate to your new field, and remember: even if you're planning self-employment in a career for which you're salaried—like accounting, retailing, contracting, or designing—you'll need courses like financial planning, which many associations offer free or at low cost (see Chapter 8).

Is entrepreneurship for you? Since investment of at least some time and money is required, get a sense of whether you're cut out for working on your own. Career counselors say that successful entrepreneurs share these characteristics: initiative, self-knowledge, self-confidence, goal orientation, perseverance, resourcefulness, and high energy levels.

If that sounds like you, train your way toward your goal. To get special help, guidance, and expertise, contact these organizations:

American Woman's Economic
Development Corp.
60 East 42d Street
New York, NY 10017
(212) 236-1100

Sponsors training and technical programs for women owning or starting small businesses.

National Association for the
Self-Employed
2324 Gravel Road
Ft. Worth, TX 76118
(817) 589-2475

Provides material and seminars.

National Small Business Association
1155 15th Street N.W.
Washington, DC 20005
(202) 293-8830

Provides education and support for entrepreneurs.

And find about other small business training and entrepreneurship information from the U.S. Small Business Administration, 1441 L Street N.W., Washington, DC 20426, (202) 652-6823.

Whether you are an independent contractor as a "temp," an independent real estate agent, or an independent franchisee or entrepreneur...whether you are independent out of choice or necessity, you can optimize the training resources that independence offers if you keep your options—and your mind—open.

# 12 Follow Up... And Up

From the most traditional of training systems—apprenticeship—through the most surprising—franchising and self-employment, this book has covered the range of free, low-cost, and salaried career training resources. You've found specific programs and resource ideas to get you thinking along new channels.

The next section offers some suggestions on how to find still more resources, to enable you to pinpoint the career training that meets your unique needs. For all of them, whether traditional or far out, you've got the four-point formula to serve as a guide to getting what you *want:*

What do I want to do?

\+ What opportunities are available?

\+ What skills are demanded?

− What skills do I have?

---

= Career training to fill the gap

Then, with the career-change checklist to rate how well each program serves your purposes, you'll figure out how to get what you *need:*

What do I want or need to learn? (What can I learn?)

Where will it get me? (Will it get me where I want to be?)

Is it suited to me? (*Why* is it suited to me?)

How much can I manage?

If you're still not sure about the answers to those questions—or if what you've seen in this book has given you some new questions to ask about career choice and career change, you may want to get help.

Expert career guidance is also available at little or no cost.

A visit to the library (it's free) to check out any of the variety of guidebooks that specialize in career inventories may be all you need. Many large libraries also have professionally run career guidance services—as do the publicly funded centers listed in Chapter 7 and the adult-focused colleges in Chapter 4.

If you're working for a company you want to stay with, check with your human resources (personnel) department for guidance to training and development opportunities you may already have access to.

Or, contact these organizations, which provide information about, and referrals to, free or low-cost career counseling in your area:

American Association for
Counseling and Development
5999 Stevenson Avenue
Alexandria, VA 22304
(703) 823-9800

American Society for Training and
Development
Box 9443
Alexandria, VA 22313
(703) 683-8100

National Employment and Training
Association
9300 East Imperial Highway
Downey, CA 90247
(310) 922-6665

Plenty of free or low-cost high-quality career guidance is available. In fact, *beware* of costly services: Opportunists abound, especially in times of great change like this decade. Some highly touted—and high-priced—guidance "experts" may actually be charging clients for information available free to all from government sources. You shouldn't have to pay to find free training—and you don't have to.

Whatever form of training you choose, apply for it with the same seriousness you would a job: Follow instructions and present yourself in your best light. (See some of the sources listed at the end of this book if you need guidance or a pep talk.)

Once you've started training, make the most of it. If you've chosen a program on top of your regular work, manage your time carefully. You may have to eliminate some of your "leisure" activities for a while. And, if you find you're working so hard at that temp job to support yourself during training that you're overextended, you may need to change your timetable so that you have enough energy to make the training worthwhile. On the other hand, don't assume that training is too much to add to your life. Managed wisely, it can change your life for the better.

Or if you've chosen a job just for the training, or are volunteering or interning, treat it like a job that you're completely committed to.

And no matter how basic some of your new projects seem, never assume you know how to do it or that you "should" know how. Nor should you assume you're getting all you can from your program: if it's lacking, explore and discuss ways in which it could be made better.

Training experts and career counselors say that the biggest block to succeeding at finding and making the most of training is often a negative attitude—or, more simply, fear. How's *your* attitude? Is fear of change holding you back from training into a new career? Think about this: How many people do you know who are doing the jobs they were originally trained for? Not many.

But how many people do you know (including yourself) who are worried? Who are afraid to leave the trap of dead-end jobs for fear of not finding other work, or afraid their current jobs will come to a sudden dead end? Such thinking is especially common when finances are tight.

Fear of change or fear of training itself can create a tighter trap than any combination of outside forces. So think about how to make change work *for* you. People just like you are turning to training by the millions. Changes in the work force and the workplace are bringing adults back to school in record numbers. Given those facts, and the facts about the variety of *free* training available, if you "can't find" what's right for you, you may be making assumptions guided by fear.

Well, *never* assume. Never assume that you can't manage training...that you're not eligible for training that's useful to you...that you can't train...that you can't change. Instead, assume that you *can.* All you need to do is ask.

Many people don't ask—or don't know where to ask. You do, now. You may have to be patient, persistent, and politely insist when you ask the sources in this book for or about training and training information, but it *is* there for the asking.

# Find Out More

Though each chapter in this book includes information on where to find more information on each topic, there's always more to find—especially once you've decided which specific paths you want to pursue. Listed here are some particularly valuable resources of across-the-board interest to career finders and career changers.

## At the Library

The library itself is a sterling resource—especially a large, central library, or one at a four-year or community college. Librarians themselves are a source of great "uncataloged" knowledge, and they love being asked for help. Also, many larger libraries have access to on-line databases and even in-person career-guidance experts; smaller ones have files of unbound materials on local jobs and training opportunities.

Library shelves hold reference books whose size and cost is beyond the reach of most individuals. Among the most useful:

*Directories in Print* (Gale Research, Inc., Detriot). An annotated, regularly updated guide to over 10,000 directories and databases, including those related to every aspect of careers and training.

*Dun's Career Guide.* An annual employment opportunities directory produced by Dun's Marketing Services, Inc., part of the Dun & Bradstreet Corporation. Its extensive descriptive lists of employers is one of the very few directories that includes reference to training programs offered. Also available in regional editions.

*Encyclopedia of Associations* (Gale Research). A three-volume annual listing of virtually every small and large membership group existing, with reference to training and clearinghouse services of many.

*Encyclopedia of Business Information Sources* (Gale Research). A biennial guide to groups and books offering facts and guidance on specific business- and career-related topics.

*National Trade and Professional Associations of the United States* (Columbia Books, Inc., Washington, DC). An annual listing. Less comprehensive than the Gale guides, but focused on groups of career-related interest. Regional editions available.

## Databases

If you have access to on-line services via your own personal computer and modem, take advantage of all the business-related databases you can. But be aware that many services are accessible through larger libraries, which also have useful reference sources on CD-ROMs. Among the most useful career-related databases are:

ABI Inform. Business practices and trends.

ERIC. Government-compiled education resources.

*Encyclopedia of Associations.* The same data as in the print version; on Dialog(r) database or on CD-ROM.

Public Affairs Information Service (PAIS). Background and current information on education and other topics.

Ask the librarian what's available to meet your needs.

## In the Bookstore

Since virtually all of the training possibilities listed in this book require that you present yourself as though you were applying for a job (in many instances, you *are* applying for a job), you may decide you need help for that procedure, from targeting through resume preparation to interview and follow-ups. Many of the groups listed in this book—especially those in Chapters 7 and 12—can provide that help.

Also available are a seemingly infinite and constantly changing supply of published guides to successful job seeking. The best approach to selecting from among them is to browse in a large bookstore (try a nearby college bookstore, too) until you find ones that best fit your personal style and career goals.

You may also find useful one or more compendiums of information on the current workplace and job market. In considering such books, be sure to check the publication date: the worthwhile ones are updated each year. Among the most thorough and accurate:

Matthew Lesko
*Lesko's Info-Power*
Information USA, Inc.
P.O. Box E
Kensington, MD 20895

A huge, well-organized, detailed collection of resources available free from government sources. Regular updates promised; get the most recent, or contact the publisher directly.

Kathryn Petras and Ross Petras
*Jobs '92*
Simon & Schuster
1230 Avenue of the Americas
New York, NY 10020

Detailed name-and-address lists of specific job opportunities by career, industry, and region, with overview of current trends and outlooks. Annual editions.

*The National Directory of Addresses and Telephone Numbers*
Omnigraphics, Inc.
Penobscot Building
Detroit, MI 48226

Addresses, phone, and fax numbers for nearly 250,000 businesses, organizations, institutions, and government agencies throughout the United States. Also sold as *The American Phone Book.* Get only this year's, direct from the publisher if necessary.

*U.S. Government Printing Office (GPO) Catalog*
Superintendent of Documents
U.S. GPO
Washington, DC 20402
(202) 783-3238

The federal government is the best and lowest-priced source for published information on *many* career-related topics. Check your phone book for the nearest GPO bookstore. To receive a catalog or get on a mailing list, use the address given here.

The best way to keep current on trends in specific career areas is to get on the mailing lists of relevant associations, like those listed in Chapter 8, since it's to their advantage to keep ahead of the trends in their fields. And it's to your advantage to stay current with the continuous change that makes career training an ongoing necessity for the 1990s.

# Index



*Index note: An *f* after a page number refers to a figures; a *t* to a table.

## About the Author

Sara D. Gilbert, an administrator at New York University's School of Continuing Education, is the author of 18 practical life and career guides, which have been critically praised as "extremely useful, practical, sensible." Her articles have appeared in numerous magazines, including *Ms.*, *Careers*, and *National Businesswoman*.